Facebook Application Development with Graph API Cookbook

Over 90 recipes to create your own exciting Facebook applications at an incredibly fast pace with Facebook Graph API

Shashwat Srivastava

Apeksha Singh

BIRMINGHAM - MUMBAI

Facebook Application Development with Graph API Cookbook

First published: November 2011

Production Reference: 1091111

Published by Packt Publishing Ltd.
Livery Place
35 Livery Street
Birmingham B3 2PB, UK.

ISBN 978-1-84969-092-8

www.packtpub.com

Cover Image by Siddharth Ravishankar (siddharthr@LNTEBG.com)

About the Authors

Shashwat Srivastava has been an avid coder since high school and has acquired technical proficiency in various programming languages with an experience of over twelve years. He is a strong advocate of open source tools and hosts his projects at SourceForge. He has successfully participated in Google Summer of Code programs 2010 and 2011.

Shashwat has graduated as a Bachelor of Electronics and Communication from Delhi College of Engineering in 2011. During his college days, he has published websites for several clients including his college library and electronics department.

Currently, he is working as an application developer at Oracle. He actively contributes to Drupal and has developed modules such as DrupalChat, DXMPP, and Chatroom. His keen interest lies in web application development and as a result he has built several Facebook and Twitter applications. Passionate about programming he loves to blog about PHP, JavaScript, MySQL, Linux, Android, and other insanities at `http://www.botskool.com/`. When unplugged, he enjoys playing chess and computer games.

First of all, I need to thank my mother and father for being a constant source of inspiration and their endless support during the book writing process. Also, I would like to thank my dear brother Anmol for all the love and care.

A huge thanks to all my friends who have given their valuable inputs on this book.

Also, I would like to thank the team at Packt Publishing, along with David, Wilson, Swapna, Shubhanjan, and other editors and reviewers. Without them you wouldn't be reading this book.

Finally, I want to thank most my friend and co-author, Apeksha, who has been with me since the beginning. She has put in a lot of efforts and worked diligently to make sure this book is complete.

Thank you for reading this book. I hope you find it interesting and useful.

Credits

Authors

Shashwat Srivastava

Apeksha Singh

Reviewer

Deepak Vohra

Acquisition Editor

Wilson D'Souza

Development Editor

Swapna Verlekar

Technical Editors

Kedar Bhat

Vanjeet D'souza

Merwine Machado

Project Coordinator

Shubhanjan Chatterjee

Proofreader

Linda Morris

Indexer

Rekha Nair

Production Coordinator

Alwin Roy

Cover Work

Alwin Roy

Apeksha Singh is a software engineer and an open source hobbyist and enthusiast. She has recently graduated as a Computer Science Engineer from Jaypee Institute of Information Technology and has extensive experience in web development and search engine optimization. She has authored articles and research papers in these fields. She has seven years of experience in the field of programming and loves data structures.

Obsessed with new technology, Apeksha keeps track of the latest developments in the world of technology and likes to update others and share her views by blogging at http://www.botskool.com/. She has also worked in the field of embedded systems and robotics. In her free time, she reads novels and plays sports such as badminton and tennis. She can be reached at her personal blog (http://apeksha0701.blogspot.com).

I would like to thank the three most important people in my life, my dad for being my role model, my mom for all the love and support and my brother Abhinav for making me believe in myself.

Also, I would like to thank my dear friends for coping with my occasional absence during the book writing stage and helping me whenever required. Most important, I would like to thank, my co-author Shashwat Srivastava for making this dream come true.

A special thanks to the team at Packt Publishing without whom this book wouldn't have been possible.

About the Reviewer

Deepak Vohra is a consultant and a principal member of the NuBean.com software company. Deepak is a Sun Certified Java Programmer and Web Component Developer, and has worked in the fields of XML and Java programming and J2EE for over five years.

Deepak is the co-author of *Pro XML Development with Java Technology, Apress* and was the technical reviewer for *WebLogic: The Definitive Guide, O'Reilly Media,* and also the technical reviewer for *Ruby Programming for the Absolute Beginner, Course Technology PTR,* and the technical editor for *Prototype and Scriptaculous in Action, Manning Publications.* Deepak is also the author of *JDBC 4.0 and Oracle JDeveloper for J2EE Development, Processing XML documents with Oracle JDeveloper 11gh,* and *EJB 3.0 Database Persistence with Oracle Fusion Middleware 11g,* all books published by *Packt Publishing.*

www.PacktPub.com

Support files, eBooks, discount offers and more

You might want to visit www.PacktPub.com for support files and downloads related to your book.

Did you know that Packt offers eBook versions of every book published, with PDF and ePub files available? You can upgrade to the eBook version at www.PacktPub.com and as a print book customer, you are entitled to a discount on the eBook copy. Get in touch with us at service@packtpub.com for more details.

At www.PacktPub.com, you can also read a collection of free technical articles, sign up for a range of free newsletters and receive exclusive discounts and offers on Packt books and eBooks.

http://PacktLib.PacktPub.com

Do you need instant solutions to your IT questions? PacktLib is Packt's online digital book library. Here, you can access, read and search across Packt's entire library of books.

Why Subscribe?

- ► Fully searchable across every book published by Packt
- ► Copy and paste, print and bookmark content
- ► On demand and accessible via web browser

Free Access for Packt account holders

If you have an account with Packt at www.PacktPub.com, you can use this to access PacktLib today and view nine entirely free books. Simply use your login credentials for immediate access.

Table of Contents

Preface   1

Chapter 1: Creating a New Facebook Application   5
Introduction   5
Downloading PHP-SDK and setting up your environment   8
Registering a new Facebook application   10
Configuring a Facebook application   13
Getting authorization and a valid session for the user   15
Requesting specific permissions from the user   17
Logging out a user   20
Handling navigation in an iFrame Facebook application   21
Handling form submission in an iFrame Facebook application   23
Dynamically resizing an iFrame Facebook application   24
Determining whether a Facebook page has been liked by a user   27

Chapter 2: Be a part of Social Graph   31
Introduction   32
Retrieving a user's information   34
Liking a post   36
Commenting on a given post   38
Setting status message   41
Deleting a picture, post, or comment of a user   43
Retrieving the current user's friendlist   44
Creating a post on the wall of a user's friend   46
Posting a picture to a specific album of the user   49
Retrieving the names of the user's friends who have liked a particular
status message   53
Creating an event   55
Paging through a user's friends   57
Searching through a user's feed   59

Tagging users in a picture   60
Adding a subscription for real time updates related to a user object   63
Creating a callback for handling real time updates   65
Deleting subscriptions   69

Chapter 3: Querying Facebook   73
Introduction   74
Returning information about a user   76
Getting the status messages of a user   78
Retrieving profile pictures of a user's friends   81
Getting the links posted by a user   84
Getting the Facebook pages followed by a user   86
Determining if two users are friends   89
Retrieving information of a group   91
Retrieving members of a group   93
Retrieving friends from a specific friend list   95
Getting all the messages in a thread   98
Checking the status of permissions for an application   100
Getting notifications, and their senders, for the current user   102
Retrieving video details associated with a user   104
Getting the five latest photos in which a user has been tagged   106
Retrieving the latest photos published by a user   109
Retrieving details of an event   111
Retrieving details of a user's friends by using the multiquery method   114

Chapter 4: Using FB Script   117
Introduction   117
Getting the current user status and performing session validation   121
Setting up extended permissions during login   124
Logging out a user   126
Resetting the size of iframe   127
Making a Graph API call   129
Executing an FQL query   131
Subscribing to an event change   133
Unsubscribing to an event change   135
Retrieving a profile picture using XFBML   137
Adding bookmarks using XFBML   139
Authentication and setting up extended permissions using XFBML   142

Chapter 5: Expressing Yourself   147
Introduction   147
Prompting the user to publish a story   150
Using Dialog to add someone as a friend   153

Using the OAuth Dialog to request permissions for your application   157
Prompting the user to send a request to friends   161
Processing requests sent to the user by friends   164

Chapter 6: Bringing Facebook to your Website   169
Introduction   169
Setting up the Like button on your web page   170
Adding a Like box   173
Setting up the Activity Feed plugin   177
Setting up the Facepile plugin on your web page   180
Integrating the Live Stream plugin using XFBML   183
Integrating the Comment box using XFBML   185
Integrating the Send button using XFBML   187
Login with Faces   192

Chapter 7: Connecting Websites to the Social Graph   195
Introduction   195
Integrating web pages into the social graph   196
Integrating audio and video data   200
Administering your page   204
Publishing stream updates to the users   207

Chapter 8: Fiddling with Virtual Currency   211
Introduction   211
Setting up the application for Facebook Credits   212
Setting up an application callback for Facebook Credits   215
Creating Facebook Credits frontend using JavaScript SDK   221
Getting the order details   226
Implementing custom offers   229
Refunding the order   233
Developing a "Send a Gift" application and integrating with
Facebook Credits   236

Chapter 9: Creating Advertisements and Analyzing Metric Data   251
Introduction   251
Retrieving impressions of the Like Box plugin   254
Retrieving a page's stream views and wall posts using batch request   258
Getting the number of installations of an application using FQL   261
Getting statistics about visitors using FQL multiquery   263
Creating a new ad for your Facebook application   269

Chapter 10: Creating Instant Applications   275
Introduction   275
Creating a "Your Good Luck Charm of the Day" Facebook application   279

Designing a "My Fast Friends" Facebook application   **284**
Setting up a photo collage   **292**
Building a birthday calendar   **299**
Developing an application to classify friends according to the cities
they live in   **308**

Chapter 11: Using Facebook Open Graph Beta   313
Introduction   **313**
Setting up your application for using Facebook Open Graph Beta   **314**
Defining actions, objects, and aggregations for your application   **317**
Customizing the Facebook Auth Dialog box   **325**
Requesting permission for publishing to the user's timeline   **328**
Defining your web page as a a Facebook graph object   **332**
Publishing actions of a user to Facebook   **334**

Index   339

Preface

With a user base of nearly 800 million people, Facebook is the number one social networking platform. Applications can be created to interact with this huge user base in various ways both inside and outside Facebook. These applications, if developed effectively and efficiently, offer a free medium for promotion and publicity of a product or an organization.

This book focuses on both the concepts and implementations necessary to develop Facebook applications and provides ready-to-use code for common scenarios faced by a developer while creating these applications. It incorporates the newly launched Facebook Graph API along with Facebook Open Graph Beta and also presents the reader with some intuitive ready-to-use applications. This book guides the reader step-by-step, from start to finish, through various stages of Facebook application development.

What this book covers

Chapter 1, Creating a New Facebook Application describes the first step towards developing a Facebook application which includes Facebook application registration process and downloading its PHP - SDK. Here, we will learn how to set up the environment and perform basic authentication to begin with Facebook application development process.

Chapter 2, Be a part of Social Graph presents some recipes to perform the most commonly encountered tasks of application development using the Facebook Graph API through PHP. Here, we will get accustomed to Facebook objects and connections and ways to use them to retrieve data.

Chapter 3, Querying Facebook demonstrates how to use the Facebook Query Language to query Facebook's humongous database for retrieving complex user data.

Chapter 4, Using FB Script shows us how we can access all the features of Graph API using Facebook JavaScript SDK such as to performing authentication and retrieving user data directly at the client side.

Chapter 5, Expressing Yourself provides an insight into Facebook Dialogs. Here, we will learn how to integrate Facebook Dialogs which provide a consistent interface to our applications. Publishing streams, sending friend requests, requesting permissions and so on will become seamlessly easy with these Facebook popup boxes.

Chapter 6, Bringing Facebook to your Website introduces us to the all time favorite Social Plugins. Here we will learn how to integrate Facebook' Social Plugins to a third party application and connect with the Facebook world from virtually anywhere and anytime.

Chapter 7, Connecting Websites to Social Graph shows the users Facebook Open Graph and ways to specify structured information about a webpage which determines how it will be rendered in Facebook. Learn all about Facebook `meta` tags, their uses, and how to incorporate them into your own web pages.

Chapter 8, Fiddling with Virtual Currency demonstrates how to integrate and use Facebook Credits with our application. This chapter will show us how to use Facebook Credits as a currency to sell our goods and services. It will also teach us how to handle transactions via Facebook Credits API.

Chapter 9, Creating Advertisements and Analyzing Metric Data talks about Facebook Metrices and Ads and recipes to retrieve metric data about our applications. Here, we will learn how to record statistics and understand user interaction with our application.

Chapter 10, Creating Instant Applications houses some readymade exquisite Facebook Applications. Here we will learn to develop few Facebook Applications right from scratch.

Chapter 11, Using Facebook Open Graph Beta introduces us to the newly launched Facebook Timeline and Open Graph Beta. Here, we will learn how to create Facebook objects, actions, and aggregations along with publishing user actions.

What you need for this book

In order to start with Facebook application development you should have a domain name and web hosting space. Your web server should support PHP which is a server-side language.

Who this book is for

This book is written for Facebook developers ranging from novice to expert. It uses PHP, HTML, and jQuery, the most commonly used platforms, to build applications in Facebook.

Conventions

In this book, you will find a number of styles of text that distinguish between different kinds of information. Here are some examples of these styles, and an explanation of their meaning.

Code words in text are shown as follows: "We use Facebook's in-built XFBML `<fb:comments>` tag to add the Comment plugin".

A block of code is set as follows:

```
<iframe src="http://www.facebook.com/plugins/likebox.php?
  href=http%3A%2F%2Fwww.facebook.com%2FPacktPub&amp;
  width=292&amp;colorscheme=light&amp;show_faces=true&amp;
  allowTransparency="true">
</iframe>
```

When we wish to draw your attention to a particular part of a code block, the relevant lines or items are set in bold:

```
<iframe src="http://www.facebook.com/plugins/likebox.php?
  href=http%3A%2F%2Fwww.facebook.com%2FPacktPub&amp;
  width=292&amp;colorscheme=light&amp;show_faces=true&amp;
  allowTransparency="true">
</iframe>
```

Any command-line input or output is written as follows:

New terms and **important words** are shown in bold. Words that you see on the screen, in menus or dialog boxes for example, appear in the text like this: "Fill in the attributes details and click on **Get Code**".

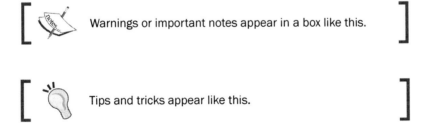

Warnings or important notes appear in a box like this.

Tips and tricks appear like this.

Reader feedback

Feedback from our readers is always welcome. Let us know what you think about this book—what you liked or may have disliked. Reader feedback is important for us to develop titles that you really get the most out of.

To send us general feedback, simply send an e-mail to feedback@packtpub.com, and mention the book title via the subject of your message.

If there is a book that you need and would like to see us publish, please send us a note in the **SUGGEST A TITLE** form on www.packtpub.com or e-mail suggest@packtpub.com.

If there is a topic that you have expertise in and you are interested in either writing or contributing to a book, see our author guide on www.packtpub.com/authors.

Customer support

Now that you are the proud owner of a Packt book, we have a number of things to help you to get the most from your purchase.

Downloading the example code

You can download the example code files for all Packt books you have purchased from your account at http://www.PacktPub.com. If you purchased this book elsewhere, you can visit http://www.PacktPub.com/support and register to have the files e-mailed directly to you.

Errata

Although we have taken every care to ensure the accuracy of our content, mistakes do happen. If you find a mistake in one of our books—maybe a mistake in the text or the code—we would be grateful if you would report this to us. By doing so, you can save other readers from frustration and help us improve subsequent versions of this book. If you find any errata, please report them by visiting http://www.packtpub.com/support, selecting your book, clicking on the **errata submission form** link, and entering the details of your errata. Once your errata are verified, your submission will be accepted and the errata will be uploaded on our website, or added to any list of existing errata, under the Errata section of that title. Any existing errata can be viewed by selecting your title from http://www.packtpub.com/support.

Piracy

Piracy of copyright material on the Internet is an ongoing problem across all media. At Packt, we take the protection of our copyright and licenses very seriously. If you come across any illegal copies of our works, in any form, on the Internet, please provide us with the location address or website name immediately so that we can pursue a remedy.

Please contact us at copyright@packtpub.com with a link to the suspected pirated material.

We appreciate your help in protecting our authors, and our ability to bring you valuable content.

Questions

You can contact us at questions@packtpub.com if you are having a problem with any aspect of the book, and we will do our best to address it.

1
Creating a New Facebook Application

In this chapter, we will cover:

- ▶ Downloading PHP-SDK and setting up your environment
- ▶ Registering a new Facebook application
- ▶ Configuring a Facebook application
- ▶ Getting authorization and a valid session for the user
- ▶ Requesting specific permissions from the user
- ▶ Logging out a user
- ▶ Handling navigation in an iFrame Facebook application
- ▶ Handling form submission in an iFrame Facebook application
- ▶ Dynamically resizing an iFrame Facebook application
- ▶ Determining whether a Facebook page has been liked by users

Introduction

If you want to develop applications that connect to the social web, then Facebook is the place from where you should begin your journey. Over the past six years, Facebook has completely revolutionized the concept of social networking and transformed the way people interact over the web with each other. With a more than 800 million user base, this is definitely the place you won't want to miss.

The social network

Today, Facebook has become the synonym for social networking and it has surpassed its competitors, such as Myspace and Friendster, by huge margins in the world of the social web. The structured form, the simulated interaction, and the dedicated platform provide users with a seamless sharing experience. *Facebooking* has become the 'key phrase' among people of all social domains. From college students to the entrepreneurs, from the elite to hoi-polloi, everyone happens to be a part of a web-based social graph and Facebook connects them all.

What makes Facebook tick?

What is it about Facebook that catapulted it from a member influx of a few thousands during the first month of its launch in 2004, to a staggering 800 million people by the end of the decade?

1. **It's simply cool!**: Keep in touch with friends, make groups for entertainment, search for people, view pictures, send messages, share wall posts, create forums, advertise, play games, and create applications; name any social activity and Facebook is already equipped with it. Facebook caters to the needs of virtually everyone and has everything for its users.

2. **It's different**: Facebook stands out from its competitors, such as Myspace and Friendster, and has done something which no other social networking site has done before. It has introduced the concept of page and millions of third-party applications, hosted both inside and outside Facebook, which gives users a complete social experience. It has moved beyond the social aspect of strictly being just a site by allowing being in touch with an always-changing network of friends and colleagues.

3. **It inspires**: Facebook is not just about sharing a similar interest, it's about networking. It allows users to express themselves, communicate, and assemble profiles that highlight their talents and experience, and also advertise and market inexpensively.

4. **It's not stopping**: Facebook has continued to grow from the start. With the humongous increase in its user base, it has been constantly updating itself with all the technological changes taking place. Facebook, with the introduction of Graph API, Open Graph protocol, Facebook Credits, Facebook Ads API, and Social Plugins, has taken care of the changing technology.

5. **It's stated everywhere**: The popularity of Facebook has been acknowledged worldwide. A brief look into some of the Facebook statistics, as taken from the official Facebook page (http://www.facebook.com/press/info.php?statistics) is as follows:

   - More than 800 million active users
   - People spend over 700 billion minutes per month on Facebook
   - More than 30 billion pieces of content (web links, news stories, blog posts, notes, photo albums, and so on) shared each month

- More than 70 translations available on the site

- More than 7 million websites have integrated with Facebook, including over 80 of comScore's U.S. Top 100 websites and over half of comScore's Global Top 100 websites

- People on Facebook install applications more than 20 million times every day

What's in it for the developers?

With more than 800 million active users and integration of more than 7 million websites, Facebook has a lot of potential for the third-party application developers. It is an attractive platform to promote a particular idea or business and spread it among the millions of users. Facebook offers its users as potential customers, making it fascinating and potentially profitable for the developers. The introduction of the Facebook Developers Platform has provided developers with many new and exciting ways to engage Facebook users. So, the benefits for the developers are as follows:

- **Make money**: Apart from advertising, Facebook allows developers to earn money by running their applications on other websites.

- **It's free**: Developing a Facebook application is exciting and free.

- **Allows collection of data**: As part of the application, Facebook allows developers to collect selected information from their users. For example, you can collect users' views on a particular interest by using polling.

- **Spreading your word through millions of users**: Updates by the Facebook application on a user's wall is another attractive way to publicize your idea or product. These updates, when viewed by friends and friends of friends, expose your application virally to the millions out there.

- **Integrate with Facebook**: Facebook social plugins, such as the Likebox and Recommendation plugin, make it possible to draw more traffic.

- **Building business**: An application provides a personalized interface to interact with people and caters to their specific needs. This, in turn, can help to promote and facilitate marketing of certain products and services.

- **Advertisement**: You can promote Facebook applications easily and efficiently. Facebook aims at making its advertisers happier and more satisfied. The introduction of the CPC advertising, which allows its advertisers to take control on the amount that advertisements generate per click, is by far its boldest and bravest move.

Truly dedicated to its developers, Facebook also incorporates a number of key elements in its Developer's Platform. Its transition from Old REST API to the new, highly efficient, and simpler Graph API speaks about Facebook's effort to meet the ever increasing needs of its developers, making it a lot more interesting for them. Supporting multiple SDKs is another effort to make it more accessible.

Technology is about change and Facebook incorporates those changes even before they are acknowledged. It changes not just to be better, but to become the best.

In this chapter, we take our first step towards Facebook application development and learn how to set up an environment for the same. So, let's delve into the Facebook world and see how we connect to it.

Downloading PHP-SDK and setting up your environment

Facebook Application Development Platform supports a lot of SDKs for the ease of its developers. One such SDK is PHP-SDK, which supports all the PHP-based web applications. PHP-SDK has been released under Open Source License and is hosted at GitHub.

Getting ready

In order to develop, create, and launch a Facebook application, you need to have a domain name and a web hosting space. From here on, we will refer to this web hosting space as the server.

Before we begin, we need to make sure that the following two PHP extensions are installed on our server:

1. PHP cURL extension
2. PHP JSON extension

PHP cURL extension provides us with a powerful library for making HTTP requests, known as **cURL**, and has been specifically designed to fetch data from remote sites. This library is used to post requests to Facebook servers using Facebook Graph API. Similarly, we need **PHP JSON (JavaScript Object Notation) extension** to convert JSON encoded data to PHP arrays for our logic processing and data mining.

There is an easy way to check for these dependencies. First, create a new file `test.php` and upload it to your server. Next, add the following code to it:

```php
<?php
  if (!function_exists('curl_init')) {
    throw new Exception('PHP cURL extension is not present.');
  }
```

```
    if (!function_exists('json_decode')) {
     throw new Exception('PHP JSON extension is not present.');
    }
 ?>
```

Now, save this file and run it on your server. If you do not get an error message, it means everything is fine and you have these extensions already installed. Otherwise, you need to install the appropriate extension(s) accordingly. Check out the following links for more information regarding installation of these extensions:

- ▶ PHP cURL: `http://php.net/manual/en/curl.installation.php`
- ▶ PHP JSON: `http://php.net/manual/en/json.installation.php`

Now let's set up Facebook PHP-SDK on the server.

How to do it...

Once we have made sure that we have the cURL and JSON extensions installed, we need to download PHP-SDK. Follow these steps:

1. Go to `https://github.com/facebook/php-sdk/` and download the latest stable version of Facebook PHP-SDK in the compressed format.
2. Create a new folder on your server where you want to host your Facebook application. We will call this new folder `my_app`.
3. Extract the content of the archive file on your local computer. Now, go inside the `src` folder and you will see a file named `facebook.php` along with another file. Upload the `facebook.php` file to your server inside the `my_app` directory.

How it works...

The `facebook.php` file contains a class named `Facebook`, which helps us to connect to the Facebook servers and post various requests. This class has inbuilt functions and we simply need to put them to use.

There's more...

The Facebook PHP SDK is available under Open Source License. So, developers can contribute to it by filing bugs and suggesting improvements. Also, Facebook offers a number of developers tools, which can help us in the debug process. These are available at the URL: `http://developers.facebook.com/tools/`.

Registering a new Facebook application

What is a Facebook application? Fundamentally, a Facebook application is a code snippet written by a developer, which extracts Facebook data of the users (who use this application) and performs some meaningful task on this data. Facebook assigns each application a unique ID and private key. This helps it to distinguish between various applications and manage security. To obtain them is the very first step towards creating a new Facebook application.

Also, for creating an application inside Facebook, we need to specify a **Canvas Page**. This is the URL of our application inside Facebook and is of the form: `http://apps.facebook.com/your_canvas_page`. The Canvas Page is like a blank canvas within Facebook on which our application will run. We can populate the Canvas Page by providing a **Canvas URL** that contains the HTML, JavaScript, and CSS for our application. The Canvas URL should point to our server. When a user requests our application, Facebook renders our predefined Canvas Page. The application content is extracted from the Canvas URL. It is like loading the application content, from our web server, within an iFrame inside Facebook.

Getting ready

Before we register a new Facebook application, we need to make sure we have verified our Facebook account. Facebook does this in order to limit spamming. There are two ways to verify ourselves for a developer account:

1. We can confirm our phone number by going to the following URL: `http://www.facebook.com/confirmphone.php`.

2. Or, we can go to the URL: `https://secure.facebook.com/cards.php` and add a credit card to our Facebook account for verification.

How to do it...

The following steps will outline how to register a new Facebook application:

1. Go to `https://developers.facebook.com/apps` and click on the **+ Create New App** button, present on the top right corner just below the Facebook top bar.

2. A pop up, as shown in the next screenshot, will appear. Key in your application name, accept the terms and conditions of Facebook, and click on **Continue**:

3. Next, you will be redirected to fill in the basic information for this application. Enter the details such as **Description**, **Contact Email**, **Privacy Policy URL**, **Terms of Service URL**, and so on. You can also upload an icon and logo for your application.

4. Additionally, you will find your application ID and application Secret. These two form a very important part of the Facebook application. You must never disclose your application's secret key to anyone. Refer to the following screenshot:

5. In the **Roles** section, you can add additional users as Administrator, Developer, Tester or Insights User.

6. Next, we need to define our Canvas Page and Canvas URL. For this, click on the **On Facebook** tab, present on the left hand side of the page. By default, the **Canvas Settings** sub tab will be loaded, as shown in the following screenshot:

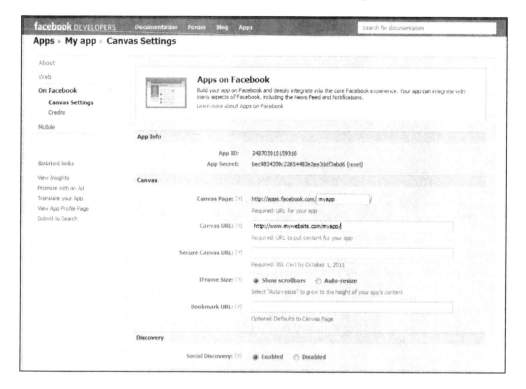

7. Now, under the **Canvas** section, type in your desired **Canvas Page** name. This will be your application's base URL on Facebook. It will be something similar to: `http://apps.facebook.com/your_canvas_page`. Next, type in your **Canvas URL**. This will be the URL from which Facebook will render your application and this URL should be of your server or domain. It will be something such as: `http://www.example.com/your_application_name/index.php`.

8. Now, click on **Save Changes**. That's it. We have registered a new application on Facebook and done some basic configuration.

How it works...

The application ID and application secret key are unique for every Facebook application. The application ID and the application secret key are required while requesting any data from Facebook. These are used to verify that the request is being made from a trusted source.

There's more...

Apart from the basic application configuration, there are some tips given below, which the developers may find useful.

Secure connection

If your application is going to have secure content, then you can set **Secure Canvas URL** in the **Canvas** section under the **On Facebook** tab. Typically, this secure version of the Canvas URL is used by Facebook when your application is accessed by a user over a secure connection (https).

Sandbox mode

Sandbox mode restricts the access of an application to only its developers. This can be used by developers in the development and testing phase. You can enable Sandbox mode by going to the **Advanced** sub tab, inside the **About** tab, on the application's settings page.

Resetting an application's secret key

If you feel that your application's secret key has been compromised, then you can easily reset it. Follow these steps:

1. Go to https://developers.facebook.com/apps/ and choose your application from the list of apps given on the sidebar on the left-hand side.

2. Next, go to the application's settings page and click on the **reset** link present adjacent to the application's secret key.

 In Facebook, the Canvas Page name must be at least seven characters long, otherwise it gives a validation error.

Configuring a Facebook application

Before we begin writing the code for our application, we need to configure certain settings in our PHP code in order to make it communicate effectively and securely with the Facebook servers. Thus, after registration, configuration is the first step that we need to perform.

Getting ready

You should have registered your Facebook application before starting with this. Also, you should have your application ID and secret key ready. These form an integral part of the configuration process.

How to do it...

We will assume that we are hosting our application in a directory named `my_app` on some server.

Create a new file and name it `config.php`, and upload it to the `my_app` directory. Also, copy the `facebook.php` file, present in PHP-SDK, in the same directory.

Copy the following code in `config.php`:

```php
<?php
  require_once 'facebook.php';
  $facebook = new Facebook(array(
    'appId'  => 'your_application_id',
    'secret' => 'your_application_secret',
    'cookie' => true,
  ));
?>
```

You need to replace `your_application_id` and `your_application_secret` in the preceding code with your Facebook application ID and secret key respectively. Now, save the file. We will need this file often as we proceed through the application development procedure.

How it works...

In `config.php`, we have created an instance of our Facebook application by declaring a new object, `$facebook`, of the `Facebook` class. We pass an array with various settings as an argument to the constructor. These parameters are `appId`, `secret`, and `cookie`. Here, `appId` refers to the application ID and `secret` refers to the secret key that we have obtained during registration. The cookie value `true` simply implies that the cookie will be used to store the session information after authentication.

Usually, a Facebook application consists of various pages and hence there are multiple PHP files. Instead of specifying the Facebook configuration parameters again and again, we have created a file named `config.php` and we will include this file in the rest of our PHP files. This will make it easy and remove unnecessary duplication of code.

See also

> ► The *Registering a new Facebook application* recipe for information on the registration process.

Getting authorization and a valid session for the user

A Facebook application is all about giving its users a personalized experience. That is why authentication and session verification form an important aspect of a Facebook application development process. There are two ways to render a Facebook application. One is inside Facebook and the other is to use it on a third party website. We will show how to get started with an application inside Facebook.

Getting ready

You should have registered your Facebook application and created `config.php`.

How to do it...

Add the following code to the top of your PHP file, which contains the application code, and name it `index.php`:

```php
<?php
  require_once 'config.php';

  /* Get a valid session */
  $session = $facebook->getSession();
  $me = null;
  if($session) {
    /* Check if session is valid */
    $me = $facebook->api('/me');
  }
  if($me) {
    echo 'User is logged in and has a valid session';
  }
  else {
    echo 'Session expired or user has not logged in yet.
          Redirecting...';
    echo '<script>top.location.href="'. $facebook->getLoginUrl()
.'";</script>';
  }
?>
```

Now, save this file and run it. An appropriate message will be displayed depending on whether the session is a valid one or has expired.

How it works...

In our main application file `index.php`, we first include `config.php`, which contains the basic configuration information. To perform authorization, we need to check for the following things:

1. First we check whether a valid user session already exists or not. This has been done by making a call to the `getSession()` function. If it returns a null value, it means either the session has expired or the user has not logged in yet.

2. However, if the session exists, we need to check if it is still valid or has expired. For this, we make a call to the **Facebook Graph API** URL `https://graph.facebook.com/me`. Here, `me` specifies the session of the active user and making a call to this returns the information of the current logged in user. If the user's session still persists, then it does not return a null value and the message **User is logged in and has valid session** is displayed, otherwise we will know that a valid session doesn't exist.

3. Upon detection of an invalid session, we redirect the user to a predefined authorization URL given by the `getLoginUrl()` function. The Facebook application login screen will look as shown in the following screenshot:

There's more...

Facebook uses the OAuth 2.0 protocol for authentication and authorization. It involves three steps:

1. User authentication
2. App authorization
3. App authentication

In the user authentication step, the user is prompted to login to Facebook if he/she is not already logged in. It ensures that the user is logged in to Facebook and has a valid session. App authorization informs the user about the data and capabilities they are providing to an application. Finally, in the App authentication step, Facebook ensures that the user is giving the information to the desired application only. After successful App authentication, a user access token is issued that enables us to access the user's information and take actions on his/her behalf.

Usually, user authentication and app authorization are handled one after another by redirecting the user to **Facebook OAuth Dialog**, discussed in detail in *Chapter 6*. This dialog can be invoked by directing the user to this URL: `https://www.facebook.com/dialog/oauth?client_id=YOUR_APP_ID&redirect_uri=YOUR_URL`.

After the user logs in and authorizes the application, Facebook redirects the user to the `redirect_uri` URL along with a query parameter named `code`, which contains a Facebook server generated authorization code.

Finally, the last step consists of application authentication, where we need to pass the authorization code and application secret to the Graph API token endpoint at this URL:

```
https://graph.facebook.com/oauth/access_token?

    client_id=YOUR_APP_ID&redirect_uri=YOUR_URL&

    client_secret=YOUR_APP_SECRET&code=THE_SERVER_CODE_FROM_ABOVE
```

Upon successful validation from Facebook, we receive an access token on behalf of the user, which we can use to perform various actions on his/her behalf.

This whole process is automatically handled internally by the `Facebook` class, present in `facebook.php`, and we just need to follow the steps discussed in the *How to do it* section.

Requesting specific permissions from the user

Facebook incorporates certain security measures to maintain the privacy of its users. There is a certain set of basic information which is publicly available, but for more information, we need to take specific permissions from the user. Thus, Facebook includes a multi-level permission structure. Initially, when a user authorizes any Facebook application, a certain set of basic permissions are provided to that application for that particular user. However, if we need to perform actions or retrieve data, which lies outside this basic permission set, then we need to request for these specific permissions. For example, to publish on a user's wall, you need to have the *publish_stream* permission from the user.

Getting ready

You should have registered your Facebook application and created `config.php`.

How to do it...

If the user is accessing our application for the first time and we have not set any extended permissions, a screen will appear asking for the default access permissions and would look as shown in the following screenshot:

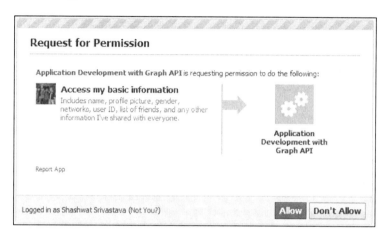

We can ask the user to grant specific permissions to our application initially when he or she first uses it. Open `index.php` and copy the following code at the appropriate location as shown:

```php
<?php
  require_once 'config.php';

  $session = $facebook->getSession();
  $me = null;
  if($session) {
    try {
      $me = $facebook->api('/me');
    } catch (FacebookApiException $e) {
    }
  }
if($me) {
    echo 'User is logged in and has a valid session';
  }
  else {
      $loginUrl = $facebook->getLoginUrl(array('req_perms' =>
      'publish_stream',));
```

```
    /**Use this code for iframe application*/
    echo '<script> top.location.href="'. $loginUrl .'"; </script>';
    /**Use this code for third party application*/
    //header('Location: '.$loginUrl);
 }
?>
```

Save the file and run it. A permission screen asking for the required permission will appear before the user and will be as shown in the following screenshot:

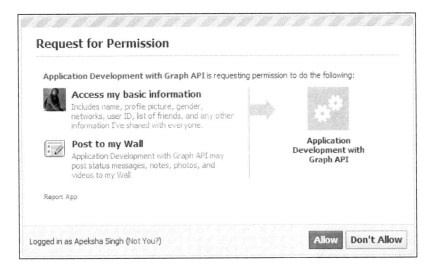

If the user clicks on the **Allow** button, the application will be authorized to do all the jobs it has requested for.

How it works...

In the `getLoginUrl()` function of the `Facebook` class, we pass an array as an argument. This array contains an index named `req_perms`, which stands for requested permissions. This index can have multiple values if we want to request multiple permissions from the user simultaneously. For example, to request permission to post on the wall, as well as access user's photos, use the following code:

```
$loginUrl = $facebook->getLoginUrl(array('req_perms' =>
  'publish_stream, user_photos',));
```

After calling this function, we store the output in a variable named `$loginUrl`. The output is a dynamically generated URL to which we should redirect the user so that he/she may grant the necessary permission. As usual, we need to use `top.location.href` (JavaScript code) for an iFrame-based application or otherwise use the `header()` function of PHP.

There's more...

Sometimes you may want to add or delete some extended permissions during the testing phase of your application. If you have authenticated with Facebook once, you won't be able to re-authenticate using the preceding code since you'll be detected as a logged in user. There is a way to achieve this.

1. Delete that application from the list of installed applications. For this, log in to your Facebook account, go to **Privacy Settings** at the top right. Under the **Apps and Websites** section, click on **Edit your settings** at the right bottom.

2. Next, you will see a list of all the installed applications. Simply click the **x** button next to the application name to remove it from the user's application list.

3. Now modify your code to re-authenticate.

Additionally, you can visit
http://developers.facebook.com/docs/authentication/permissions/.

Logging out a user

At times, we may need to destroy the current session of the user and safely log him/her out of our Facebook application. Here's how we will do that.

Getting ready

You should have registered your Facebook application and created `config.php`. Also, the user should have been logged in and must have a valid and unexpired session.

How to do it...

Add the following code to the PHP code of your Facebook application file `index.php`:

```php
<?php
  require_once 'config.php';
  $logoutUrl = $facebook->getLogoutUrl(array('next' => 'http://apps.
    facebook.com/[your_app_canvas_name]/',));
?>
<a href ="#" onclick="top.location.href='<?php echo $logoutUrl; ?>';
  return false;">Logout</a>
```

You need to replace `[your_app_canvas_name]` according to your Facebook application URL. If you want to redirect the user to some other URL, then just replace `http://apps.facebook.com/[your_app_canvas_name]/` with the intended URL.

How it works...

The `getLogoutUrl()` function of the Facebook class returns the URL, to which we should send the user, in order to log him/her out of the Facebook network. We pass an array as a parameter to this function. The array has an element named `next`, which determines where the user will be redirected after he/she has been successfully logged out of the Facebook network. We store this formed URL in a variable named `$logoutUrl`.

Next, we use the JavaScript `onclick` event to redirect the user to this URL when he/she clicks on it. We need to use the `onclick` event because the Facebook application is normally present in an iFrame. If the application would have been directly run on a third party server instead of Facebook, then we could have directly set the `href` parameter equal to the logout URL without using the JavaScript `onclick` event.

There's more...

There is also an alternate method to redirect the user. Instead of using the `onclick` event, we can also use the `target` parameter of the hyperlink and set it to `_top`. This will, in turn, change the location of the iFrame's parent. It can be implemented as shown in the following code snippet:

```
<a href ="<?php echo $logoutUrl; ?>" target = "_top">Logout</a>
```

Handling navigation in an iFrame Facebook application

Navigation for applications, which run inside Facebook, has to be handled differently. In a multi-page based application, which runs inside Facebook, when a user clicks on a hyperlink, it will be loaded inside the iFrame. Suppose you want to direct the user to an external URL, in this case, you won't want it to appear in the same iFrame. Thus, navigation becomes ineffective and has to be implemented efficiently.

Getting ready

You should have registered your application and created `config.php`.

How to do it...

Suppose we have two files, `index.php` and `about.php`. We want to create a hyperlink for `about.php` in `index.php`, as well create a hyperlink to an external site, say `www.example.com`. Simply follow these steps:

1. Open `config.php` and add the following highlighted line to it:

```php
<?php
  require_once 'facebook.php';

  $facebook = new Facebook(array(
    'appId'      => 'your_application_id',
    'secret'     => 'your_application_secret',
    'cookie'     => true,
  ));
  $appBaseUrl = 'http://apps.facebook.com/[your_app_canvas_name]';
?>
```

2. Replace `[your_app_canvas_name]` accordingly and save the file.

3. Now, add the following code to `index.php`:

```php
<?php
  require_once 'config.php';
?>
<a href='<?php echo $appBaseUrl?>/about.php' target='_top'>
  About Us</a>
<a href='http://www.example.com' target='_top'>External Link</a>
```

4. Save `index.php`. Also, add some HTML code to `about.php`. Now run `index.php`.

How it works...

Suppose our domain name is `http://www.example.com` and we have uploaded `index.php` and `about.php` inside a directory named `my_app`. If we specify `http://www.example.com/my_app/` as our Canvas URL in Facebook, then by default when we access the application base URL, `index.php` is rendered inside the iFrame. If we wish to open some other page of our application inside Facebook, we just need to add the name of the file after the base URL of our application. For example, to open `about.php` inside Facebook, we need to go to: `http://apps.facebook.com/[your_app_canvas_name]/about.php`. Facebook automatically does this mapping. Whenever you enter a filename after your application's base URL, Facebook searches for it inside the predefined directory and renders that file inside its iFrame.

Here we have defined our application's base URL in `config.php` and while forming hyperlinks, we just concatenate the filename after this base URL if the file is in the same directory as `index.php`, otherwise we can form links accordingly. We have also set the `target` attribute of the hyperlink as `_top`. This makes sure that when we click on it, the URL of iFrame's parent changes.

Now, when we click on **About us**, we will be directed to `http://apps.facebook.com/ [your_app_canvas_name]/about.php`, whereas clicking on **External Link** will direct us to the external site `www.example.com`.

Handling form submission in an iFrame Facebook application

It's common for an application to display a form to the users and ask them to fill it in. Hence, form processing is a very important aspect of the Facebook application development and it turns out that it needs to be done differently again in the case of iFrame-based applications.

Getting ready

You should have registered your application and created `config.php`.

How to do it...

We will create a form in `index.php`, which will ask the user to enter his/her favorite movie. Add the following code to the main application file `index.php`:

```php
<?php
  require_once 'config.php';
?>
<form method='post' action='http://www.example.com/my_app/process_
form.php' target='_top'>
  <input type='text' name='movie' />
  <input type='submit' value='Submit' />
</form>
```

Save `index.php`. Now create a new file, name it `process_form.php`, and add the following code to it:

```php
<?php
  if($_POST['movie']) {
    //Do form processing here...
  }
  header('Location: http://apps.facebook.com/[your_app_canvas_name]');
?>
```

How it works...

In the main application file (`index.php`), we have created a form, which takes the user's favorite movie as the input, as shown in the following screenshot:

The important thing to note here is that in the `action` tag, we need to specify the URL which will process the data and save it on our server. If we use Facebook's application URL, we will not get the form data. Here, `target` is again set to `_top` so that when we click on it, the iFrame's parent changes and it gets redirected to: `http://www.example.com/my_app/process_form.php`.

`process_form.php` simply processes the form data and redirects the user to the application URL, `http://apps.facebook.com/[your_app_canvas_name]`.

Dynamically resizing an iFrame Facebook application

In an application, which runs in an iFrame inside Facebook, horizontal and vertical scroll bars may appear in the iFrame if the content exceeds a predefined height and width of the canvas. Fortunately, Facebook provides a ready to use method to dynamically resize an iFrame inside it.

Getting ready

You should have registered your Facebook application and created `config.php`.

How to do it...

Open the main file (`index.php`) of your application and add the following code to it:

```php
<?php
  require_once 'config.php';
?>
<div id="fb-root"></div>
<script>
  window.fbAsyncInit = function() {
    FB.Canvas.setAutoResize();
  };
```

```
(function() {
  var e = document.createElement('script'); e.async = true;
  e.src = document.location.protocol +
    '//connect.facebook.net/en_US/all.js';
  document.getElementById('fb-root').appendChild(e);
}());
</script>
```

Put your application's content inside a `div` named `fb-root` and save the file. Now, when you will load your application, it will have no scrollbars inside the iFrame.

If our content contains a collage of profile pictures of the current user's friends and has not been resized, then it will look as shown in the following screenshot:

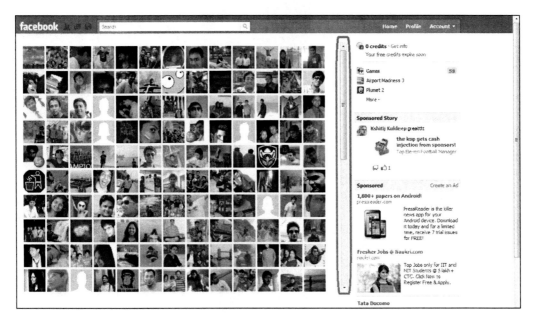

Here, the highlighted region shows the scrollbar inside the iFrame, which we want to remove. After, using the resize code, this is how the above content will appear:

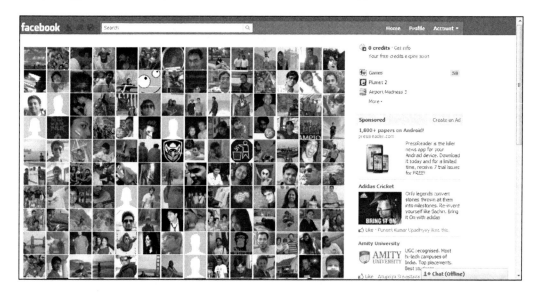

How it works...

First, we load the **JavaScript SDK** using the standard `<script>` element. Moreover, the most efficient way to load the SDK in an application is to load it asynchronously so that it does not block loading of other elements of the application's page. This is particularly important to ensure fast page loads for users and SEO robots/spiders. Also, we have specified a `<div>` element named `fb-root` within the document. It is important to include a `div` with this name; otherwise the JavaScript SDK will not load and report an error.

In the previous code snippet, the function assigned to `window.fbAsyncInit` is run as soon as the Facebook JS SDK is loaded. The function contains a line:

```
FB.Canvas.setAutoResize();
```

This starts a timer, which keeps on resizing the iFrame every few milliseconds. The default duration is 100 milliseconds.

There's more...

By default, the timer will keep on running after regular intervals and will keep on resizing the iFrame. If we want to stop this timer, we can do so by passing `false` as an argument as shown:

```
FB.Canvas.setAutoResize(false);
```

If we want to change the default interval (100 ms), we can do so by passing an integer as a parameter to this function as shown:

```
FB.Canvas.setAutoResize(200);
```

 If there is only one parameter and it is a number, it is assumed to be the interval.

Parameters

The parameters of `FB.Canvas.setAutosize()` have been outlined in the following table:

Name	Type	Description
onOroff	Boolean	Turn timer on or off. Default is on.
Interval	Integer	Set the time interval of the timer. Default is 100 ms.

Determining whether a Facebook page has been liked by a user

If your Facebook application supports its own custom tab, then it becomes imperative to know whether the user, who opens the tab, is already a fan of your page or not. And if not, then we can display different content to him/her suggesting doing so. This can tremendously help an application to gain popularity.

Getting ready

You should have defined your **Page Tabs** settings present under the **On Facebook** tab on the application settings page. Here, we have used a file named `tab.php` to display the tab content. Also, you should have created `config.php`.

How to do it...

The following steps will demonstrate how to determine if a Facebook page has been liked:

1. Open `tab.php` and add the following PHP code to it:
   ```php
   <?php
     Include config.php:
     require_once 'config.php';
   ```

2. Retrieve and decode the `signed_request` parameter:
   ```php
   $decodedSignedRequest = $faccbook ->getSignedRequest();
   ```

3. Check if the page has been liked by the user:

```
if ($decodedSignedRequest['page']['liked'] == 1){
  echo "User like this page";
}
else{
  echo "No, User doesn't like this page";
}
?>
```

4. Save and open your custom tab inside a Facebook page. A screenshot is shown next:

How it works...

Whenever a user opens our custom tab, Facebook sends us the `signed_request` parameter, which contains a sub parameter called `page`. We can use this parameter to determine whether the user is a fan of our page/application or not. We don't need to have any permission from the user for accessing this parameter. Even if the user is using our tab for the first time, Facebook sends us this parameter with limited information.

We use the inbuilt `getSignedRequest()` of the **Facebook** class to retrieve and decode the `signed_request` parameter. It is then stored in the PHP array named `$decodedSignedRequest`. This `$decodedSignedRequest` array contains a sub array with the `key` page. Next, we check for an element named `liked` in this sub array. If it is set to 1, then it means that the current user is a fan of our page. This has been done by the following code:

```
if ($decodedSignedRequest['page']['liked'] == 1){
    echo "User like this page";
}
else{
    echo "No, User doesn't like this page";
}
```

Finally, we display an appropriate message depending on whether the user has liked the page or not. In the actual scenario, we can display different content to users using the above code.

There's more...

The same tab of a Facebook application can be used on multiple Facebook pages.

Customizing an application's tab content based on Facebook page

We can customize the content of an application's tab based on which Facebook page it has been added to. For this, we need to retrieve the page ID of the current Facebook page. This can be done by the following code:

```php
<?php
  require_once 'config.php';
  $decodedSignedRequest = $facebook->getSignedRequest();
  print_r($decodedSignedRequest)
  if ($decodedSignedRequest['page']['id'] == 1234){
    echo "Content for a specific Facebook page";
  }
  else{
    echo "Content for other Facebook pages";
  }
?>
```

2
Be a part of Social Graph

In this chapter, we will cover:

- ▸ Retrieving a user's information
- ▸ Liking a post
- ▸ Commenting on a given post
- ▸ Setting a status message
- ▸ Deleting a picture, post, or comment of a user
- ▸ Retrieving a current user's friendlist
- ▸ Creating a post on the wall of a user's friend
- ▸ Posting a picture to a specific album of the user
- ▸ Retrieving the names of the user's friends who have liked a particular status message
- ▸ Creating an event
- ▸ Paging through a user's friends
- ▸ Searching through a user's feed
- ▸ Tagging users in a picture
- ▸ Adding a subscription for real time updates related to a user object
- ▸ Creating a callback for handling real time updates
- ▸ Deleting subscriptions

Introduction

Facebook provides its own API for application developers. Facebook API is ever changing and has a rapid pace of development. Facebook has changed its core development platform and now it uses Graph API for reading and writing data.

Facebook Graph API

Facebook introduced the Graph API to make application development simpler and easier for its developers. Facebook Graph API is all about objects and connections. The whole concept of Open Graph is to put people in the centre of the web and help establish meaningful connections between them and retrieve information from this setup in an easy manner.

In Facebook Graph API, every object has a unique ID and a lot of connections which developers can utilize to build successful web applications. The thing that makes Facebook Graph API so simple and easy is the fact that it provides access to Facebook objects like events, people, and photos through a consistent and uniform URL. Every object can be accessed using the URL—`https://graph.facebook.com/ID`, while for connections we have `https://graph.facebook.com/ID/CONNECTION_TYPE`.

Facebook Graph API also has a special identifier named as `me`, which refers to the current user. A call to the Graph API at `https://graph.facebook.com/me` would return all the information about the current user which is publicly accessible. The authentication is based on the OAuth 2.0 protocol and makes it simple to connect to Facebook in order to access user information.

Facebook Graph API supports a variety of features. For example:

- Authorization
- Reading
- Searching
- Publishing
- Deleting
- Analytics

Prerequisites for this chapter

This section will introduce you to the basic configuration that you must do before starting with the recipes, discussed in this chapter. There are two main prerequisites that need to be fulfilled before implementing the recipes.

First, you need to create a `config.php`, and add the following code to it:

```php
<?php
  require_once 'facebook.php';
  /** Create our Application instance. */
  $facebook = new Facebook(array(
    'appId' => 'your_application_id',
    'secret' => 'your_application_secret_key',
    'cookie' => true,
  ));
```

Here, `facebook.php` is the file containing `Facebook` class and can be downloaded from GitHub. We have created an object, `$facebook`, of this class and will use it in our `index.php`. You need to provide your application ID and secret key here. For more information, read the first chapter.

Next, create a file named `index.php` and add the following code to it:

```php
<?php
```

Include the configuration file:

```php
require_once 'config.php';
```

Get the current user's session using the `getSession()` function and perform session validation:

```php
$session = $facebook->getSession();
$me = null;
if ($session) {
  try {
    $me = $facebook->api('/me');   /*Check whether the current
            session is valid by retrieving user information.*/
  } catch (Exception $e) {}
}
/* If the current session is invalid or user has not authorized
    the application then redirect to a authorization URL.*/
```

Redirect the user to the authorization URL if session is not valid:

```php
if (!($me))
  {
  echo '<script>
    top.location.href="'.$facebook->getLoginUrl
    (array('req_perms' => 'publish_stream',
    'next' => 'http://apps.facebook.com/[your_app_url]
    /',)).'";
```

```
      </script>';
      exit;
    }
  ?>
```

Here, we first retrieve a valid session for a user by calling the `$facebook->getSession()` function and storing the response in `$session` variable. Next, we try to retrieve the basic information of the current user by posting a GET request to `https://graph.facebook.com/me`. We use the `$facebook->api()` function to do so. `https://graph.facebook.com` is automatically prefixed by the `api()` function to its first argument, that is why we have passed `/me` as its first argument. The returned data is stored in the `$me` variable.

Finally, we check whether `$me` variable is null or not. If it is null, then we need to redirect the user to the authorization URL in order to get appropriate permission(s) and a valid session token for the user. To redirect the user, we use JavaScript code. We set `top.location.href` to the URL where we want to redirect the user. This URL is given by the function `$facebook->getLoginUrl()`. Also, this function takes array as its argument. The index `req_perms` is used to request from the user specific permissions. Multiple permissions can be requested by separating them a comma. Additionally, the `next` index specifies where the user will be redirected after successful authorization and session generation.

Once you have created these two files, you can use them directly in the subsequent recipes.

Retrieving a user's information

Facebook allows us to retrieve the profile information of a user directly by using its Graph API. However, by default, Facebook limits the extraction to only those fields which are public. For all the other fields, we need to ask for some extended permissions from the user.

Getting ready

If we want to access the profile information of the user, then we need to make sure that his/her session is a valid and authenticated one and has not expired. To ensure this, we should have set up `config.php` and `index.php` as explained in the beginning of the chapter.

How to do it...

The following steps will show how to retrieve a user's information:

1. Open `index.php` and append the following code to the end of the file:

```
<html>
  <body>
    <?php
      $me = $facebook->api('/me');
      print_r($me);
```

```
        ?>
      </body>
    </html>
```

2. A successful execution of this code will return a JSON object which is converted to PHP array by the `api()` function with all the public details of the current logged-in user. This is how an output may look like:

```
Array
(
    [id] => 786017563
    [name] => Shashwat Srivastava
    [first_name] => Shashwat
    [last_name] => Srivastava
    [link] => http://www.facebook.com/shashwat12
    [username] => shashwat12
    [gender] => male
    [locale] => en_US
)
```

How it works...

Facebook Graph API allows us to access its objects through a uniform URL `https://graph.facebook.com/[object_id]`. To retrieve the profile information of the current logged-in user, we need to query the user object of the Graph API as explained as follows:

► In `$me = $facebook->api('/me')`, we make a call to the Graph API by using the `api()` function.

► It makes a GET request to `https://graph.facebook.com/me` to retrieve the required information. The argument that is passed in the `api()` function gets concatenated to `https://graph.facebook.com`.

► The `/me` gets automatically appended and the URL, to which the GET request is made, becomes `https://graph.facebook.com/me`.

 The me in Facebook terminology refers to the current authenticated user.

► The `api()` function will return all the profile information of the logged-in user and will store it in the `$me` variable.

There's more...

The Facebook objects are inter-connected to each other by **connections**. With every Graph API object you will have some connections. Connections are also objects that are somehow related to the current object under introspection. It is just a bridge between one object and another and tells us how any two given objects are related to each other.

 To retrieve all objects which are related to an object with a particular connection, we just need to make a GET request to the following URL—`https://graph.faceboook.com/[object_id]/[connection_type]`.

For example, if you want to get the books listed on the user's profile, you need to make a GET request to the following URL—`https://graph.facebook.com/me/books`. However, we should also keep in mind that in order to retrieve connected objects, we require appropriate **permissions**. In this case, we need to have the `user_likes` or `friends_likes` permission for retrieving the list.

Liking a post

Facebook Graph API allows us to programmatically like any given post item for a particular user. This enables us to take a decision on behalf of the user, thereby providing a better user experience.

Getting ready

Before we begin, you should have registered your application and set up `config.php`. You should know the ID of the post item that you want to like on behalf of the user. Also, you need to make sure that the user has given the **publish_stream** permission to the application.

How to do it...

In order to easily demonstrate the task, we will take up the most recent item from the current user's feed and like it. For a better understanding, the code to retrieve the ID of the first feed item is shown in a separate function `getFirstPostId()` in the following code snippet:

1. Open `index.php` and append the following lines to the already existing code:
   ```php
   <?php
   ```

2. Get the ID of the first post in the user's feed:
   ```php
   function getFirstPostId($feeds) {
     return $feeds['data'][0]['id'];
   ```

```
}
//The id of the post to like
$id = getFirstPostId($facebook->api('/me/posts'));
```

3. Make a **POST request** using the `api()` function:

```
$like_id = $facebook->api('/'.$id.'/likes', 'POST');
?>
```

4. Upload this edited file to the server in the directory where you have hosted your Facebook application.

5. Now go to the following URL—`http://apps.facebook.com/[your_canvas_name]/`. The first post of your feed will be automatically liked by you as shown in the following screenshot:

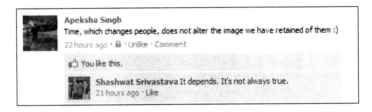

How it works...

In `index.php`, we have first defined a function named `getFirstPostId()`. As its name suggests, it returns the ID of the post item from the user's feed. The user's feed is retrieved by making a GET request to `https//graph.facebook.com/me/posts`. Once we have the post ID, we make a POST request to the following URL—`https://graph.facebook.com/[post_id]/likes`. To do so, we use the `api()` function of the `Facebook` class.

Once the Facebook successfully executes the like request, it returns the ID of the newly created like object back to us, which we can store in our database for future reference. Here, this newly generated object's ID is stored in the variable `$like_id`.

There's more...

If we are using our Facebook application to like a particular object, then a possibility to unlike it at a later stage is always there. For this, we should store the returned like ID in our database. This will enable us to provide our users with the option to "dislike" the already liked posts if they are not happy with it or they change their mind.

Deleting a like

To delete a particular like, we need to issue a DELETE request to the URL of the form—`https://graph.facebook.com/[LIKE_ID]`, where `[LIKE_ID]` is the ID of the like that has to be deleted. You can delete a like as shown in the following code snippet:

```
$facebook->api('/'.$id, 'DELETE');
/* $id is the id of the like to be disliked */
```

Commenting on a given post

In Facebook, comments make it easier for us to communicate, share, and discuss ideas with our friends. It allows us to post our opinions in the form of comments on every post of our friends.

Getting ready

You should have set up `config.php` and `index.php` as explained in the beginning of the chapter. The user must have granted **publish_stream** permission to your application. Also, you should know the ID of the post on which you want to comment.

How to do it...

The following steps will demonstrate how to add a comment

1. Create a new file named `action_comment.php` and add the following code to it:

    ```
    <?php
    ```

2. Include the configuration file:

    ```
    require_once 'config.php';
    ```

3. Enter the Post ID on which you want to comment on:

    ```
    $post_id='[your_post_id]';
    ```

4. Get the comment from POST array:

    ```
    $message = $_POST['message']);
    ```

5. Post the message by using the `api()` function:

    ```
    $comment_id = $facebook->api('/'.$post_id.'/comments','POST',
                    array('message' => $message,));
    ?>
    ```

6. Now append the following code in the main application file (`index.php`). We will use AJAX to post to `action_comment.php` for creating a new comment:

```
<script type="text/javascript"
```

7. Include JQuery library using Google CDN:

```
    src="https://ajax.googleapis.com/ajax/libs/jquery/
        1.5.0/jquery.min.js"></script>
```

8. Create a text area and button to get the comment:

```
<textarea id="txtcomment">the comment to be posted</textarea>
<br />
<input type="button" id="comment" value="click to post comment" />
<br />

<script type="text/javascript">
```

9. Use the `ready()` function to add the jQuery event:

```
  $(document).ready(function() {

    $('#comment').click(function() {
      $.post("action_comment.php",
        {message:$('#txtcomment').val()});
    });

  });
</script>
```

10. Now when you will run `index.php`, you will see a textbox as shown in the following screenshot:

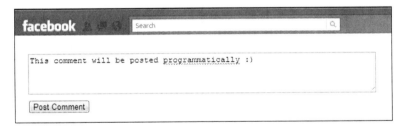

11. And once you have clicked on the **Post Comment** button, the comment will be successfully published on the specified post.

How it works...

In order to post a comment on a particular post, we need to make a POST request to the URL of the form—`https://graph.facebook.com/[POST_ID]/comments`, where `[POST_ID]` is the ID of the post on which we want to comment. This post request should include `message` as a query parameter. The value of the `message` parameter is the comment which we want to make on the post.

The `index.php` has a textbox and button with IDs `txtcomment` and `comment` respectively. We use jQuery to bind the click event of the button. When a user clicks on this button, after typing in his comment in the textbox, we make an AJAX request to `action_comment.php`. We post the text typed by the user in the textbox with the help of the `$.post()` function. The first argument of the function is the name of the file to which the request has to be made and the second argument is the data to be posted in the JSON format. We retrieve the text typed by the user by using the code—`$('#txtcomment').val()` and then we post it to `action_comment.php`.

In `action_comment.php`, this posted message is retreived as as `$_POST['message']`. Here `$post_id` is the ID of the post on which we want to comment. Next, we use `api()` of the `Facebook` class to make a POST request along with the user's message. This finally posts the comment.

There's more...

When a comment is successfully posted, the ID of the newly created comment is returned. In the above code, this ID is stored in `$comment_id`. We can store this comment ID in a database for future reference.

Deleting a comment

We can delete a comment on a particular post on behalf of the user. We should know the ID of the comment which we want to delete. Once we know this, we can make a `DELETE` request as shown in the following code snippet:

```
$delete = $facebook->api('/'.$comment_id.'', 'DELETE');
/* The comment will be deleted.*/
```

If the comment is deleted successfully, then 1 will be returned as the response from the server and stored in `$delete`.

Setting status message

Facebook Graph API enables us to set a new status update for the user on his/her behalf. This status update is immediately reflected in the user's feed, thereby improving the popularity of our application.

Getting ready

For setting a new status message, we should have the **publish_stream** permission. This extended permission can be requested from the user when he first visits the application. Also, you should have set up `config.php` and acquired a valid session for the current user.

How to do it...

The following steps will show how to set a status message:

1. Open `index.php` of the application and append the following code to it:

```
<html>
  <body>
    <?php
```

2. Store the status message in a variable:

```
$message = 'message we want to set as status update';
```

3. Post the status message by using the `api()` function:

```
$status_id = $facebook->api('/me/feed', 'POST',
              array('message' => $message));
    ?>
  </body>
</html>
```

4. Now, if you will run the Facebook application, you will see that the value of `$message` is set as the status message of the current user. The following screenshot explains what it will look like:

How it works...

First, we store the status message we want to set in the `$message` variable. Next, we set the status message by using the `api()` function of the Facebook class. The `api()` function takes the following three arguments:

▶ The first argument is concatenated to `https://graph.facebook.com` to form a complete URL to which a request has to be made. Here, our argument is `/me/feed` and it is appended to `https://graph.facebook.com`. So the complete URL becomes `https://graph.facebook.com/me/feed`.

▶ The second argument is a type of request that should be made. Here, `POST` is mentioned because we need to make a POST request to set a status message for the current user.

▶ The third argument is an array which contains the parameters that we want to set. These parameters are then appended to the URL formed as a result of the first argument. Here, the parameter `message` specifies the message that we want to set as the status of the user.

Once the status message is set successfully, the server returns the ID of the newly set status, and this is stored in `$status_id`.

There's more...

If we want to post something else, along with the status message, then we can do so by adding more parameters to the array, which is the third argument of the `api()` function. For example, if we want to display a link along with the status message, we need to add the following index into the array `'link' => 'http://link.to.something'`. Thus, the code will now become:

```
$status_id = $facebook->api('/me/feed ', 'POST ',
          array('message ' => 'message we want to post ',
          'link' => 'http://link.to.something'));
```

This will display the status message along with the link we have mentioned. For a complete list of arguments, visit this URL—`http://developers.facebook.com/docs/reference/api/post`.

Deleting a picture, post, or comment of a user

Sometimes we may want to delete a picture, post, or comment that has got posted by mistake or contains some unwanted content. Facebook Graph API allows this to be done programmatically.

Getting ready

You should have setup `config.php` and `index.php` as discussed in the beginning of the chapter. Also, you should know the ID of the object (picture, comment, and so on), which you want to delete.

How to do it...

The following steps will show how to delete content added by a user:

1. Open `index.php` and append the following code to the already existing code of the file:

```
<html>
  <body>
    <?php
```

2. Enter the object ID which you want to delete:

```
$id='[custom_object_id]';
```

3. Send the DELETE request using the `api()` function:

```
$delete = $facebook->api('/'.$id, 'DELETE');
?>
  </body>
</html>
```

How it works...

For deleting any post, we need to make a DELETE request to Facebook. Here, once we know the ID of the object which has to be deleted, we make a call to the URL of the form – `https://graph.facebook.com/[custom_object_id]` and issue a DELETE request. This has been done by passing them as parameters in the `facebook->api()` function through the following line of code:

```
$delete = $facebook->api('/'.$id, 'DELETE');
```

Replace `[custom_post_id]` with the ID of the post you want to delete.

Retrieving the current user's friendlist

Facebook allows its users to create and manage custom friendlists. This gives the users the option to classify their friends on some basis. We can create a friendlist of our choice and name it accordingly. For example, we can differentiate between our business and social contacts by creating two different friendlists for them. To get access to the friendlist of a user is in many ways important for an application. It allows us to publish and send notifications to only specific contacts of the user.

Getting ready

You should have set up `config.php` and `index.php` as explained in the beginning of the chapter. Moreover, the application must have requested **read_friendlists** permission from the user. Without this, the friendlist of the current user can't be retrieved.

How to do it...

Facebook Graph API provides us with a URL-based interface for retrieving information:

1. Open `index.php` and append the following PHP code:

   ```
   <?php
   ```

2. Access the user's friendlist using the `api()` function and print it:

   ```
   $friendlists = $facebook->api('/me/friendlists');
   print_r($friendlists);
   ?>
   ```

This will display all the friendlists of the current user in array format along with the list ID and name. For a user who has two friendlists, such as school friends and best buddies, the output could be something as follows:

```
Array ( [data] => Array ( [0] =>
    Array ( [id] => 10150102062889898
    [name] => school friends )
    [1] => Array ( [id] =>
      10150101962859898
      [name] => best buddies )
    )
  )
```

We can use the friendlist ID from the above array to retrieve all the friends belonging to a particular friendlist.

How it works...

`$facebook` is an object of the `Facebook` class declared in `config.php`. We use the `api()` to make a GET request to the URL—`https://graph.facebook.com/me/friendlists` and we store the returned data in the variable named `$friendlists`. The returned data from the server is in JSON format, which is automatically converted to PHP array by the `api()` function. Thus, `$friendlists` will now contain all the friendlists, along with their IDs and names, of the current user.

There's more...

Apart from getting the friendlist of the current user, we may at times want to perform some other operations on friendlists, such as getting its members, deleting it, and so on. We will show you how to perform some of these operations now.

Getting a friendlist's members

If we know the friendlist's name, then we can easily get its corresponding ID from the `$friendlists` PHP array. Once we know the ID of the friendlist, it becomes very easy to get its members. To get the members of a particular friendlist, copy the following code in `index.php` and run it:

```php
<?php
  $friendlist_id = 'xyz'; //Your friendlist id
  $friendlist = $facebook->api('/' . $friendlist_id.
    '/members');
  print_r($friendlist);
?>
```

We will have to replace `friendlist_id` with a valid friendlist ID. Here, `$friendlist` is a PHP array and it contains the list of all members.

Creating a new friendlist

We need to have `manage_friendlists` permission for creating a new friendlist. We can create a new friendlist by adding the following snippets of code:

```php
<?php
  $create = $facebook->api
  ('/me/friendlists?name=childhoodfriends', 'POST');
?>
```

Here, we have created a new friendlist with the name `childhoodfriends`. For this, we issue a POST method to the following URL—`https://graph.facebook.com/[User ID]/frien dlists?name=[FriendListName]`.

Adding a new member to a friendlist

To add members to a friendlist, we need to issue a POST request to the following URL—`https://graph.facebook.com/[FriendList_ID]/members/[USER_ID]`. See the following code:

```php
<?php
  $add = $facebook->api('/me/'.$friendlist_id.
    '/members/'.$user_id, 'POST');
?>
```

Deleting a friendlist

To delete a friendlist, all that needs to be done is to issue a DELETE request to the URL `https://graph.facebook.com/[FriendList_ID]`. The following code will let you do so:

```php
<?php
  $delete = $facebook->api('/me/'.$friendlist_id, 'DELETE');
?>
```

Again, we need to make sure that we have the **manage_friendlists** permission.

Creating a post on the wall of a user's friend

Many a time, we need to post on the wall of a user's friend to either update them with the latest development or inform them about what their other friends have been doing. For example, in a quiz application, we may need to tell the friends what the user has answered about them. The best way to go about this is to post on their wall. This, in turn, gets reflected in their feed, thereby increasing the popularity of the application.

Getting ready

To create a post on the wall of a user's friend, first we need to make sure that our application has acquired **publish_stream** permission from the current user. Once this permission is given by the user, then we can post on the wall of any user's friend. The important thing to note here is that it is not necessary that the user's friend may have given us the required permission or even added our application. When a user gives an application **publish_stream** permission, it means it is authorizing the application to make a post on his/her friend's walls too.

Additionally, you must have created `index.php` and `config.php` as explained in the section at the beginning of this chapter.

How to do it...

The following steps will demonstrate how to create a poste on a friend's wall:

1. Open `index.php` and append the following code to the already existing content:

```
<html>
  <body>
    <?php
```

2. Create a function to get the Friend ID:

```
function getFriendId($name, $friends) {
  foreach($friends['data'] as $friend) {
    if(strcasecmp($name,$friend['name'])==0)
      return $friend['id'];
  }
  return NULL;
}
```

3. Make a call to the friend's connection object using the `api()` function:

```
$friends = $facebook->api('/me/friends');
```

4. Make a call to the `getFriendId()` function and store the friend's ID:

```
$id = getFriendId('[Friend_Name]',$friends);
```

5. Post the message using the `api()` function:

```
$post_id = $facebook->api('/'.$id.'/feed', 'POST',
  array('message' => 'This post has been made on a
    friend\'s wall',));
  ?>
  </body>
</html>
```

6. If we will now execute `index.php`, then a message will be posted on the wall of the current user's friend, whose name is `[Friend_Name]`. The following screenshot shows what the message on a friend's wall looks like:

How it works...

For demonstration purposes, we have created a function named `getFriendId()` which gives the ID of a user corresponding to his/her name from the list of the current user's friends. Initially, we get this list of friends by calling the `$facebook->api()` function. It gets the list of the current user's friends from this URL—`https://graph.facebook.com/me/friends`. We save the response in `$friends`, which is a PHP array.

Then, we call the `getFriendId()` function and retrieve the ID of the user with the name `[Friend_Name]`. Once we have the ID of the user's friend, we can post to his/her wall by using the `$facebook->api()` function, which takes in three parameters. The first is the URL to which we make a request; second is the type of the request and third is an array which contains certain properties in the index such as value format. Here, we make a POST request to the feed of the user's friend. The value of the `message` array index becomes the actual content which is posted on the wall of the user's friend.

There's more...

Although the earlier mentioned code snippet will post on to a user's wall, in practice we may want to perform this post action dynamically, that is, when a user performs some action, then as a result we post to his/her friend's wall. To do so, we place the PHP post code in a separate file named `action_post.php`; when we want to make a POST request on the wall of the user's friend, as a result of some action taken by him/her, then we issue an AJAX call through jQuery to `action_post.php`:

1. Add the following lines of code to `action_post.php`:

   ```php
   <?php
     //Code for action_post.php
   ```

2. Include the configuration file:

   ```php
   require_once('config.php');
   ```

3. Check if POST data is available, and then post the message using the `api()` function:

   ```php
   if($_POST['message']) {
     $status = $facebook->api('/me/feed', 'POST',
     array('message' => $_POST['message'],));
   }
   ?>
   ```

4. Next, add the following code to `index.php` after the code given in the beginning of the chapter:

   ```html
   <html>
     <head>
       <script type="text/javascript"
   ```

5. Include the jQuery library using the Google CDN:

   ```
           src="https://ajax.googleapis.com/ajax/libs/jquery/
               1.5.0/jquery.min.js"></script>
   ```

6. Use the `ready()` function to add the jQuery click event:

   ```javascript
       <script type="text/javascript">
         $(document).ready(function() {
   ```

```
      $('#post').click(function() {
        $.post("action_post.php",
          {message: "Facebooking can be fun! :-)"});
      });
    });
  </script>
</head>
<body>
```

7. Create a div on which we will use jQuery's `click()` event:

    ```
    <div id='post'>Post something on my friend's wall!</div>
    </body>
    </html>
    ```

In `index.php`, we have used jQuery's `click()` event for div, which has `post` ID , to make an AJAX call to `action_post.php`. This call is made by the `$.post()` function. The first argument is the URL to which the request is made and the second argument is the data which is posted. This data is in JSON format.

Posting a picture to a specific album of the user

Using Facebook Graph API, we can programmatically post a picture to any album of the user. We can use this to create images and post them on behalf of the user.

Getting ready

You should have the album ID to which you want to post the picture. Additionally, you must have created `config.php` and `index.php` as explained in the beginning of this chapter. Also, the application needs to have the **publish_stream** permission for posting the picture.

How to do it...

We can upload a picture to an album by following these steps:

1. Create a new file and name it as `action_postpic.php`. Add the code given below to this file:

    ```
    <?php
    ```

2. Include the configuration file:

    ```
    require_once 'config.php';
    ```

3. Use the `realpath()` function to return the canonicalized absolute pathname of the location of the picture:

```
$pic = realpath("/home/server_name/path/to/picture.jpg");
```

4. Enter the album ID:

```
$album_id='[custom_album_id]';
```

5. Enable the file upload to the Facebook server using the `setFileUploadSupport()` function:

```
$facebook->setFileUploadSupport("http://" .
  $_SERVER['SERVER_NAME']);
```

6. Get the message to be posted along with the picture and post the picture by using the `api()` function:

```
$message = ($_POST['message'])?$_POST['message'] :
  'This picture looks awesome';
$pic_id = $facebook->api('/'.$album_id.'/photos', 'POST',
  array('message' => $message ,'source' => '@' . $pic,));
?>
```

7. Next, we append the following code to our main application file (`index.php`), which will use jQuery to call `action_postpic.php`:

```
<!doctype html>
```

8. Extend the current XML notations to FBML to enable Facebook tags to be used in the application:

```
<html xmlns:fb="http://www.facebook.com/2008/fbml">
  <head>
    <script type="text/javascript"
```

9. Include jQuery library using the Google CDN:

```
          src="https://ajax.googleapis.com/ajax/libs/jquery/
              1.5.0/jquery.min.js"></script>
  </head>
  <body>
```

10. Create a text area for the picture description and a button to post the picture:

```
      <textarea id="pictext">description of the pic</textarea>
      <br />
      <input type="button" id="postpic" value="Post Picture" />
      <br />
      <script type="text/javascript">
```

11. Use the `ready()` function to add the jQuery click event:

```
$(document).ready(function() {
  $('#postpic').click(function() {
    $.post("action_postpic.php",
    {message: $('#pictext').val()});
  });
});
</script>
</body>
</html>
```

12. Now, upload both the files to the server. Once we run `index.php`, a textbox asking for the image description will get displayed as shown in the following screenshot:

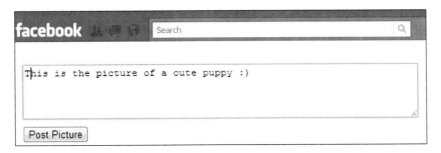

If a user clicks on the **Post Picture** button, then the picture, which is present at `home/server_name/path/to/picture.jpg` on the server, will be posted to the user's album.

The picture will be published in the album with ID `[custom_album_id]`. The following screenshot shows of a sample picture after it has been published:

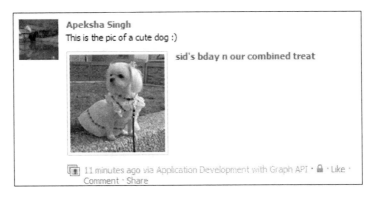

If you are not dynamically creating the picture, which has to be posted to Facebook for the user, then you need to employ a suitable picture upload mechanism in order to upload pictures from the user's local computer to your server. Only then you will be able to post that picture to Facebook on behalf of the user.

How it works...

In `index.php`, we have a text area with `pictext` ID, which gives the user an option to provide the description of the picture being uploaded. This text will appear along with the picture when it gets posted.

Next, we use jQuery to bind a function to the `click` event of the `postpic` button. We use the `$.post()` function to make a `POST` request to `action_postpic.php`. Here, we have passed two arguments to the `$.post()` function. The first one specifies the URL to which the request is made and the second one specifies the JSON data to be posted. The JSON data contains an index named `message`. Its value is the description of the picture, which will be posted, and will appear along with it.

Now, let us have as look as how the picture gets posted to an existing album. This has been done in `action_postpic.php`. First, we need to specify the path of the image which we want to post. Usually, this path would be of our server where the picture resides. Next, we have the following line of code:

```
$pic = realpath("/home/server_name/path/to/picture.jpg ");
```

This `realpath()` function removes all symbolic links (such as `'/./'`, `'/../'`, and extra `'/'`) and returns the absolute pathname which is stored in `$pic`. Once we have the picture path, the next step is to upload this picture to Facebook. For this, we need to enable the file upload, which is disabled by default. This is done by this line of code:

```
$facebook->setFileUploadSupport("http://" . $_SERVER
    ['SERVER_NAME']);
```

The `setFileUploadSupport` actually takes in the server name as the parameter and makes Facebook ready to allow file uploads.

Now, the final step is to make a POST request through Facebook Graph API. For posting a picture to an existing album, we need to make a call with the POST method to the following URL type—`http://graph.facebook.com/ALBUM_ID/photos`. Assuming that we already know the album ID where we want the picture to be uploaded to, we make a POST request with the following line of code:

```
$pic_id = $facebook->api('/'.$album_id.'/photos', 'POST',
    array('message' => $message ,'source' => '@' . $pic,));
```

Here, we use the `$facebook->api()` function to post picture to the Facebook . It has the following three arguments:

- The first argument is the URL to which the POST request has to be made. `https://graph.facebook.com` is automatically prefixed to this argument.

- The second argument is the type of request to make. Here, we need to make the POST type request.

- The third request is an array which passes additional options. Here the array has two indexes—`message` and `source`. The value of the message becomes the picture description after it has been posted. The source contains the picture that has to be uploaded or posted. An important thing to note here is that @ before the path of the image. This is here to indicate that we want to post the **"contents"** of the file and not pass the file name as a string to the source.

After the picture is successfully posted, `$pic_id` contains the ID of the newly created picture. We can save this picture ID along with the user ID in our database for future reference.

There's more...

In case we do not know any album ID and still we want to upload the picture, then we can do so by posting the picture to `https://graph.facebook.com/me/photos`. Facebook automatically creates a new album with your application name and uploads the picture there. To do so, you need to change only the following portion of the code in `action_postpic.php`:

```
$pic_id = $facebook->api('/me/photos', 'POST',
   array('message' => $message ,'source' => '@' . $pic,));
```

The rest of the code will remain the same.

Retrieving the names of the user's friends who have liked a particular status message

Sometimes we may want to retrieve details of the people who have liked a particular status of a user. This can be used to get the top followers of a user based on these interactions.

Getting ready

We should have created `config.php` and `index.php` as explained in the beginning of this chapter. Also, we need to have the ID of the status message on which we want to perform this operation.

The following steps will retreive the names of the user's friends who have liked a particular status message:

1. To retrieve the likes of a particular status message, we need to add the following code to the already existing code in `index.php`, which has been discussed in the beginning of the chapter:

```html
<html>
  <body>
    <?php
```

2. Enter the status message ID and get the likes using the `api()` function:

```php
$status_id='[custom_status_id]'; //Your status id here
$get_likes = $facebook->api('/' . $status_id . '/likes');
```

3. Print the name of the users who have liked the status message:

```php
foreach ($get_likes['data'] as $user) {
  echo $user['name'] . '<br />';
}
?>
  </body>
</html>
```

4. Now, if you will run `index.php` it will list the names of all the users who have liked the status message whose ID is `[custom_status_id]` and will look something similar to the following screenshot:

How it works...

To retrieve the names of the users who have liked a particular status, we have used the `api()` function of the Facebook Graph API. Here, we have made a GET request to `https://graph.facebook.com/STATUS_ID/likes` through the `$facebook->api()` function. Facebook returns a JSON array containing a list of users who have liked that particular status message along with their respective user ID and name. This is automatically converted to a corresponding PHP array by the `api()` function and stored in `$get_likes`.

Next, we have used a `foreach` loop of PHP to print the names of the users who have liked that particular status message. Once we have the user names along with IDs, we can use this data to determine the people who are most involved with the user.

Creating an event

Facebook events allow us to let other people know about the upcoming events. These can be used to organize gatherings, parties with your friends, send an invite for an occasion, and make last minute plans. We can create an event, attend a previously created event, or decline the invitation. Using Facebook Graph API, we can easily create new events through our application for the user.

Getting ready

Creation of an event requires the **create_event** permission. Also, you should have created `index.php` and `config.php` as explained in the beginning of this chapter.

How to do it...

The following steps will show how to create an event:

1. Open `index.php` and append the following code to the file:

```
<html>
  <body>
    <?php
```

2. Post the event information using the `api()` function:

```
$event = $facebook->api('/me/events', 'POST',
  array('name' => 'This is a new event',
  'start_time' => '2011-04-01T14:00:00+0000',
  'end_time' => '2011-04-02T14:00:00+0000'));
?>
  </body>
</html>
```

3. Now run `index.php`. The event with the specified date, `start_time`, and `end_time` will be created. A sample screenshot is as follows:

An important thing to note here is that the event's `start_time` and `end_time` should be in ISO-8601 formatted date/time or UNIX timestamp. Moreover, if it contains a time zone, which is not recommended, it is converted to Pacific Time before being stored and displayed.

How it works...

To create a new event, we have to use the `$facebook->api()` function. It takes in the following three parameters:

▸ The first is the URL to which the request has to be made. For creation of an event, we need to make a POST request to the connection object `/me/events`. `https://graph.facebook.com` automatically gets prefixed to this, so the complete URL becomes—`https://graph.facebook.com/me/events`.

▸ The second is the type of request we want to make, which in our case is the POST request.

▸ The third is an array in which we pass the additional properties such as details of the event, its start time, and end time. `name` field is used to specify the title of the event while the `start_time` and `end_time` refer to the respective times when the event will start and end.

More parameters can also be added to the array to specify additional information about the event such as `location`, `venue`, and so on. A complete list of such parameters can be viewed from the **events** table provided at `http://developers.facebook.com/docs/reference/api/event/`.

An important thing to note here is that in the array where we pass information of the event, at least two parameters, that is, event's title and `start_time` are necessary. If we remove any of these, then the event will not get created.

There's more...

Apart from creating an event, we may at times want to perform some other operations on the event object, such as deleting it. The process to delete an already created event programmatically is explained in the next section.

Deleting an event

To delete an event, all that needs to be done is to issue a DELETE request to the URL of the form—`https://graph.facebook.com/`[Event_ID]. This is how it would be done:

```php
<?php
  $event_id = '[event_id_to_be_deleted]';
  $delete = $facebook->api('/me/'.$event_id, 'DELETE');
?>
```

Moreover, a Facebook event object has a lot of connection objects associated with it. Using these objects we can easily know the statistics of the event created by us, such as the number of people attending, event's profile picture, and so on.

Paging through a user's friends

For certain Facebook applications, paging through data is a very important concept and comes in a lot handier than other features. For example, if we have an application where we require only a certain number of names of the user's friends to get displayed at a time, then we need to have a method to access the next page and set limits to the number of data objects that can be displayed at a time. This is when paging comes into picture.

Getting ready

You should have created `index.php` and `config.php` as explained in the beginning of this chapter.

How to do it...

The following steps will demonstrate paging through a user's friends:

1. Create a new file and name it as `action_paging.php` and save it inside the Facebook application directory. Next copy the following code in it:

    ```php
    <?php
    ```

2. Include the configuration file:

    ```php
    require_once('config.php');
    ```

3. Get the offset value and set the limit of the content to be displayed per page:

```
$offset = ($_GET['offset'])?$_GET['offset']:0;
$limit = 100;
$friends = $facebook->api('/me/friends?offset=' .
                          $offset . '&limit=' . $limit);
print_r($friends);
```

4. Create a hyperlink for the previous page:

```
if($friends['paging']['previous']) {
    echo '<br><a target="_top" href="http://apps.facebook.com/
        [your_application_url]/action_paging.php?offset=' .
        ($offset-$limit) . '">Previous</a>';
}
```

5. Create a hyperlink for the next page:

```
if($friends['paging']['next']) {
    echo ' <a target="_top" href="http://apps.facebook.com/
        [your_application_url]/action_paging.php?offset=
        '.($offset+$limit).'">Next</a>';
}
?>
```

6. Make sure to replace `[your_application_url]` with the appropriate canvas name of your application. To execute this code snippet, go to `http://apps.facebook.com/[your_application_url]/action.paging.php` after uploading the file to the server.

How it works...

While accessing Graph API data through the URL, we can add some additional parameters which can control the total size of the data on a single page and its chronological order. We have used the `limit` and `offset` parameters here to display certain numbers of user's friends at a time and page through the complete data set.

We pass the `offset` parameter through the GET request to the `action_paging.php`. If the `offset` parameter has not been set, then we initialize the `$offset` variable to 0. We do this by the following line of code:

```
$offset = ($_GET['offset'])?$_GET['offset']:0;
```

The `limit` parameter is used to limit the number of results displayed on a single page. So, with the combination of `offset` and `limit` parameters we can page through the complete data set displaying certain limited set of data at a time. To create the next and previous hyperlinks, we add or subtract the `$limit` variable to the `$offset` variable respectively and set this value as the `offset` parameter along with default URL. The following lines of code do this:

```
//Hyperlink code for Previous Link
echo '<br><a target="_top" href="http://apps.facebook.com/
  [your_application_url]/action_paging.php?offset=' .
  ($offset-$limit) . '">Previous</a>';
//Hyperlink code for Next Link
echo ' <a target="_top" href="http://apps.facebook.com/
  [your_application_url]/action_paging.php?offset=
  '.($offset+$limit).'">Next</a>';
```

There's more...

We can also use some other parameters apart from `offset` and `limit`. These are `until` and `since`. The value of these parameters should be a UNIX timestamp or any date accepted by `strtotime`. For example, check out the following URLs:

▶ `https://graph.facebook.com/search?until=yesterday&q=orange`

▶ `https://graph.facebook.com/search?until=1299070237&q=orange`

The first URL will retrieve all the results until yesterday and the second URL will fetch all the data prior to the UNIX timestamp 1299070237.

Searching through a user's feed

Facebook enables you to search through a user's feed. We can query for a particular term in the user's feed.

Getting ready

You should have created `index.php` and `config.php` as explained in the beginning of this chapter.

How to do it...

The following steps will demonstrate how to search through a user's feeds

1. Create a file named `action_search.php` and add the following code to it:

    ```
    <html>
      <body>
        <?php
    ```

2. Include the configuration file:

    ```
    require_once 'config.php';
    ```

3. Enter the search term and search through the user's feeds using the `api()` function:

```
$search_term = 'facebook';
$results = $facebook->api('me/feed?q='.$search_term);
```

4. Display the messages in which the search term is present:

```
foreach ($results['data'] as $result)
    echo $result['message'] . '<br>';
    ?>
  </body>
</html>
```

5. Upload the file to the application directory and go to `http://apps.facebook.com/[your_application_url]/action_search.php`. Here, replace `[your_application_url]` with the appropriate canvas name of your application.

How it works...

To search for a particular term in the user's feed, we make a GET request to the URL—`https://graph.facebook.com/me/feed` along with a query parameter `q`. This parameter is used to specify our search term. Facebook automatically searches the user's feed according to this term and returns the result in JSON format. In `action_search.php`, we have used the `api()` function to make the GET request after adding the `q` query parameter to the URL. This is done by the following line of code:

```
$results = $facebook->api('me/feed?q='.$search_term);
```

The data returned is stored in the `$results` array. Next, we print the individual messages from the returned array using the `foreach` loop.

Tagging users in a picture

Tagging is used to identify different people present in a picture. It is an effective way to notify and involve user's friends while posting a picture, thereby increasing popularity of your application. For applications such as Polaroid, Best Friends, and so on, it becomes imperative to tag user's friends in the picture.

Getting ready

You should have created `config.php` and `index.php` as explained in the beginning of this chapter. You should know the IDs of the users you want to tag in a picture. Generally, an application dynamically creates a picture and then tags various users in it. If it is not the case, then you need to implement a suitable upload mechanism and should know the path where you have uploaded and saved the picture, which you want to post on behalf of the current user. Additionally, you need **publish_stream** permission for successfully publishing the picture.

How to do it...

The following steps will demonstrate how to tag users in a picture:

1. Open `index.php` and append the following code to the bottom of the file:

    ```php
    <?php
    ```

2. Include the configuration file:

    ```php
    require_once 'config.php';
    ```

3. Use the `realpath()` function to return the canonicalized absolute pathname of the location of the picture:

    ```php
    $pic_path = realpath("/home/server_name/public_html/
                         path/to/picture.jpg");
    ```

4. Enter the album ID and enable the file upload to the Facebook server using `setFileUploadSupport()` function:

    ```php
    $album_id='[custom_album_id]';
    $facebook->setFileUploadSupport("http://" .
      $_SERVER['SERVER_NAME']);
    $message = 'This picture looks awesome!';
    ```

5. Mention the ID of the people to be tagged, and the location of the tag box, and store it in the `$tags` array:

    ```php
    $tags[] = array(
      'tag_uid' => $facebook->getUser(), /*Current user's id*/
        'x' => 0,'y' => 0
    );
    $tags[] = array(
      'tag_uid' => 7000678, /*Id of another user to be tagged */
        'x' => 0,'y' => 0
    );
    ```

6. Publish the picture along with the tagged users using the `api()` function:

    ```php
    $pic_id = $facebook->api('/'.$album_id.'/photos',
      'POST', array('message' => $message, 'source' =>
      '@' . $pic_path, 'tags' => $tags,));
    ?>
    ```

7. Now, if we run `index.php` we will find that the current user gets tagged in the picture. The following screenshot is a sample snapshot:

For tagging a particular user in a picture, first we need to successfully publish the picture from our server to the desired album where we want this picture to be. We first get the absolute path of the picture on our server by using the `realpath()` function. You should know the path where the picture is present on your server. Usually, you would be creating the picture dynamically by using PHP GD library. Next, we enable the upload and make the Facebook server ready to handle picture uploads. This has been done by the following line of code:

```
$facebook->setFileUploadSupport ("http://" .
    $_SERVER['SERVER_NAME']);
```

Now, for tagging the users, we create an array named `$tags`. This array contains sub-arrays where each array carries the tag information for a particular user. This sub-array consists of three indices as listed below:

- `tag_uid`: It represents the ID of the user whom we want to tag in the picture
- `x`: It represents the percentage from the left edge of the photo and decides the position of the tag box
- `y`: It represents the percentage from the top edge of the tag box and decides the position of the tag box

So the complete code will look as the following:

```
$tags[] = array('tag_uid' => $facebook->getUser(),
    'x' => 0,'y' => 0
);
```

Once we have defined this array and included all the users whom we want to tag, we simply pass it as an additional argument in the array parameter of the `$facebook-api()` function while publishing the picture through the following piece of code:

```
$pic_id = $facebook->api('/'.$album_id.'/photos',
    'POST', array('message' => $message ,'source' =>
    '@' . $pic, 'tags' => $tags,));
```

All the users that have been specified in the $tags array will get tagged in the picture that has been published.

See also

- For more details on how to upload a picture to a specific album, you should refer to the *Posting a picture to a specific album of the user* recipe in this chapter.

Adding a subscription for real time updates related to a user object

Facebook allows us to subscribe to real time updates for certain objects. This way we don't need to poll the Facebook servers continually for detecting updates in user data. It saves a lot of processing time and resources. There are various objects to which we can subscribe:

- ▶ `user`: Using Facebook user object, we can get notifications when certain properties and fields of the user change. For example, we can subscribe to a change in a user's e-mail ID, photos, activities, interests, and so on.

- ▶ `permissions`: Sometimes a user may change certain permissions which have been granted to our application. To get notified of a change in permission levels, we can subscribe to the permission object.

- ▶ `page`: A page, which has installed our application, at times may change its public properties. We can subscribe to the page object to get notifications for these changes.

For each object you can subscribe to some of its properties. Here we will subscribe to the feed and friends properties of the object user.

Getting ready

You should have registered your application and should have created `config.php` as explained in the beginning of this chapter.

How to do it...

We will create a PHP code snippet and use it to post our subscription request to the Facebook server.

1. Create a file named `action_subscribe.php` and add the following code to it:

   ```php
   <?php
   ```

2. Include the configuration file:

   ```php
   require_once 'config.php';
   ```

3. Specify the arguments needed to post to the authorization URL in the `$args` array:

   ```php
   $args = array('grant_type' => 'client_credentials',
       'client_id' => $facebook->getAppId(),
       'client_secret' => $facebook->getApiSecret());
   ```

4. Initialize cURL using the `curl_init()` function:

   ```php
   $ch = curl_init();
   ```

5. Set the authorization URL by using the `curl_setopt()` function:

```
$url = 'https://graph.facebook.com/oauth/access_token';
curl_setopt($ch, CURLOPT_URL, $url);
```

6. Set the POST and RETURNTRANSFER method and POSTFIELDS using the `curl_setopt()` function:

```
curl_setopt($ch, CURLOPT_HEADER, false);
curl_setopt($ch, CURLOPT_RETURNTRANSFER, true);
curl_setopt($ch, CURLOPT_POST, true);
curl_setopt($ch, CURLOPT_POSTFIELDS, $args);
```

7. Use the `curl_exec()` function to execute the POST request and `explode()` function to extract the access token:

```
$access_token = explode("=", curl_exec($ch));
curl_close($ch);
$access_token = $access_token[1];
```

8. POST the subscription request using the `api()` function:

```
$info = $facebook->api('/' . $facebook->getAppId()
    .'/subscriptions', 'POST', array('access_token' =>
    $access_token, 'object' => 'user', 'callback_url' =>
    'http://www.yoursite.co.in/app/action_callback.php',
    'fields' => 'feed, friends', 'verify_token' =>
    'your_secret_verify _token',));
?>
```

9. Now run this file.

How it works...

For making a subscription request, we first need to get an OAuth access token on behalf of the application. To do so, we need to make a POST request to the following URL—`https://graph.facebook.com/oauth/access_token`. We use PHP CURL library functions to assist us. We first use `curl_init()` which initializes and returns a cURL handle.

Next, we set certain options for configuring the request before executing it. We have configured the following attributes by using the `curl_setopt()` function:

- `CURLOPT_HEADER`: It determines whether or not to include the header in the output

- `CURLOPT_RETURNTRANSFER`: It determines whether or not to return the transfer as a string of the return value of `curl_exec()` instead of outputting it out directly

- `CURLOPT_POST`: It determines whether or not to make a normal HTTP POST request

- `CURLOPT_POSTFIELDS`: It contains the data to post when making a POST request

After this, we use `curl_exec()` to finally make the POST request and we store the result in `$access_token`, after using the `explode()` function on the returned result. We have used the `explode()` function because the data returned is something like **access_token=XXXXXX** and we have to extract the value of the access token. Once we have the access token we make a POST request using the `api()` function as follows:

```
$info = $facebook->api('/' . $facebook->getAppId()
    .'/subscriptions', 'POST', array('access_token' =>
    $access_token, 'object' => 'user', 'callback_url' =>
    'http://www.yoursite.co.in/app/action_callback.php',
    'fields' => 'feed, friends', 'verify_token' =>
    'your_secret_verify _token',));
```

We make a POST request to the URL of the form—`https://graph.facebook.com/[app_id]/subscriptions`. The third argument of this function contains an array, which is used to configure the subscription we want to make. It has the following attributes:

- `access_token`: This contains the access token obtained for the application

 This token is different from the access token requested on behalf of a user for getting a valid session.

- `object`: It determines what type of object we want to subscribe to
- `callback_url`: It is the URL to which Facebook will post notifications
- `fields`: These contain the list of the fields, separated by a comma, to which you want to subscribe to but not all fields can be subscribed to
- `verify_token`: This is the secret token which is used in `callback_url` for security purposes

Once we have successfully made our subscription request, Facebook will post notifications to the specified callback URL.

Creating a callback for handling real time updates

When we subscribe to any object for real time updates, we need to create a callback URL where Facebook will ping us whenever the subscribed data gets updated. This URL should be capable of receiving both HTTP GET (for performing subscription verification) and POST (for getting change notifications) requests from Facebook.

Getting ready

You should have registered your application and should have the application ID and secret key ready.

How to do it...

The following steps will deal with creating callbacks:

1. Create a PHP file and name it as you want your callback URL to be. We will call it `action_callback.php` here. Now add the following code in it:

   ```php
   <?php
   ```

2. Specify your secret verification token:

   ```php
   define('VERIFY_TOKEN', 'your_secret_verification_token');
   ```

3. Retrieve the request method made:

   ```php
   $method = $_SERVER['REQUEST_METHOD'];
   ```

4. If this is a GET request, then verify the VERIFY_TOKEN:

   ```php
   if ($method == 'GET' && $_GET['hub_mode'] == 'subscribe'
     && $_GET['hub_verify_token'] == VERIFY_TOKEN) {
       echo $_GET['hub_challenge'];
   }
   ```

5. If this is a POST request containing the updates notifications, then save it to a file:

   ```php
   else if ($method == 'POST') {
     $updates = json_decode(file_get_contents("php://input"),
       true);
     /**Your own code to take action based upon the update
       notification should be put here*/
     $myFile = "log.txt";
     $fh = fopen($myFile, 'a');
     fwrite($fh, 'updates = ' . print_r($updates, true));
     fclose($fh);
   }
   ?>
   ```

6. Save this file. Now, if we have mentioned this file as a callback URL for a certain subscription, then whenever there is any update related to that subscription Facebook will make subsequent GET and POST requests to this file.

How it works...

Whenever there is any update for an object that we have subscribed to, then Facebook pings the callback URL, associated with that subscription, and makes two types of requests. The first is the HTTP GET request to verify the subscription and the next is the POST request for posting any changes that have taken place to the callback URL. Facebook makes an HTTP GET to our callback URL with the following parameters: `hub.mode`, `hub.challenge`, and `hub.verify_token`.

 In PHP, dots and spaces in query parameter names are automatically converted to underscores. For example, `hub.mode` gets converted to `hub_mode`.

These three parameters have been discussed in detail:

- `hub_mode`: The string `subscribe` is passed in this parameter.
- `hub_challenge`: It is a random string which we have to print back as an output to the GET request. Facebook reads this output to cross check that we are following the proper protocol and have indeed posted back the same challenge.
- `hub_verify_token`: We must use the value of this parameter to match against our private verification token, which we had passed earlier while creating the subscription. This helps us in indentifying that the request we have received is indeed from Facebook.

In `action_callback.php` we first check the type of the request made. This can be determined by looking at the value of `$_SERVER['REQUEST_METHOD']` as shown in the following code:

```
$method = $_SERVER['REQUEST_METHOD'];
if ($method == 'GET' && $_GET['hub_mode'] == 'subscribe'
  && $_GET['hub_verify_token'] == VERIFY_TOKEN) {
    echo $_GET['hub_challenge'];
  }
```

If it is a GET request, we check if our `VERIFY_TOKEN` matches with the one passed by Facebook (`hub_verify_token`). If it does, then we simply return back the value of `hub_challenge`. Facebook requires us to do this for verification purposes.

Once, we have returned the challenge to Facebook, it then makes a POST request containing the update notifications. This we handle in the `elseif` condition as shown in the following code:

```
else if ($method == 'POST') {
  $updates = json_decode(file_get_contents("php://input"),
    true);
```

```
/**Your own code to take action based upon the update notification
should be put here*/
  $myFile = "log.txt";
  $fh = fopen($myFile, 'a');
  fwrite($fh, 'updates = ' . print_r($updates, true));
  fclose($fh);
}
```

We convert the posted JSON data into a PHP array by using the json_decode() function and then we store this in $updates. A sample value of $updates may look similar to the following snippets of code:

```
Array
(
  [object] => user
  [entry] => Array
  (
    [0] => Array
    (
      [uid] => 786017563
      [id] => 786017563
      [time] => 1300426857
      [changed_fields] => Array
      (
        [0] => friends
      )
    )
  )
)
```

Now, you must write your own code after this to take action based upon the received notification. For instance, you may have saved e-mail IDs of users in your database; upon receiving notification for any change in them, you should again get the updated values by using the api() function for corresponding users and then save them back in the database.

 The received notification just tells about the "changed fields" for a specific object (such as user). We need to retrieve on our own the "values" of these "changed fields" by using Facebook Graph API.

Here, for demonstration purpose's we keep on logging the updates received by Facebook in a text file named log.txt.

The `log.txt` should have read, write, and execute (777) permissions assigned to it.

Deleting subscriptions

Facebook Graph API gives an option to delete subscriptions of our application, if we may find them redundant. Moreover, we can also delete subscriptions pertaining to a particular object, user, permissions, or page.

Getting ready

We should have already subscribed to some updates so that we can delete them.

How to do it...

We will create a PHP code snippet and use it to post our subscription deletion request to the Facebook server:

1. Create a file named `action_delete_subs.php` and add the following code to it:

   ```php
   <?php
   ```

2. Include the configuration file:

   ```php
   require_once 'config.php';
   ```

3. Specify the arguments needed to post to the authorization URL in the `$args` array:

   ```php
   $args = array('grant_type' => 'client_credentials',
     'client_id' => $facebook->getAppId(),
     'client_secret' => $facebook->getApiSecret());
   ```

4. Initialize cURL using the `curl_init()` function:

   ```php
   $ch = curl_init();
   ```

5. Set the authorization URL using the `curl_setopt()` function:

   ```php
   $url = 'https://graph.facebook.com/oauth/access_token';
   curl_setopt($ch, CURLOPT_URL, $url);
   ```

6. Set the POST and RETURNTRANSFER method and POSTFIELDS using the `curl_setopt()` function:

   ```php
   curl_setopt($ch, CURLOPT_HEADER, false);
   curl_setopt($ch, CURLOPT_RETURNTRANSFER, true);
   curl_setopt($ch, CURLOPT_POST, true);
   curl_setopt($ch, CURLOPT_POSTFIELDS, $args);
   ```

7. Use the `curl_exec()` function to execute the POST request and the `explode()` function to extract the access token:

```
$access_token = explode("=",curl_exec($ch));
curl_close($ch);
$access_token = $access_token[1];
```

8. Make the subscription DELETE request using the `api()` function:

```
$delete = $facebook->api('/'. $facebook->getAppId() .
  '/subscriptions', 'DELETE', array('access_token' =>
  $access_token,));
?>
```

9. Save this file and run it. All the subscriptions for our application will get deleted.

How it works...

To delete the subscriptions for our application, we need to make a DELETE request to the following URL—`https://graph.facebook.com/[APP-ID]/subscriptions`. Before we can do that, we need to request an access token for our application. This access token is different from the "user access token" which we generally use to take action on behalf of the user. Here, we want to make a change to our application data, which is independent of any user. Hence, we want an application specific access token. To get this OAuth token, we need to make a POST request to `https://graph.facebook.com/oauth/access_token`; we need our application ID (app-id) and application secret (app-secret).

In order to make this POST request for getting the access token, we use the cURL library of PHP. `$args` is an array which contains the arguments that we need to post to the authorization URL. These arguments are as follows:

- `grant_type`: It should be set to `client_credentials`
- `client_id`: It should be set to our application ID
- `client_secret`: It should be set to our application secret key

We use `curl_init()` to initialize the cURL cursor. Next, we use the `curl_setopt()` function to set certain options, such as setting the URL to the authorization URL and setting the method POST to true. Then, we use the `curl_exec()` function to execute the POST request and the `explode()` function to extract the `access_token` from the returned data.

Once we have a valid access token, we make a DELETE request to Facebook by using the `api()` function. Upon successful deletion, 1 is returned as a response from the server and stored in `$delete`.

There's more...

If we want to delete a subscription pertaining to a particular object such as user, permission, or page, we can do so by simply specifying the object parameter in the array. For example, if we want to delete a subscription for a user object, then we can do so as shown in the following code snippet:

```
$delete = $facebook->api('/'. $facebook->getAppId() .
   '/subscriptions', 'DELETE', array('access_token' =>
   $access_token, 'object' => 'user'));
```

As we have specified the user object, all the subscriptions pertaining to the user object will get deleted.

3
Querying Facebook

In this chapter, we will cover:

- ▸ Returning information about a user
- ▸ Getting the status message of a user
- ▸ Retrieving profile pictures of a user's friends
- ▸ Getting the links posted by a user
- ▸ Getting the Facebook pages followed by a user
- ▸ Determining if two users are friends
- ▸ Retrieving information of a group
- ▸ Retrieving members of a group
- ▸ Retrieving friends from a specific friend list
- ▸ Getting all the messages in a thread
- ▸ Checking the status of permissions for an application
- ▸ Getting notifications for the current user and the sender of the notifications
- ▸ Retrieving video details associated with a user
- ▸ Getting the five latest photos in which a user has been tagged
- ▸ Retrieving the latest photos published by a user
- ▸ Retrieving details of an event
- ▸ Retrieving details of a user's friends by using multiquery method

Introduction

We all are familiar with **SQL (Structured Query Language)** which provides a convenient way to query a database containing some relevant information. Facebook has its own SQL like language for querying its database. It is known as **Facebook Query Language**, abbreviated as FQL. While Facebook Graph API provides an easy to use interface, FQL on the other hand provides more control over what, and how much, data we want to extract.

It provides access to the data exposed by the Graph API through a structured SQL type interface. Facebook supports a lot of tables which can be queried via FQL to retrieve meaningful information. Using FQL we can even run some complex queries which can't be done by using Graph API all alone.

There are a few important points to be noticed in FQL:

- FQL queries are executed by fetching the URL `https://api.facebook.com/method/fql.query?query=QUERY`. We can specify a response format as either XML or JSON with the `format` query parameter.

- FQL queries are always written in this form:

  `SELECT [fields] FROM [table] WHERE [conditions]`

- Moreover, unlike SQL the FQL `FROM` clause can have only one table name.

- Another important thing to note is that the `WHERE` clause can only have attributes which are indexable. Each FQL table has certain fields which are marked as * meaning they are indexable. The query can be run only if we index them by these fields.

Prerequisites

We need to do some basic configuration before starting with the recipes discussed in this chapter. Follow these steps:

1. First, create a `config.php` file and add the following code to it:

```php
<?php
  require_once 'facebook.php';
  /** Create our Application instance. */
```

2. Initialize the Facebook application:

```php
$facebook = new Facebook(array(
  'appId'  => 'your_application_id',
  'secret' => 'your_application_secret_key',
  'cookie' => true,
    ));
```

Here, the `Facebook` class is defined in `facebook.php` and can be downloaded from GitHub. `$facebook` is an object of this class and we will use it in our `index.php` file. You need to provide your application ID and secret key here. For more information, refer to *Chapter 1*. Now to continue:

1. Create a file named `index.php` and add the following code to it:

   ```
   <?php
   ```

2. Include the configuration file:

   ```
   require_once 'config.php';
   ```

3. Get the current user's session information by using the `getSession()` function and then validate the session:

   ```
   $session = $facebook->getSession();
   $me = null;
   if ($session) {
     try {
       $me = $facebook->api('/me');
         /*Check whether the current session is valid by
            retrieving user information.*/
     }
   }
   /* If the current session is invalid or user has not authorized
       the application then redirect to a authorization URL.
       If session is invalid redirect the application to the
       authorization URL */
   if(!($me))
     {
     echo '<script>
       top.location.href="'.$facebook->getLoginUrl(
       array('req_perms' => 'publish_stream',
       'next' => 'http://apps.facebook.com/[your_app_url]
       /',)).'";
       </script>';
       exit;
     }

   ?>
   ```

Here, we first retrieve a valid session for the user by calling the `$facebook->getSession()` function and storing the response in the `$session` variable. Next, we try to retrieve the basic information of the current user by posting a GET request to `https://graph.facebook.com/me`. We use the `$facebook->api()` function to do so. `https://graph.facebook.com` is automatically prefixed by the `api()` function to its first argument, that's why we have passed `/me` as its first argument. The returned data is stored in the `$me` variable.

Finally, we check whether the `$me` variable is null or not. If it's null, then we need to redirect the user to the authorization URL in order to get appropriate permission(s) from, and a valid session token for, the user. To redirect the user, we use JavaScript code. We set `top.location.href` to the URL where we want to re-direct the user. This URL is given by the function `$facebook->getLoginUrl()`. Also, this function takes array as its argument. The index `req_perms` is used to request specific permissions from the user. Multiple permissions can be requested by separating them using a comma. Additionally, the index `next` specifies where the user will be redirected after successful authorization and session generation.

Once you have created these two files, you can use them directly in the subsequent recipes.

Returning information about a user

FQL supports multiple tables with a number of attributes. The Facebook **user** table can be queried via FQL to retrieve all the information details of a particular user. For example, a user's name, relationship status, and other profile information can be easily retrieved provided we have the necessary permissions.

Getting ready

You should have setup `config.php` and `index.php` as explained in the beginning of the chapter. Also, you cannot access all the fields in the **user** table. Some require you to have extended permissions. Thus, the prerequisite is that you should have acquired all the permissions for accessing required fields from the user, otherwise you will get empty values for fields against which you don't have extended permissions. For example, to access the birthday of the user you need to have the `user_birthday` permission.

The available permissions can be seen from the Facebook permissions table provided at http://developers.facebook.com/docs/reference/api/permissions/. You just have to choose the ones required by your application and ask for extended permissions for them.

How to do it...

The following steps will demonstrate how to retrieve information from the **user** table:

1. Open `index.php` and append the following code to it:

```
<html>
  <body>
    <?php
```

2. Retrieve a user's information by executing the following FQL query:

```
$users = $facebook->api(array('method' => 'fql.query',
    'query' => "SELECT uid, first_name, last_name, sex,
    pic_square FROM user WHERE uid = me() OR uid = 637089897"));
```

3. Display the result in a table format:

```
echo "<table width='70%'>";
echo "<tr><th align='LEFT'>User Id</th>
        <th align='LEFT'>First Name</th>
        <th align='LEFT'>Last Name</th>
        <th align='LEFT'>Sex</th>
        <th align='LEFT'>Picture</th></tr>";

foreach ($users as $user) {
  echo "<tr><td>" . $user['uid'] . "</td>
        <td>" . $user['first_name'] . "</td>
        <td>" . $user['last_name'] . "</td>
        <td>" . $user['sex'] . "</td>
        <td><img src='". $user['pic_square'] . "' /></td>
      "</tr>;
}

echo "</table>";
?>
</body>
</html>
```

4. Now run `index.php` and you will get something like this as the output:

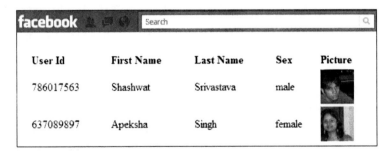

How it works...

Facebook FQL has a `user` table from which we can retrieve information about a user. Here we run the following query:

```
SELECT uid, first_name, last_name, sex, pic_square FROM user WHERE uid
= me() OR uid = 637089897
```

In this we retrieve the user ID, first name, last name, sex, profile picture of the logged in user, as well as a user with ID **637089897** from the user table.

Using the `api()` function we make a call to this query. The returned user information gets stored in the `$users` PHP variable. Next, using the `foreach()` PHP loop we print the user's information one by one.

There's more...

The FQL user table contains another field which is **family**. However, for retrieving a user's family's result we need to query the **family** table instead of the **user** table. Moreover every attributes can be returned either as an integer, string, or array. All this information has been provided in the tables given in the *Appendix*.

Also, we need to check the **permissions** table to see which attributes require which permissions and grant them before querying for them. We can also get the publicly available attributes for a user, provided we have the user's ID and the necessary permissions.

See also

▸ *Getting the status message of a user*

▸ *Getting the Links posted by a user*

▸ *Getting the Facebook pages followed by a user*

▸ *Retrieving the latest photos published by a user*

Getting the status messages of a user

We can query using FQL to retrieve the status messages of a user, as well as his/her friends.

Getting ready

You should have already set up `config.php` and `index.php` as explained in the beginning of the chapter. Also, to be able to access the status message of a user, the application needs to have the `user_status` permission. If we even want to access the status messages of friends, then we need the `friends_status` permission as well.

How to do it...

The following steps will demonstrate how to get the status messages of a user:

1. Open `index.php` and append the following code to it:

```
<html>
  <body>
```

```
Status messages of <?php echo $me['name']; ?> are listed below
- <br>
<?php
```

2. Retrieve the status messages of the user by executing the following FQL query:

```
$statuses = $facebook->api(array('method' => 'fql.query',
    'query' => "SELECT message FROM status WHERE uid = me()"));
```

3. Display the status messages of the user:

```
$i=1;

echo '<table>';
foreach ($statuses as $status) {
    echo "<tr><td width = '5%'>" . $i . "</td>
        <td width = '95%'>" . $status['message'] . "</td></tr>";
    $i++;
}

echo '</table>';
?>
</body>
</html>
```

4. Run the file. A screenshot of the output of the code would be something like this:

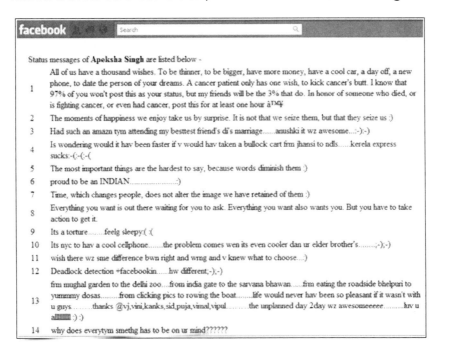

How it works...

In `index.php`, we use the `api()` function of the `Facebook` class in order to execute our FQL query. In the `api()` function, we pass an array as an argument. It has two indexes—`method` and `query`. We set the method to `fql.query` and this indicates that we want to execute an FQL query by making a GET request to the URL of the form `https://api.facebook.com/method/fql.query?query=QUERY` where the FQL query to be executed is given by the value of the index named `query`. In an FQL query, we simply select the status messages from the **status** table. It has been done through the following FQL query:

```
SELECT message FROM status WHERE uid = me()
```

The retrieved status messages are, by default, in reverse chronological order, that is, most recent ones are present at the top. These are stored in an array named `$statuses`. We use a `foreach` loop to extract one status message, given by `$status['message']`, at a time and display it in a new row inside a table.

There's more...

We can also query the **status** table to return status messages of more than one user. Suppose, if we want to retrieve the status messages of the current user's friends, we can do so by executing the following FQL query:

```
SELECT uid, status_id, message FROM status WHERE uid IN (
    SELECT uid2 FROM friend WHERE uid1 = me())
```

Here, first the sub-query will be executed—`SELECT uid2 FROM friend WHERE uid1 = me()`. It will retrieve all the uids of the friends of the current user from the **friend** table. Then corresponding to these uids the values of `uid`, `status_id`, and `message` fields from the **status** table will be returned, that is, we will get the status messages of the friends of the current user.

Moreover, for better optimization we can limit the results to within the last week by querying like this:

```
SELECT uid, status_id, message FROM status WHERE uid IN (
    SELECT uid2 FROM friend WHERE uid1= me()) AND
    time > {time_of_last_week}
```

Here, we need to replace `{time_of_last_week}` with a suitable Unix timestamp during that period.

 The **status** table returns the result of either the last 30 days or 50 posts, whichever is more.

If we want to retrieve just the current status message of the user, then we can do so by executing an FQL query on the **user** table instead. The corresponding FQL query will be:

```
SELECT status FROM user WHERE uid = me()
```

It extracts the value of the **status** field from the **user** table for the current user. The **status** field contains the latest status message for the corresponding user ID.

See also

▶ *Getting the latest five photos in which a user has been tagged*

Retrieving profile pictures of a user's friends

Many a time, our application requires the profile pictures of some of the user's friends. For example, if we have an interface where we want to list a user's friends, then we could use their profile pictures as well, for providing a better user experience. By using a simple FQL query, it is possible to retrieve the profile pictures of a user's friends.

Getting ready

You should have already set up `config.php` and `index.php` as explained in the beginning of the chapter.

How to do it...

The following steps will demonstrate how to retrieve friends' profile pictures:

1. Open `index.php` and append the following code to it:

```
<html>
  <body>
    Profile pictures of friends of <?php echo $me['name']; ?> are
      displayed below (as a collage) - <br><br>
    <?php
```

2. Retrieve the profile pictures of the user's friends by executing the following FQL query:

```
$profile_pics = $facebook->api(array('method' => 'fql.query',
  'query' => "SELECT pic_square, uid FROM user WHERE uid IN (
  SELECT uid2 FROM friend WHERE uid1= me())"));
```

3. Display the profile pictures of the user's friends:

```
foreach($profile_pics as $pic) {
  echo '<image src="' . $pic['pic_square'] . '" width="40"
    height="40" />';
```

```
        }
      ?>
    </body>
  </html>
```

4. Now run `index.php` and you will see a collage of all your friends' profile pictures, as shown in the following screenshot:

How it works...

In order to execute an FQL query, we need to pass two parameters, together as an array, to the `api()` function of the `Facebook` class. The index `method` should be set as `fql.query` to indicate that we want to execute an FQL query and `query` should contain the actual FQL query. Let's discuss the FQL query we have executed:

```
SELECT pic_square, uid FROM user WHERE uid IN (
    SELECT uid2 FROM friend WHERE uid1= me())
```

This FQL query consists of a sub-query and main query. The sub-query, `SELECT uid2 FROM friend WHERE uid1 = me()`, is executed first. In this sub-query, we select all the IDs of the current user's friends from the **friend** table. The **friend** table has two columns—`uid1` and `uid2`. Each set of values of `uid1` and `uid2` represents a pair of friends. So, here we set the `uid1` as the uid of the current user and retrieve all the values of the `uid2` column present against this. Once we have these IDs, then in the main query we retrieve the corresponding profile picture of all the friends of the current user. This we do by querying the **user** table. It has a field named `pic_square` which gives the URL of the profile picture of a user in square format.

Next, we use the HTML `img` tag to display these profile pictures. We use `foreach` loop to iterate over results and set the returned URL of the profile pictures as the value of the `src` attribute in the `img` HTML tag. You can similarly use these profile pictures in your application to provide a more personalized experience to the user.

 Here, we have executed a nested FQL query to retrieve the profile pictures of friends of the current user.

There's more...

Instead of using the `pic_square` field of the **user** table, we can use also try `pic`, `pic_small`, and `pic_big`. The profile picture will remain the same as returned by these fields, but will have different dimensions as is obvious from the field names.

Suppose, we want to sort the profile picture of the user's friends in alphabetical order according to their name, we can do so by using the ORDER BY clause in the following FQL query. It is illustrated in the following query:

```
SELECT pic_square, uid FROM user WHERE uid IN (
    SELECT uid2 FROM friend WHERE uid1= me()) ORDER BY first_name
```

The ORDER BY clause, by default, just orders the result based on the field specified in ascending order. Here, it will order it by the first name of the user's friends. If we want it to be sorted in descending order we need to add DESC in the ORDER BY clause as shown:

```
SELECT pic_square, uid FROM user WHERE uid IN (
    SELECT uid2 FROM friend WHERE uid1= me())ORDER BY first_name DESC
```

The query will return the profile pictures after sorting them according to `first_name` in descending order alphabetically.

Getting the links posted by a user

Facebook gives us the opportunity to share status, photos, links, and videos. If we want to retrieve the links a user has posted, then we can do so by using FQL.

Getting ready

You should have already created `config.php` and `index.php` as explained in the beginning of this chapter.

How to do it...

The following steps will demonstrate how to get the links posted by a user:

1. Open `index.php` and append the following code to it:

```html
<html>
  <body>
    Links posted by <strong><?php echo $me['name']; ?></strong>
    are listed below - <br><br>
      <?php
```

2. Retrieve the links posted by a user by executing the following FQL query:

```php
$links = $facebook->api(array('method' => 'fql.query',
    'query' => "SELECT owner_comment, title, summary, link_id,
    url FROM link WHERE owner = me()"));
```

3. Display the links posted in a table format:

```php
echo '<table>';
    foreach ($links as $link) {
        echo '<tr><td>' . $link['link_id'] . '</td>
                <td>' . $link['title'] . '</td>
                <td>' . $link['owner_comment'] . '</td>
                <td>' . $link['summary'] . '</td>
                <td>' . $link['url'] . '</td></tr>';
    }
    echo '</table>';
  ?>
  </body>
</html>
```

4. Now, run `index.php` and all the links by the current user will be retrieved and displayed in tabular format, as shown in the following screenshot:

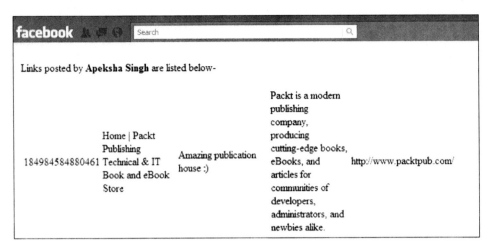

These table columns display link ID, title, comment, summary, and URL respectively. We can use this information about the different links posted by user in various ways in our application.

How it works...

In `index.php`, we have run the following FQL query:

```
SELECT owner_comment, title, summary, link_id, url FROM link
    WHERE owner = me()
```

Here, we have selected the following fields from the **link** table:

- `owner_comment`: It gives the comment the owner has made about the link
- `title`: It gives the title of the link which is extracted from the metadata of the site
- `summary`: It gives the summary which is usually a small piece of text extracted from the link
- `link_id`: It's the ID of the link as assigned by Facebook
- `url`: It's the actual URL

To actually execute this FQL query, we use the `api()` function of the `Facebook` class. In the `api()` function, we pass an array as argument with two indexes—`method` and `query`. Here, the method is defined as `fql.query` which means that we want to execute an FQL query by posting a `GET` request to the URL of the form `https://api.facebook.com/method/fql.query?query=QUERY` and the `query` decides the actual FQL query that we want to execute by posting it to this URL. The result is returned in JSON format from Facebook which is converted to a corresponding PHP array and stored in `$links`. After this we use a `foreach` loop to print all the links one by one in tabular format.

There's more...

The link table has two indexable fields—`link_id` and `owner`, that is, we can use either of these fields to query the whole table for particular information. Also, if we want to extract the image linked with a particular link we can do so by using `image_urls` field. Similarly, we can use the `created_time` field to get the time when a particular link was posted by the user.

See also

▶ *Retrieving the latest photos published by a user*

Getting the Facebook pages followed by a user

Facebook uses the concept of **Page** for grouping together the similar activities and interests of users. It has a separate page dedicated for every personal characteristic and activity of a user. Facebook users like these pages which give an insight into their personality. We can retrieve the list of Facebook pages liked by a user, in order to know him/her better, which in turn will help us to give him/her a more personalized experience.

Getting ready

You should have set up `config.php` and `index.php`, as explained in the beginning of this chapter. Also, you should know the ID of the user whose list of liked pages you wish to retrieve. Usually, you will do this for the current user whose ID can be specified by using the special identifier `me()` in the FQL query.

How to do it...

The following steps will demonstrate how to retrieve the pages a user likes:

1. Open `index.php` and append the following code to it:

```
<html>
```

```
<body>
  Pages followed by <strong> <?php echo $me['name']; ?></strong>
  are listed below - <br><br>
  <?php
```

2. Retrieve the pages followed by the user by executing the following FQL query:

```
$pages  =  $facebook->api(array('method' => 'fql.query',
  'query' => "SELECT page_id, name, type, pic_square,
  fan_count FROM page WHERE page_id IN (SELECT target_id
  FROM connection WHERE source_id = me()
  AND is_following = 1)",));
```

3. Display the page information in table format:

```
echo '<table>';
echo '<tr><th>Page Name</th>
          <th>Type</th>
          <th>Picture</th>
          <th>Fans</th>
          <th>Page id</th></tr>';

foreach ($pages as $page) {
  echo '<tr><td>' . $page['name'] . '</td>
          <td>' . $page['type'] . '</td>
          <td><img src = "' . $page['pic_square'] .
                    '" /></td>
          <td>' . $page['fan_count'] . '</td>
          <td>' . $page['page_id'] . '</td></tr>';
}
echo '</table>';
?>
</body>
</html>
```

4. Once you have added the code to `index.php`, then it's time to run the code. A screenshot of a sample output is shown:

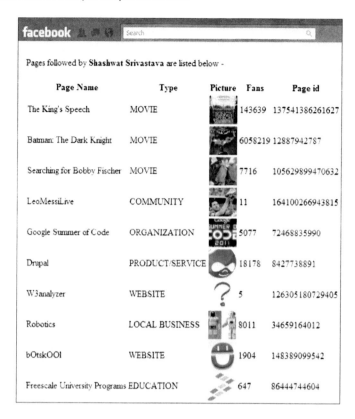

How it works...

For retrieving the pages followed by a user, we use a nested FQL query and retrieve the data from two tables, namely, **connections** and **page**. We use the **connection** table to get the ID of the pages of which the current user is a fan and is following them. We do this by using the following sub-query which is highlighted:

```
SELECT page_id, name, type, pic_square, fan_count
 FROM page WHERE page_id IN (
SELECT target_id FROM connection WHERE source_id = me() AND
 is_following = 1)
```

We get the values of `target_id` which are basically the IDs of the pages that the user is following. Here, in the `WHERE` clause of the sub-query we set `source_id` as `me()`, that is, the current user's ID and `is_following` as `1` which ensures that the user is following the pages being retrieved.

Next, we use these page IDs in the main query to get the following data from the **page** table:

- ▶ `page_id`: It is the ID of the retrieved page
- ▶ `name`: The public name associated with the page
- ▶ `type`: It identifies the category of the page such as website, organization, movie, and so on
- ▶ `pic_square`: It gives the URL of the public picture of the page, which is shaped as a square
- ▶ `fan_count`: This gives the total number of followers of the page

The retrieved data is stored in a PHP array, `$pages`. We use a `foreach` loop to print all the pages followed by the user one after another in tabular fashion.

There's more...

The FQL **page** table can be queried to get information about any page. The only prerequisite is to know the ID or name of the page. Both the attributes `page_id` and `name` are indexable, that is, we can use them in the `WHERE` clause of an FQL query.

Determining if two users are friends

Many a time, an application may want to ascertain if any two given users are linked together as friends or not. We can do so by using FQL in Facebook. It makes it easy to determine this connection since it has a separate table, **friend**, especially for this purpose.

Getting ready

You need to set up `config.php` and `index.php`, as explained in the beginning of the chapter. Also, you should have the IDs of both the users on whom you want to perform this operation.

How to do it...

The following steps will determine if two users are friends:

1. Open `index.php` and append the following code to it:
   ```
   <html>
     <body>
       <?php
   ```

2. The following FQL query will determine if the two users whose IDs have been provided are friends::

```
$check_friends = $facebook->api(array('method' =>
    'fql.query', 'query' => "SELECT uid1, uid2 FROM friend
    WHERE uid1 = me() AND uid2='637089897'"));
```

3. Check if users are friends or not and display the results accordingly:

```
if($check_friends)
    echo "Both the users are friends.";
else
    echo "Users are not friends.";
?>
</body>
</html>
```

4. Save `index.php` and run it.

5. Change the values of `uid1` and `uid2` in the FQL query. You may want to set them programmatically. An appropriate message will be displayed depending on whether the users are friends or not:

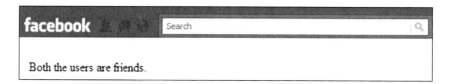

How it works...

Here, we have used the **friend** table in an FQL query to determine whether the users are friends or not. We do so by executing the following FQL query:

```
SELECT uid1, uid2 FROM friend WHERE uid1 = me() AND uid2='637089897'
```

Here, `uid1` and `uid2` will vary depending on the ID of the users for whom we are running this query. Both these attributes are indexable. If the query runs successfully and both the users under inspection turn out to be friends, then the IDs of both will be returned and stored in `$check_friends`. A sample value of it could be:

```
Array ([0] => Array ([uid1] => 786017563 [uid2] => 637089897))
```

If the users are not friends then a null value is returned. We use an `if else` condition on `$check_friends` to test this and print the results accordingly.

Retrieving information of a group

One of the most important features that Facebook supports is **Groups**. Groups allow people with similar interests or backgrounds to connect and share information with each other. A user may have subscribed to different groups, with each group having some definite purpose. By using FQL we can retrieve the detailed information of the groups being followed by a user.

Getting ready

You should have already set up `config.php` and `index.php` as explained in the beginning of the chapter. If we want to find out the information of a particular group, then we need to know the corresponding group ID. Also, if we want to list the groups a user follows, then the application should have `user_groups` extended permission. To access the list of groups of user's friends we should have `friends_groups` extended permission.

How to do it...

The following steps will demonstrate how to retrieve group information:

1. Open `index.php` and append the following code to it:

   ```
   <html>
     <body>
       <?php
   ```

2. Specify the group ID:

   ```
       $gid = '116511191758694';
   ?>
   Group information for id <?php echo $gid; ?> created by
   <strong><?php echo $me['name']; ?></strong> is listed below -
   <br><br>
   <?php
   ```

3. Retrieve the group information by executing the following FQL query:

   ```
       $groups = $facebook->api(array('method' => 'fql.query',
         'query' => "SELECT name, description, privacy, creator,
         pic_small FROM group WHERE gid='" . $gid . "'",));
   ```

4. Display the group information in a table format:

   ```
       echo '<table>';
       echo '<tr><th>Name</th>
               <th>Description</th>
               <th>Privacy</th>
               <th>Creator</th>
               <th>Picture</th></tr>';
   ```

```
        foreach ($groups as $group) {
          echo '<tr><td>' . $group['name'] . '</td>
                  <td>' . $group['description'] . '</td>
                  <td>' . $group['privacy'] . '</td>
                  <td>' . $group['creator'] . '</td>
                  <td><img src = "' . $group['pic_small'] .
                      '" /></td>
              </tr>';
        }
        echo '</table>';
      ?>
    </body>
</html>
```

5. Change the value of the $gid variable with the group ID for which you want to run the query and retrieve the details. Save and run index.php and you will get something like this as the output:

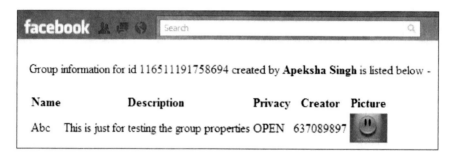

How it works...

To retrieve information about a particular group, you must change the value of $gid which indicates the ID of the group for which you want to retrieve information. We execute the following FQL query to retrieve information of a group:

```
SELECT name, description, privacy, creator, pic_small FROM group WHERE
gid=[GID]
```

Here, [GID] has to be replaced with the value of the $gid variable which we have defined earlier. Upon successful execution of this query we get the following information about the group:

- ▸ `name`: The name of the group whose information we want to retrieve
- ▸ `description`: The description of the group
- ▸ `privacy`: The privacy status of the group whether it is OPEN, CLOSED, or SECRET
- ▸ `creator`: The user ID of the person who has created the group
- ▸ `pic_small`: The URL of a small photo of the group being queried

The retrieved data is stored in a PHP array called $groups. We use a `foreach` loop to print all the pages, followed by the user one after another in tabular fashion.

Retrieving members of a group

Facebook supports an independent **group_member** table from where all the members of a particular group can be retrieved.

Getting ready

You should have set up `config.php` and `index.php` as explained in the beginning of the chapter. If we want to find out any information about a particular group, then we need to know the corresponding group ID. Also, if we want to know the list of groups being followed by a user, then the application should have `user_groups` extended permission. To access the list of groups of user's friends we should have `friends_groups` extended permission.

How to do it...

The following steps will demonstrate how to retrieve group members:

1. Open `index.php` and append the following code to it:

```
<html>
  <body>
    <?php
```

2. Specify the group ID:

```
        $gid = '116511191758694';
    ?>
    Group members for id <?php echo $gid; ?> created by
    <strong><?php echo $me['name']; ?></strong> is listed below -
    <br><br>
    <?php
```

3. Retrieve the group members by executing this FQL query:

```
$grp_members = $facebook->api(array('method' => 'fql.query',
    'query' => "SELECT uid, name, pic_square FROM user
    WHERE uid IN (SELECT uid FROM group_member
    WHERE gid='" . $gid . "')",));
```

4. Display the group member information in a tabular format:

```
echo '<table width="100%">';
echo '<tr><th>User Id</th>
         <th>Name</th>
         <th>Profile pic</th></tr>';
foreach ($grp_members as $grp_member) {
  echo '<tr><td>' . $grp_member['uid'] . '</td>
           <td>' . $ grp_member['name'] . '</td>
           <td><img src = "' . $ grp_member['pic_square'] .
               '" /></td></tr>';
}
echo '</table>';
  ?>
 </body>
</html>
```

5. Replace the $gid with the group ID for which you want to retrieve information. Now save the file and run it. Successful execution of the code will return the user name, user ID, and profile picture of all the members belonging to a particular group, as shown in the following screenshot:

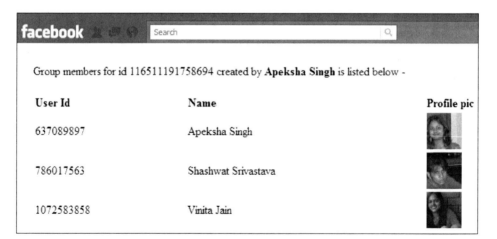

How it works...

Here, we have used a nested FQL query which involves **group_member** and **user** tables. First, we get the user IDs of all the members of a particular group. This we do by using the following sub-query:

```
SELECT uid FROM group_member WHERE gid='GROUP_ID'
```

Next, we use all the retrieved IDs of the users to get their name, ID, and profile picture from the **user** table. So, the complete query becomes:

```
SELECT uid, name, pic_square FROM user WHERE uid IN (SELECT uid FROM
group_member WHERE gid='GROUP_ID')
```

We use the `api()` function to actually execute the FQL query. It takes an array as an argument with two indexes `method` and `query`. The first index has its value as `fql.query` and it means that we want to execute an FQL query. The second index contains the actual FQL query as its value. The returned result is stored in `$grp_members`. We use a `foreach` PHP loop to print the details of all the users along with their name, ID, and profile picture one by one.

See also

▶ *Retrieving information of a group*

Retrieving friends from a specific friend list

Facebook provides its users with an option to create friend lists in order to categorize their friends. For example you can have a friend list named 'office' which contains all your work colleagues in it. Basically, a friend list allows users to segregate their friends in different groups. A Facebook application may require targeting only certain sections of a user's friends, in this case retrieving friends from a specific friend list becomes important.

Getting ready

You should have set up `config.php` and `index.php` as explained in the beginning of the chapter. Also, the application should have `read_friendlists` permission.

How to do it...

The following steps will retrieve friends from a specific friend list:

1. Open `index.php` and append the following code to it:

```html
<html>
  <body>
    Members and the respective Friendlist to which they belong as
    created by <strong><?php echo $me['name']; ?></strong> are
    listed below - <br><br>
    <?php
```

2. Retrieve the user's friend list information by using the following FQL query:

```php
$friendlists = $facebook->api(array('method' => 'fql.query',
    'query' => "SELECT flid, uid FROM friendlist_member
    WHERE flid IN (SELECT flid FROM friendlist
    WHERE owner=me())",));
```

3. Display the friendlist information in a table format:

```php
echo '<table width="100%">';
echo '<tr><th ALIGN=LEFT>User Id</th>
        <th ALIGN=LEFT>Friendlist Id</th></tr>';
foreach ($friendlists as $friendlist) {
  echo '<tr><td>' . $friendlist['uid'] . '</td>
        <td>' . $friendlist['flid'] . '</td></tr>';
}
echo '</table>';
?>
  </body>
</html>
```

4. Save the file and run it. A successful execution of the code will give us a list of the different friend lists created by the user, as friend list IDs and the user IDs of their corresponding members. A screenshot of the output is as follows:

facebook   🔍   Search   🔍

Members and the respective Friendlist to which they belong as created by **Apeksha Singh** are listed below -

User Id	Friendlist Id
1332656337	10150102062889898
745975216	10150102062889898
694401363	10150102062889898
786017563	10150102062889898
1100946856	10150101962859898
786017563	10150101962859898
769907659	10150101962859898
1072583858	10150101962859898
680479538	10150101962859898
665520814	10150101962859898
550312069	10150101962859898
545308195	10150101962859898

How it works...

Here, we retrieve information using two tables—**friendlist** and **friendlist_member**—and thus, run a nested query. First, we fetch the friend list ID (`flid`) from the **friendlist** table for the current user by using the following query:

```
SELECT flid FROM friendlist WHERE owner=me()
```

This returns us the IDs of all the friend lists which have been created by the current user. Then, for these obtained friend lists we query the **friendlist_member** table to fetch the user ID of the members. The complete query then becomes this:

```
SELECT flid, uid FROM friendlist_member WHERE flid IN (
SELECT flid FROM friendlist WHERE owner=me())
```

We use Facebook's `api()` function to make a call to execute this query. The returned information is stored in the `$friendlists` variable. We use a `foreach` PHP loop to print the ID of all the members of the friend list(s), as well as their corresponding friend list ID to which they belong.

There's more...

If, at any stage, we want the user's name, along with the user ID of the people belonging to a particular friend list, then we need to query the **user** table as well. There are multiple ways to do this. We can either save the user IDs obtained by querying the **friendlist_member** table and then use them to query the **user** table for their names. Or, we can execute a multiquery, explained in the last recipe of this chapter.

Getting all the messages in a thread

Facebook has messaging system for all its users which gives them a personalized mail system experience. They have an inbox where they can receive messages and reply to them. The messages from each user get stored in threads and thus, different threads are formed when different users interact. By using FQL we can retrieve the messages that belong to a particular thread.

Getting ready

You should have set up `config.php` and `index.php` as explained in the beginning of the chapter. Also, the application should have `read_mailbox` permission and you should know the thread ID whose messages you want to retrieve.

How to do it...

The following steps will demonstrate how to retrieve all the messages in a thread:

1. Open `index.php` and append the following code to it:

   ```
   <html>
     <body>
       <?php
   ```

2. Specify the thread ID:

   ```
         $tid = '1892443481437';
       ?>
   ```

3. Retrieve the messages belonging to the thread by using the following FQL query:

   ```
         Messages belonging to the thread <?php echo $tid; ?> are
         listed below - <br><br>

         <?php
   ```

```
$messages = $facebook->api(array('method' => 'fql.query',
    'query' => "SELECT body, author_id FROM message
        WHERE thread_id = '" . $tid . "'",));
```

4. Display the messages in tablular format:

```
echo '<table width="100%">';
echo '<tr><th ALIGN=LEFT>Author Id</th>
        <th ALIGN=LEFT>Message Content</th></tr>';

foreach ($messages as $message) {
echo '<tr><td>' . $message['author_id'] . '</td>
        <td>' . $message['body'] . '</td></tr>';
}
echo '</table>';
?>
</body>
</html>
```

5. Replace the `$tid` variable with the thread ID corresponding to which you want to retrieve the messages. Now, save `index.php` and run it. Upon successful execution of the code a list of all the messages belonging to the specified thread ID will be displayed as shown:

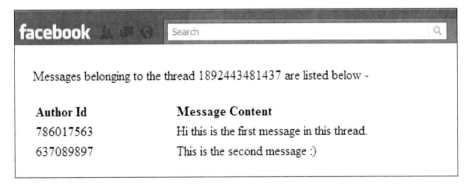

How it works...

Here, we retrieve the message details from Facebook's **message** table. The query that we run is `SELECT body, author_id FROM message WHERE thread_id = [tid]` by which we retrieve the content of the message as `body` and the user ID of the person who has created that message as `author_id` by querying the **message** table.

We use the `api()` function to make a call to execute this query. The retrieved contents gets stored in the `$message` variable. We use a `foreach` PHP loop to print the retrieved message information in a tabular layout.

There's more...

We can also retrieve individual messages if we know the corresponding message ID. This is because the **message** table also has `message_id` as an indexable field. This can be done by using the following query:

```
SELECT body, author_id FROM message WHERE message_id = [MSG ID]
```

Checking the status of permissions for an application

A user may grant many extended permissions to an application. Many a time it becomes necessary to check if the user has granted the application a specific permission or not. We can easily do this using FQL.

Getting ready

You should have set up `config.php` and `index.php` as explained in the beginning of the chapter. Also, you should know the permissions for which you want to check the status granted by the user. This can be looked at from the **permissions** table.

How to do it...

The following steps will check the permission for an application:

1. Open `index.php` and append the following code:

```
<html>
  <body>
    <strong>Permission statuses</strong> - <br><br>
    <?php
```

2. Retrieve the status of permissions by executing the following FQL query:

```
$permissions = $facebook->api(array('method' => 'fql.query',
    'query' => "SELECT publish_stream, user_checkins, sms,
    read_mailbox FROM permissions WHERE uid = me()",));
```

3. Display the permission statuses in tabular format:

```
echo '<table width= "50%">';
foreach ($permissions as $permission) {
    echo '<tr><td>' . 'publish_stream'. '</td>
            <td>' . $permission['publish_stream'] .
                '</td></tr>';
    echo '<tr><td>' . 'user_checkins'. '</td>
            <td>' . $permission['user_checkins'] .
                '</td></tr>';
    echo '<tr><td>' . 'sms'. '</td>
            <td>' . $permission['sms'] . '</td></tr>';
    echo '<tr><td>' . 'read_mailbox'. '</td>
            <td>' . $permission['read_mailbox'] .
                '</td></tr>';
}
echo '</table>';
?>
</body>
</html>
```

4. Replace the permissions mentioned in the SELECT clause of the query with the permissions of your choice. Now, save the file and run it. Upon successful execution of the code, a list containing the permission statuses will be displayed and will appear something like this:

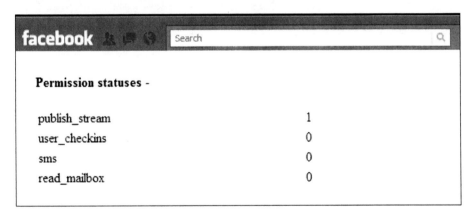

5. Here 1 stands for permission being granted while 0 implies permission has not been granted.

How it works...

Facebook contains a **permissions** table from which we can find the status of certain permissions given by a particular user. In the code, we run the following query:

```
SELECT publish_stream, user_checkins, sms, read_mailbox
  FROM permissions WHERE uid = me()
```

Here, in the `SELECT` clause we write the names of the queries for which we want to check the status. We have checked the status for the following permissions:

- `publish_stream`: It is required to enable an application to post content, comments, and so on
- `user_checkins`: It provides authorized read access to a user's checkins
- `sms`: It enables the application to send and receive messages to and from the user
- `read_mailbox`: It enables the application to read a user's Facebook inbox

We can replace these permissions with any of our choice. We run this query through the `api()` function of the `Facebook` class. The status of these permissions, which is either `0` for *not granted* and `1` for *granted*, is returned and stored in `$permissions`. We use a `foreach` PHP loop to print the permission statuses.

Getting notifications, and their senders, for the current user

Facebook has a very important feature through which it notifies the user whenever his/her friend interacted with him/her, called the notification section. We can retrieve the notifications for the current user for our application by using Facebook FQL.

Getting ready

You should have set up `config.php` and `index.php` as explained in the beginning of the chapter.

How to do it...

The following steps will demonstrate how to get the notifications for the current user:

1. Open `index.php` and append the following code to it:

```
<html>
  <body>
    Notifications for the user <strong><?php echo $me['name'];
    ?></strong> are listed below - <br><br>
```

```
<?php
```

2. Retrieve the notification information by executing the following FQL query:

```
$notifications = $facebook->api(array('method' =>
   'fql.query', 'query' => "SELECT notification_id,
   body_text,sender_id FROM notification WHERE
   recipient_id=me()",));
```

3. Display the notification and its sender in a table format:

```
echo '<table width= "100%">';
echo '<tr><th ALIGN=LEFT>Notification Id</th>
         <th ALIGN=LEFT>Body</th>
         <th ALIGN=LEFT>Sender Id</th></tr>';
foreach ($notification as $notification) {
  if($notification['body_text'])
    echo '<tr><td>' . $notification['notification_id'] .
                '</td>
            <td>' . $notification['body_text'] . '</td>
            <td>' . $notification['sender_id'] .
                '</td></tr>';
}
echo '</table>';
?>
</body>
</html>
```

4. Save the file and run it. A list of the notifications of the current user will be displayed in the descending order of the time with the latest appearing at top. A snapshot of the output of the code is shown in the following screenshot:

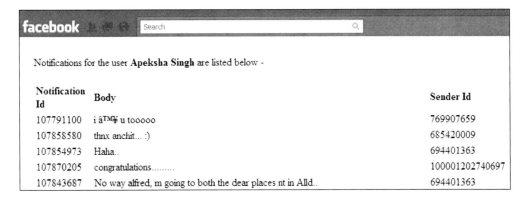

How it works...

To retrieve the notifications of the current user we make use of the **notification** table. Here, we run the following FQL query:

```
SELECT notification_id, body_text, sender_id FROM notification
  WHERE recipient_id = me()
```

The attributes of the `SELECT` clause may vary depending on our choice and can be looked up from the **notification** table. In the previous code, we have retrieved the notification ID, body of the notification, and the ID of the sender.

The query is executed by making a call to the `api()` function of the `Facebook` class. The information returned gets stored in the `$notifications` variable. We use a `foreach()` loop to iterate through the array and display the obtained results one by one.

 An important thing to note here, is that Facebook deletes notifications that are more than seven days old. Thus, notifications which are only less than a week old will get displayed.

Retrieving video details associated with a user

A user may be tagged in a number of videos published on Facebook. To retrieve the information of the videos associated with a user we can use FQL and fetch the videos in which the user has been tagged.

Getting ready

You should have set up `config.php` and `index.php` as explained in the beginning of the chapter. Also, you need to have `user_photo_video_tags` extended permission.

How to do it...

The following steps will retrieve video details in which the user has been tagged:

1. Open `index.php` and append the following code to it:

```
<html>
  <body>

    Videos in which user <strong><?php echo $me['name']; ?></
    strong> has been tagged are listed below - <br><br>
    <?php
```

2. Get the video information pertaining to the current user using the following FQL query:

```
$videos = $facebook->api(array('method' => 'fql.query',
  'query' => "SELECT vid, title, description, thumbnail_link
  FROM video WHERE vid IN(SELECT vid FROM video_tag
  WHERE subject=me())",));
```

3. Display the video details in tabular format:

```
echo '<table width= "100%">';
echo '<tr><th align="LEFT">Video Id</th>
         <th align="LEFT">Title</th>
         <th align="LEFT">Description</th>
         <th align="LEFT">Thumbnail</th></tr>';
foreach ($videos as $video) {
  echo '<tr><td>' . $video['vid'] . '</td>
           <td>' . $video['title'] . '</td>
           <td>' . $video['description'] . '</td>
           <td><img src="' . $video['thumbnail_link'] . '"
               height="50" /></td></tr>';
}
echo '</table>';
?>
</body>
</html>
```

4. Save the file and run the application. A list of the videos, with their details, in which the current user has been tagged will be displayed as shown in the following screenshot:

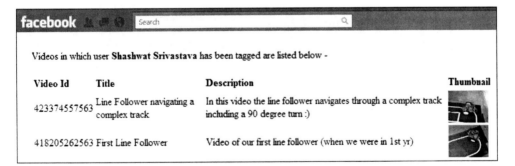

How it works...

Here, we use a nested query as we have to retrieve the video details from two tables—`video_tag` and `video`. First, we retrieve the ID of all the videos in which a user has been tagged. This has been done by executing the following query:

```
SELECT vid FROM video_tag WHERE subject = me()
```

The next step is to get the video details such as title, description, and so on from the **video** table for all the retrieved video IDs. Thus, the complete query becomes:

```
SELECT vid, title, description, thumbnail_link FROM video
    WHERE vid IN (SELECT vid FROM video_tag WHERE subject = me()
```

We make a call to Facebook to execute this query by using the `api()` function of **Facebook** class. Upon running the code, the details of all the videos in which the user has been tagged get stored in the `$videos` variable. We use a `foreach()` loop to iterate through the array and display the obtained video information one by one.

There's more...

In the code, the `subject` field can even accept the ID of a *group* or *event*. In such cases it will give the ID of the videos belonging to that particular group or event. For example to get the details of videos associated with a particular group we can simply run the following query:

```
SELECT vid, title, description, thumbnail_link FROM video
    WHERE vid IN(SELECT vid FROM video_tag WHERE subject=[gid])
```

Here [gid] has to be replaced with the ID of the group whose videos we want to retrieve.

Getting the five latest photos in which a user has been tagged

A Facebook user may have his/her own photos, or may appear in someone else's album. In the latter case, the user is usually tagged or marked in a box and this is reflected as a tagged picture in his/her profile. By using FQL, we can query Facebook to get the five latest pictures in which a user has been tagged.

Getting ready

You should have set up `config.php` and `index.php` as explained in the beginning of the chapter. Also, you need to have `user_photo_video_tags` extended permission.

How to do it...

The following steps will demonstrate how to get the five latest photos of the user:

1. Open `index.php` and append the code given below to it:

```html
<html>
  <body>
    Latest <strong>five</strong> pictures in which <strong>
    <?php echo $me['name']; ?></strong> has been tagged are listed
    below - <br><br>
    <?php
      $i=0;
```

2. Retrieve the tagged pictures of the user by executing the following FQL query:

```php
$tagpics = $facebook->api(array('method' => 'fql.query',
    'query' => "SELECT src_small FROM photo WHERE pid IN (
    SELECT pid,created FROM photo_tag WHERE subject = me()
    ORDER BY created DESC)",));
```

3. Display the latest five tagged pictures:

```php
foreach ($tagpics as $tagpic) {
    echo $tagpic['pid']." ".$tagpic['created'].
        '<img src="' . $tagpic['src_small'] . '" />';
    $i++;
    if($i==5)
        break;
}
?>
  </body>
</html>
```

4. Now save the file and run the application. The five latest pictures, in which the current user has been tagged, will be displayed as shown in the following screenshot:

How it works...

FQL contains a **photo_tag** table in which the details of the pictures in which a specific user has been tagged are present. It contains x and y coordinates of the tag, created time, subject ID, and so on.

Here, we have written a nested FQL query in which first, by using the **photo_tag** table we get the photo ID (pid) of the tagged pictures. We order the pictures by the time they were created in descending order so that we get the latest pictures first. This was done by the following line of code:

```
SELECT pid, created FROM photo_tag WHERE subject = me()
   ORDER BY created DESC
```

Next, to display the pictures we need to fetch their URL. For this, we query the **photo** table for all the picture IDs that we have obtained using the previous query. Thus, the complete query becomes:

```
SELECT src_small FROM photo WHERE pid IN (SELECT pid, created
   FROM photo_tag WHERE subject = me() ORDER BY created DESC)
```

The retrieved picture information gets stored in $tagpics. On traversing this array we simply display the first five among the obtained pictures using a foreach() PHP loop. They will be the latest ones as we have ordered them in the descending order of their created time.

There's more...

The `subject` field present in the **photo_tag** table does not only refer to the user ID of the person we are looking for. We can even get the pictures related to a particular event or group. For this, we simply need to put the corresponding event ID or group ID in the subject field. For example:

`SELECT pid FROM photo_tag WHERE subject=[eid]`, where `[eid]` should be replaced by the ID of an event.

See also

- *Retrieving the latest photos published by a user*

Retrieving the latest photos published by a user

A Facebook user can create photo albums in his/her profile and upload and publish pictures. By using FQL we can retrieve these photographs published by the user.

Getting ready

You should have set up `config.php` and `index.php` as explained in the beginning of the chapter. Also, you need to have `user_photos` extended permission.

How to do it...

The following steps will retrieve the latest pictures published by a user:

1. Open `index.php` and append the following code given:

```
<html>
  <body>
    Latest pictures published by <strong><?php echo $me['name'];
    ?></strong> are shown below - <br><br>
    <?php
```

2. Retrieve the latest pictures published by the user by using the following FQL query:

```
$pics_published = $facebook->api(array('method' =>
   'fql.query', 'query' => "SELECT src_small, pid FROM photo
   WHERE aid IN (SELECT aid FROM album WHERE owner = me()
   ORDER BY created DESC)ORDER BY created DESC",));
```

3. Display the retrieved pictures:

```
foreach ($pics_published as $pic) {
   echo '<img src="' . $pic['src_small'] . '" />';
}
?>
</body>
</html>
```

4. Now run the application file. A series of pictures, which have been recently published by the user, will get displayed and will look something like this:

How it works...

In the code for retrieving the pictures published by a user, first of all we select the albums which the user has created. For this we query the **album** table and order the albums in descending order of their time of creation, thus, making the recent ones the first in the list. It has been done by the following FQL query:

```
SELECT aid FROM album WHERE owner = me() ORDER BY created DESC
```

Next, we need to retrieve the pictures associated with these albums and display them. Since, this should contain the latest ones at the top, we order the pictures in the descending order of their creation time. This is finally achieved through the following complete query:

```
SELECT src_small, pid FROM photo WHERE aid IN (SELECT aid
    FROM album WHERE owner = me() ORDER BY created DESC)
    ORDER BY created DESC
```

Here, `pid` refers to the picture ID whereas `src_small` is the URL of a particular picture. The pictures retrieved get stored in a PHP variable `$pics_published`. We traverse through this array through the `foreach()` loop and display the pictures using the HTML `img` tag.

There's more...

We can always limit the number of pictures that we want to display or retrieve. This can be easily done by using the `LIMIT` clause in FQL. For example to retrieve the latest five photos we can use the `LIMIT` clause as follows:

```
SELECT src_small, pid FROM photo WHERE aid IN (SELECT aid FROM album
    WHERE owner = me() ORDER BY created DESC) ORDER BY created DESC
    LIMIT 5
```

Retrieving details of an event

One of the most amazing features of Facebook is **events**. Events allow us to schedule some task at a specific time and invite people and thus, we can share our plans and ideas. We can use FQL to retrieve the details of any event created by a user.

Getting ready

You should have set up `config.php` and `index.php` as explained in the beginning of the chapter. Also, you need to have `user_events` extended permission.

How to do it...

The following steps will retrieve the event details:

1. Open `index.php` and append the code given below:

```
<html>
  <body>
    <?php
```

2. Specify the event id:

```
    $eid = 153741751357153;
?>
Event information for id <?php echo $eid; ?> created by
<strong><?php echo $me['name']; ?></strong> is listed below -
<br><br>
<?php
```

3. Retrieve the details of an event using this FQL query:

```
$events = $facebook->api(array('method' => 'fql.query',
    'query' => "SELECT eid, name, description, start_time,
    end_time, location, pic_square FROM event
    WHERE eid = $eid"));
```

4. Display event details in a table format:

```
echo '<table width = "100%">';
echo '<tr><th align="LEFT">Event Id</th>
         <th align="LEFT">Name</th>
         <th align="LEFT">Description</th>
         <th align="LEFT">Location</th>
         <th align="LEFT">Picture</th>
         <th align="LEFT">Start Time</th>
         <th align="LEFT">End Time</th></tr>';
foreach ($events as $event) {
  echo '<tr><td>' . $event['eid'] . '</td>
           <td>' . $event['name'] . '</td>
           <td>' . $event['description'] . '</td>
           <td>' . $event['location'] . '</td>
           <td><img src = "' . $event['pic_square'] .
               '" /></td>
           <td>' . date("D M j G:i:s T Y", $event
                   ['start_time']) . '</td>
           <td>' . date("D M j G:i:s T Y", $event
                   ['end_time']) . '</td>
       </tr>';
```

```
        }
        echo '</table>';
    ?>
    </body>
</html>
```

5. Replace $eid with the event ID of your choice. Now run the application file. A list containing the event detail will get displayed and will appear something like this:

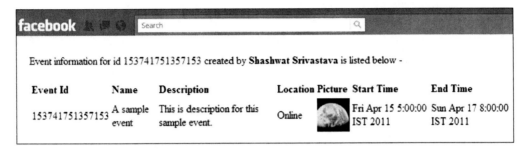

How it works...

FQL contains an **event** table which stores all the details corresponding to any event which is uniquely identified by an event ID. Here, we retrieve the following details—event ID, name, description, start time, end time, and location. This has been done by executing the following query:

```
SELECT eid, name, description, start_time, end_time, location,
    pic_square FROM event WHERE eid = [eid]
```

The [eid] in the query has to be replaced by the ID of the event for which we want to fetch the details.

We make a call to this query using the api() function of the Facebook class. The returned information gets stored in the $events variable. Next, using a foreach() PHP loop we print the obtained event details in a tabular format.

Retrieving details of a user's friends by using the multiquery method

Many a time, we want to execute multiple FQL queries in our application. If we will use the `fql.query` method to do this, then our application will make multiple requests to Facebook for executing these queries and will hamper performance. We can optimize this by using the `fql.multiquery` method which allows us to execute multiple queries together in a single call to Facebook. This improves performance tremendously and consumes less time.

Getting ready

You should have set up `config.php` and `index.php` as explained in the beginning of the chapter.

How to do it...

The following steps will demonstrate how to retrieve a user's friend's details:

1. Open `index.php` and append the code to it:

   ```
   <html>
     <body>
       Details of friends of <strong><?php echo $me['name']; ?></
       strong> by using fql.multiquery are shown below - <br><br>

       <?php
   ```

2. Define multiple queries in the `$multi_queries` array:

   ```
   $multi_queries = array('query1' => 'SELECT uid2 FROM friend
       WHERE uid1 = me()', 'query2' => 'SELECT name FROM user
       WHERE uid in (SELECT uid2 FROM #query1)', );
   ```

3. Convert the `$multi_queries` array to a JSON type array using the `json_encode()` function:

   ```
   $encoded_multi_queries = json_encode($multi_queries);
   ```

4. Execute the multiple queries using the `fql.multiquery` method:

   ```
   $results = $facebook->api(array('method' => 'fql.
       multiquery', 'queries' => $encoded_multi_queries));
   ```

5. Display the results of the query:

```
echo '<strong>Query 1: Uid of friends - </strong>';
foreach ($results[0]['fql_result_set'] as $result) {
  echo $result['uid2'] . ', ';
}
echo '<br><br><strong>Query 2: Name of friends - </strong>';
foreach ($results[1]['fql_result_set'] as $result) {
  echo $result['name'] . ', ';
}
?>
</body>
</html>
```

6. Save and run the application file. A successful execution of the code will display an output like this:

How it works...

In the code, our main aim is to retrieve the user ID and name of the current user's friends and display them. `$multi_queries` is a PHP array with two indexes—`query1` and `query2` which contain one query each. Thus, we have two set of queries:

- `query1 => SELECT uid2 FROM friend WHERE uid1 = me()`: It selects the user ID of the friends of the current user
- `query2 => SELECT name FROM user WHERE uid in (SELECT uid2 FROM #query1)`: It gives the names of the users whose ID has been retrieved in the first query

We can fetch data from one query and then again use it in another query within the same call. To reference the results of a former query in any latter query within the same call, we need to specify its name in the `FROM` clause, preceded by #. Thus, we have `query2` dependent on the result of `query1`. Here, with the use of multiquery we are executing both of them in the same call.

We use the `json_encode()` function to convert array named `$multi_queries` to a JSON data type and we store this in `$encoded_multi_queries`. For executing the multiquery, we use the `api()` function. It takes an array as its argument parameter. In the array, we set `fql.multiquery` as the `method` to indicate that we want to execute multiple queries in the same call. And, the `queries` index contains the FQL queries in JSON format which we want to execute. After execution of the multiquery, the returned information gets stored in the `$results` variable. We use a `foreach()` PHP loop to print the retrieved data from both the queries.

> You can use `print_r($results)` to understand the structure of the returned data array.

4
Using FB Script

In this chapter, we will cover:

- ▸ Getting the current user status and performing session validation
- ▸ Setting up extended permissions during login
- ▸ Logging out a user
- ▸ Resetting the size of iframe
- ▸ Making a Graph API call
- ▸ Executing an FQL query
- ▸ Subscribing to an event change
- ▸ Unsubscribing to an event change
- ▸ Retrieving a profile picture using XFBML
- ▸ Adding bookmarks using XFBML
- ▸ Authentication and setting up extended permissions using XFBML

Introduction

Facebook has its own JavaScript SDK which provides a rich set of features and functionalities through JavaScript. This relieves the load off the server and makes the application load faster. The client-side authentication and rendering provides a great user experience as the content becomes dynamic in nature.

Facebook JavaScript SDK comes with a set of predefined functions and XFBML tags. We can use these functions and XFBML tags in applications which run inside, as well as outside Facebook. Facebook JavaScript SDK consists of a JavaScript file whose source URL is `http://connect.facebook.net/en_US/all.js`. We need to include this JS file in our application. This file handles all Facebook JavaScript functions as well as parsing and rendering of XFBML tags. These predefined functions are like normal JavaScript functions and they provide us with functionalities, such as performing Facebook authentication, making a Graph API call, executing FQL query, and so on. On the other hand, XFBML tags are like HTML tags which are parsed and rendered by Facebook JavaScript SDK, such as displaying a profile picture, login button, bookmark button, and so on.

Prerequisites

This section will introduce you to the basic configuration that you must do before starting with the recipes discussed in this chapter. The following is a prerequisite that must be fulfilled before implementing any recipe given in this chapter:

1. Create a file `index.php` and add the following code to it:

    ```
    <html xmlns="http://www.w3.org/1999/xhtml" xmlns:fb="http://www.
    facebook.com/2008/fbml">
    <body>
    ```

2. All the application content will be inside the following `div`:

    ```
    <div id="fb-root">
      <!-- Your application content here -->
    </div>
    ```

3. Include jQuery library from Google CDN:

    ```
    <script type="text/javascript"
      src="https://ajax.googleapis.com/ajax/libs/jquery/
      1.5.2/jquery.min.js">
    </script>
    ```

4. Initialize the application by calling `FB.init()`:

    ```
    <script type="text/javascript">
    window.fbAsyncInit = function() {
      FB.init({
        appId : 'your_app_id',
        status : true,
        cookie : true,
        xfbml : true
      });
    /* Your FB JavaScript code here. It will be loaded asynchronously.
    */
    };
    ```

5. Load FB JavaScript SDK asynchronously:

```
(function() {
  var e = document.createElement('script');
  e.type = 'text/javascript';
  e.src = document.location.protocol +
          '//connect.facebook.net/en_US/all.js';
  e.async = true;
  document.getElementById('fb-root').appendChild(e);
}());
</script>
</body>
</html>
```

Here, replace `your_app_id` in the `FB.init()` function with your own application ID.

In order to use XFBML in your application consistently across all web browsers, we need to add an XML namespace attribute to the root `<html>` element of `index.php`. This is necessary to render XFBML tags in Internet Explorer.

```
<html xmlns="http://www.w3.org/1999/xhtml"
  xmlns:fb="http://www.facebook.com/2008/fbml">
```

We load the Facebook JavaScript SDK by using the standard `<script>` element. We load SDK asynchronously so that it does not hinder the loading of other elements in our application and this ensures fast page loads for the users. Also, we have specified a `<div>` element named `fb-root` within the document. It is important to include a div with this name otherwise the JavaScript SDK will not load and report an error. The code for this is as follows:

```
<div id="fb-root">
  <!-- Your application content here -->
</div>
<script type="text/javascript">
window.fbAsyncInit = function() {
  FB.init({
    appId : 'your_app_id',
    status : true,
    cookie : true,
    xfbml : true
  });
/* Your FB JavaScript code here. It will be loaded asynchronously. */
};
(function() {
  var e = document.createElement('script');
  e.type = 'text/javascript';
  e.src = document.location.protocol +
          '//connect.facebook.net/en_US/all.js';
```

```
    e.async = true;
    document.getElementById('fb-root').appendChild(e);
}());
</script>
```

Facebook JS SDK is available over both regular and SSL connections. Apart from the protocol, the rest of the URL (`//connect.facebook.net/en_US/all.js`), used for loading FB JS SDK over regular or SSL connection, is the same. Depending on the connection type of our application, we can load FB JS SDK accordingly by appending `document.location.protocol` to this URL. The `document.location.protocol` returns the protocol of the web page which is either `http` or `https`.

As soon as the JavaScript SDK is loaded asynchronously and is ready to use, we initialize our Facebook application by calling the `FB.init()` function. Here we pass the following four parameters:

- `appId`: which is the application ID which we get after registering our application with Facebook
- `status`: its true value implies that we can perform a user login status check if required
- `cookie`: it enables the cookies to allow the server to access the session
- `xfbml`: allows us to access and parse XFBML tags, if true

Another important thing to note, is that we have called the `FB.init()` function inside the function assigned to `window.fbAsyncInit`. This function, which is assigned to `window.fbAsyncInit`, is executed as soon as the JavaScript SDK is loaded asynchronously. Thus, any code which we want to run after the SDK is loaded, should be placed within this function after the `FB.init()` function.

Additionally, we have loaded jQuery by using the following `<script>` code:

```
<script type="text/javascript"
  src="https://ajax.googleapis.com/ajax/libs/jquery/
  1.5.2/jquery.min.js">
</script>
```

We will use jQuery throughout this chapter as it is easy to use and understand, as well as it makes coding easy.

 Facebook JavaScript SDK supports different locales. The locales follow `ISO language` and `country codes` respectively, and are concatenated by an underscore. For example, `en_US` in `http://connect.facebook.net/en_US/all.js` represents US English. The complete list of Facebook locales is available in this XML file - `https://www.facebook.com/translations/FacebookLocales.xml`.

Getting the current user status and performing session validation

Almost always, your application requires performing certain operations for which we need to have an authenticated and valid user session. By using Facebook JavaScript SDK, we can check the logged in status of the user and whether the session is still valid or not.

Getting ready

You should have created `index.php` as mentioned in the beginning of this chapter.

How to do it...

Open `index.php` and add the following highlighted code inside the function assigned to `window.fbAsyncInit`, just after the `FB.init()` function:

1. Initialize the application:

```
window.fbAsyncInit = function() {
  FB.init({
    appId : 'your_app_id',
    status : true,
    cookie : true,
    xfbml : true
  });
  /* Your FB JavaScript code here. It will be loaded asynchronously.
  */
```

2. Retrieve the current user's login session using the `FB.getLoginStatus()` function:

```
FB.getLoginStatus(function(response) {
  if (response.session) {
    alert('We have confirmed that you have a
      valid session.');
  }
  else {
    FB.login(function(response) {
      if (response.session) {
        alert("User is logged in");
      }
      else {
        alert("User is not logged in");
      }
    });
```

```
        }
      });
   };
```

3. Save and run `index.php`.

How it works...

Here, after initializing our Facebook application, we make a call to the `FB.getLogin Status()` function, which retrieves the current user's login status from the Facebook server. It takes a callback function as an argument. This callback function receives a JavaScript array named `response`, which contains information about the current connection between the client and the Facebook server. This `response` array has an element named `session` which contains a Boolean type value and can be used to determine whether the user has a valid session or not. If the user has a valid session, then the code inside the `if` conditional statement gets executed which, in turn, displays an alert box with the message shown in the following screenshot:

If `response.session` is `false`, then we know that the session has either expired or doesn't exist. Thus, we need to prompt the user to login. For this, we make a call to the `FB.login()` function. It will first check whether the user is logged on to the Facebook network or not. If not so, then it will display a Facebook Login dialog box to the user. Once the user successfully logs on to Facebook, it next checks whether the user has authorized the application or not, that is, whether the user has allowed the application to access his/her basic information or not. Again, if it is not so, then it displays the **Request for Permission** dialog box as shown in the following screenshot:

After the user interacts with this dialog box, we again check for the value of `response.session` inside the callback function, which is the argument of the `FB.login()` function. If the user has authorized the application, then `response.session` will be set to `true` otherwise it will be `false`. A message is then displayed accordingly.

There's more...

In our code, `FB.login()` is triggered automatically if the user is not logged in. However, this function always launches a Facebook pop-up dialog box. This pop up will be blocked by all modern browsers as it does not have a user event, such as a click on a hyperlink or button, associated with it and this is deemed as malicious activity by them. To overcome this problem, instead of calling the `FB.Login()` function automatically when the user doesn't have a valid session, we can associate with the `onclick()` event of a button or hyperlink. This can be done by the following code snippet:

```
<input type="button" onclick="FB.login()"
  value="Click to Login" />
```

> ► *Authentication and setting up extended permissions using XFBML*

Setting up extended permissions during login

A Facebook application is often required to access the user's profile, to post messages on his/her wall as well as on his/her friends' wall, to publish pictures, and so on. However, for security reasons, all these tasks are not allowed by default by Facebook and we need to request specific permission, known as **extended permission**, for each task from the user. This can be easily done at the client side using the Facebook JavaScript SDK.

Getting ready

You should have set up `index.php`, as explained in the beginning of the chapter.

How to do it...

The following steps will help in setting up extended permissions:

1. Open `index.php` and add a login button inside the div `fb-root`:

```
<div id="fb-root">
<!-- Your application content here -->
<input type="button" id="login" value="Click to Login" />
</div>
```

2. Add the following highlighted code just after the `FB.init()` function. Here, we use FB.login() function for requesting extended permissions:

```
/* Your FB JavaScript code here. It will be loaded asynchronously.
*/
$(document).ready(function() {
  $("#login").click(function() {
    FB.login(function(response) {},
    {perms: 'read_stream, publish_stream, offline_access'});
  });
});
```

3. Save the file and run it. When the user launches the application for the first time and if he/she is already logged in to Facebook, then a dialog box asking for the above mentioned permissions will get displayed and will look like the following screenshot:

How it works...

For requesting extended permissions, when the user logs in for the first time, we use the
`FB.login()` function. The first argument of this function is a callback function and the
second argument is optional and is used to modify login behavior. The `perms` takes a string
as its value which contains extended permissions separated by a comma. Here, it is—`read_
stream, publish_stream, offline_access`.

We have asked for the read, publish, and offline permissions from the user. If more
permissions are required, then they can be simply looked up from the permission table
given at this link - `http://developers.facebook.com/docs/reference/api/
permissions/`.

See also

▸ Another way to ask for an extended set of permissions is through XFBML. For more
information, refer *Authentication and setting up extended permissions using XFBML*

Logging out a user

Facebook JavaScript SDK allows to safely logout the current user from Facebook. This is a must have feature, especially when your application is hosted outside of Facebook. Here is how we will implement this.

Getting ready

You should have set up `index.php` as explained in the beginning of the chapter.

How to do it...

The following steps will show how to log out a user:

1. Open `index.php` and add the following code inside the div `fb-root`:

   ```
   <input type="button" id="logout" value="Click to Logout" />
   ```

2. Now, inside the function assigned to window.fbAsyncInit, copy the following highlighted code right after the FB.init() function. Here, we use the `FB.logout()` function to logout a user:

   ```
   $(document).ready(function() {
     $("#logout").click(function() {
       FB.logout(function(response) {
         // user is now logged out
         alert('User has been successfully logged out.');
       });
     });
   });
   ```

3. Save and run `index.php`.

How it works...

For logging out a user, we have provided an input button with a `logout` ID. Next by using jQuery, we have registered to the `click()` event and whenever this event is fired, the callback function inside this is executed.

We make a call to the `FB.logout()` function inside the callback function. This function automatically logs out the current user from the Facebook network. It accepts an optional argument which is also a callback function. This function is invoked when the user has been successfully logged out. We use this callback function to display an alert message to the user as shown in the following screenshot:

Chapter 4

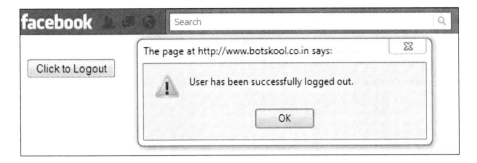

See also

▶ We can also use XFBML tag to provide a logout option for the user. It has been explained in *Authentication and setting up extended permissions using XFBML* recipe.

Resetting the size of iframe

Facebook allows us to set the size of your application's iframe inside which our content appears. This is useful whenever our content changes, that is, we can change the width and height of our iframe accordingly. Facebook Javascript SDK comes equipped with this functionality and we will show you here how to implement it.

Getting ready

You should have set up `index.php` as explained in the beginning of the chapter.

How to do it...

The following will help reset the size of iframe:

1. Open `index.php` and add the following highlighted code to the div `fb-root`:

```
<div id="fb-root">
  <!-- Your application content here -->
  Width(in pixels): <input type="text" id="width" value="640" />
  Height(in pixels): <input type="text" id="height"
    value="480" />
  <br />
  <input type="button" id="resize" value="Resize iframe" />
</div>
```

3. Add the following code after the FB.init() function. Here, we use the `FB.Canvas.setSize()` function to set the size of the iframe:

```
$(document).ready(function() {
  $("#resize").click(function() {
    FB.Canvas.setSize({
      width: $("#width").val(),
      height: $("#height").val()
    });
  });
});
```

4. Save and run `index.php`.

How it works...

Here, we have used a pair of text type input boxes to demonstrate how to reset the size of the application's iframe. The two input textboxes with IDs `width` and `height` correspond to width and height of the iframe in pixels respectively. Also, we have an input button with the `resize` ID. We have registered to use the `click()` event of this button with the help of the following code:

```
$(document).ready(function() {
  $("#resize").click(function() {
    FB.Canvas.setSize({
      width: $("#width").val(),
      height: $("#height").val()
    });
  });
});
```

We have used the `FB.Canvas.setSize()` function inside the callback function of the `$("#resize").click()`. This function takes an optional object as the argument which has two attributes—`width` and `height`. These decide the new dimension of the iframe and these values are in pixels. We use the `val()` function of the jQuery to get the values of the two input textboxes.

 The maximum value of the width of the iframe is restricted to whatever we have chosen in our application settings. However, there is no restriction on the maximum value of the height of the iframe.

Also, if we don't pass any argument inside the `FB.Canvas.setSize()` function and call it, then the iframe is automatically resized according to the current content size.

Making a Graph API call

We can make Graph API calls to the Facebook server through the JavaScript SDK. This allows us to build dynamic applications, which can load data directly from Facebook servers to the user's browser. This improves performance tremendously, in comparison to making all calls from your server, as all processing and rendering is done on the client side.

Getting ready

You should have set up `index.php` as explained in the beginning of this chapter.

How to do it...

The following steps will describe a Graph API call:

1. Open `index.php` and add the following code to it just below the `FB.init()` function. Specify the content to be posted:

    ```
    var text = 'This content is posted via the JS SDK';
    ```

2. Make a Graph API call using the `FB.api()` function:

    ```
    FB.api('/me/feed', 'post', { message: text },
    function(response) {
      if (!response || response.error) {
        alert('Error occured');
      } else {
        alert('Post ID is ' + response.id);
      }
    });
    ```

3. Save and run the file. An alert box will be displayed as shown in the following screenshot:

Also, a message will be posted on the current user's wall as shown in the following screenshot:

How it works...

Here, we have used the `FB.api()` function of JS SDK to make a Graph API based call. The syntax of the `FB.api()` function is the following code snippet:

```
FB.api(url_path, http_method, query_param, cb_fn);
```

The various parameters used inside the `FB.api()` function are as follows:

▶ `url_path`: This signifies the URL of the Graph API object whose properties we want to access. For example, to access the current user's friends, this should be set as `/me/friends` and gets automatically appended to `https://graph.facebook.com`.

▶ `http_method`: This is used to mention the type of request which we want to make. We can either make a `POST`, `GET`, or `DELETE` request to Facebook. This is an optional field with `GET` as the default request.

▶ `query_param`: This is also an optional field. It contains the necessary parameters related to the current query. For example, it can be a message which is to be published or can even be paging parameters.

▶ `cb_fn`: This is the callback function which is used to handle the response.

In the preceding code, we have published a message given by the `text` variable to the current user's wall. For this, we make a call to the `FB.api()` function as shown in the following code snippet:

```
FB.api('/me/feed', 'post', { message: text },
    function(response) { });
```

Here, we have accessed the Graph API object given by `https://graph.facebook.com/me/feed`. As we want to publish the message, a `POST` request had been made. Also, the `query_param` parameter contains the message which we want to publish. We have used the callback function to notify the user whether the `POST` request was successful or not.

Executing an FQL query

One way to execute the FQL query is by using the PHP SDK for the Graph API. However, we can even execute FQL by using the Facebook JavaScript SDK method `FB.Data.query`. This makes execution faster without putting any load on your server.

Getting ready

You should have set up `index.php` as explained in the beginning of the chapter.

How to do it...

Here we retrieve the current user's profile information using the FQL query.

1. Open `index.php` and copy the code given below just after the `FB.init()` function. Check the login status of the user by using the `FB.getLoginStatus()` function:

```
FB.getLoginStatus(function(response) {
    if (response.session) {
        fqlQuery();
    }
});
```

2. Define the FQL query inside the `fqlQuery()` function:

```
function fqlQuery(){
    var query = FB.Data.query('SELECT name, hometown_location,
        sex, pic_square FROM user WHERE uid=me()
    ');
```

3. Print the result:

```
query.wait(function(rows) {
    $("#name").html('Your name: ' + rows[0].name + "<br />" +
    '<img src="' + rows[0].pic_square + '" alt="" />' +
    "<br />");
});
}
```

4. Save the file and run it. If we have a valid user session, then the FQL query will run and we will get the output as shown in the following screenshot:

How it works...

Here, we use the `FB.Data.query()` function of Facebook JavaScript SDK to perform a parameterized FQL query. In the earlier code, first we use the `FB.getLoginStatus()` function to check whether the user's session is a valid one or not. This has been done as we are retrieving the profile information of currently logged in user. If the session is valid, then we make a call to the `fqlQuery()` function.

In the `fqlQuery()` function, we use the `FB.Data.query()` function to execute the FQL query. It takes a single argument, which is the query we want to execute, and is in the form of string. Here, it is the following code snippet:

```
SELECT name, hometown_location, sex, pic_square FROM user
WHERE uid = me()
```

This function returns an `FB.Data.Query` object, which gets stored in the `query` variable. We parse this object row by row and display the results accordingly.

Subscribing to an event change

Facebook JavaScript SDK has a beautiful feature known as **event subscription**, that is, we can subscribe to any particular event and whenever that event takes place, a callback function, which has to be specified by us, will be executed. This eliminates the need to use the traditional loop based mechanism, which checks for the event continually, and we are automatically notified when a particular event takes place. Suppose we want to subscribe to an event which gets fired whenever a user logs in. This event is known as `auth.login` and can be subscribed to as explained in this recipe.

Getting ready

You should have set up `index.php` as explained in the beginning of the chapter.

How to do it...

The following steps will demonstrate how to subscribe to an event change:

1. Open `index.php` and add the following highlighted code inside the `fb-root` div:

```
<div id="fb-root">
   <button id="login">Login</button>
</div>
```

2. Add the following highlighted code just after the `FB.init()` function inside the function assigned to `window.fbAsyncInit`. Here, we subscribe to the login event using the FB.Event.subscribe() function:

```
window.fbAsyncInit = function() {
   FB.init({appId: 'your_application_id', status: true,
      cookie: true, xfbml: true});
   /* All the events have been registered here. */
   FB.Event.subscribe('auth.login', function(response) {
      // do something when the user logs in
      alert('You have logged in.');
   });
};
```

4. Use the `ready()` function to register the jQuery `click()` event:

```
$(document).ready(function() {
   $("#login").click(function() {
      FB.login();
   });
});
```

5. Save `index.php` and launch the application.

How it works...

Here, we have used the `FB.Event.subscribe()` function to subscribe to the `auth.login` event. This function takes two arguments. The first argument is the name of the event to which we want to subscribe to and the second argument of the function is the callback function which gets executed when the event mentioned as the first argument takes place.

To demonstrate event subscription, we have used a button with `id` as `login` and `value` as `Login`. We have used jQuery to specify a callback function for the click event on this button. This function in turn calls the `FB.login()` function.

Now if a user has not logged on to the Facebook network and if he/she clicks on the login button of this application, then the `FB.login()` function gets executed. Hence, the Facebook Login dialog box will appear as shown in the following screenshot:

As soon as the user logs in, the `auth.login` event will be fired and the following screen is displayed:

There's more...

You can subscribe to the following events:

Events	Description
auth.login	This event is fired when a user logs in
auth.logout	This event is fired when a user logs out
auth.prompt	This event is fired when a user is prompted to log in or register after clicking on a Like button
auth.sessionChange	This event is fired when the user session changes
auth.statusChange	This event is fired when the status changes
xfbml.render	This event is fired when the FB.XFBML.parse() function finishes its execution
edge.create	This event is fired when the user likes something (through the fb:like XFBML tag)
edge.remove	This event is fired when the user unlikes something (through the fb:like XFBML tag)
comment.create	This event is fired when the user adds a comment (through the fb:comments XFBML tag)
comment.remove	This event is fired when the user removes a comment (through the fb:comments XFBML tag)
fb.log	This event is fired on log message.

Unsubscribing to an event change

If we have earlier subscribed to an event change, then at a later stage it may happen that we no longer need this functionality. To deal with this we can simply unsubscribe to that event by using Facebook JavaScript SDK.

Getting ready

You should have set up `index.php` as explained in the beginning of the chapter.

How to do it...

The following steps will show how to unsubscribe to an event change:

1. Open `index.php` and add the following highlighted code inside the `fb-root` div. Add login, logout, subscribe, and unsubscribe buttons:

```
<div id="fb-root">
  <input type="button" id="login" value="Login" /><br />
  <input type="button" id="logout" value="Logout" /><br />
  <input type="button" id="sub" value="Subscribe to auth.login
    event" /><br />
  <input type="button" id="unsub" value="Unsubscribe to
    auth.login event" /><br />
</div>
```

2. Declare jQuery click events for the login, logout, subscribe, and unsubscribe buttons:

```
<script type="text/javascript">
  $(document).ready(function() {
    var onAuth = function(response) {
      alert('You have logged in.');
    };
    $("#login").click(function() {
      FB.login();
    });
    $("#logout").click(function() {
      FB.logout();
    });
    $("#sub").click(function() {
      FB.Event.subscribe('auth.login', onAuth);
    });
    $("#unsub").click(function() {
      FB.Event.unsubscribe('auth.login', onAuth);
    });
  });
</script>
```

3. Save and run `index.php`.

How it works...

Here, we have used four input type buttons to demonstrate how to unsubscribe to an event. We use two buttons with `login` and `logout` IDs to login to and logout from Facebook respectively. We have added `FB.login()` and `FB.logout()` functions to the `click()` event of these buttons, which handle authentication.

Next, we have assigned a callback function to `onAuth`. This displays a message to the user that he/she has successfully logged in. We assign the `FB.Event.subscribe()` function to the `click()` event of the input button with the `sub` ID.

Finally, to unsubscribe, we have used an input button with the `unsub` ID. Once the user clicks on this, the `FB.Event.unsubscribe()` function is called. This function takes two arguments. The first argument should be the name of the event, which we want to unsubscribe, and the second argument should have a callback function, which is exactly similar to that defined in `FB.Event.subscribe()`.

Retrieving a profile picture using XFBML

For rendering the profile picture of a user, we will need to make a request through Facebook Graph API and then retrieve it. Facebook JavaScript SDK provides an easier way. We can use XFBML markup to do this. Here, we just have to write an XFBML tag to render the picture. Also, we can configure the profile picture being displayed.

Getting ready

You need to set up `index.php`, as explained in the beginning of the chapter. Also, you should know `UID` of the user, whose profile picture you want to render, if he/she is not the current logged in user.

How to do it...

The following steps will help retrieve a profile picture:

1. Open `index.php` and add the following XFBML tags inside the div named `fb-root`:

   ```
   Retrieving profile picture of users using XBFML - <br><br>
   ```

2. Use the XFBML `fb:profile-pic` tag to load the profile pictures of the users:

   ```
   <fb:profile-pic uid="loggedinuser" linked="true"
     size="square">
   </fb:profile-pic>
   <fb:profile-pic uid="{custom_uid}" linked="true"
     size="square">
   </fb:profile-pic>
   ```

3. The first `fb:profile-pic` XFBML tag will load the profile picture of the current user. The second `fb:profile-pic` XFBML tag will load the profile picture of the user whose UID is {`custom_uid`}. You can replace this accordingly.

How it works...

Here, we have used the `fb:profile-pic` XFBML tag to render the profile picture of users. For XFBML tags to be parsed and rendered, the `xfbml` attribute of the array, which is passed as an argument of the `FB.init()` function, should have been set to `true`. This has already been done in `index.php` in the beginning of the chapter. Also, XFBML tags should be present inside the div named `fb-root`. The `fb:profile-pic` takes the following attributes:

- ▸ `uid`: This attribute contains the UID of the user whose profile picture has to be loaded. To display the profile picture of the current user, set the value of this attribute as `loggedinuser`.
- ▸ `size`: It decides the size of the rendered profile picture. The default value is `thumb`. Other valid values are `small`, `normal`, and `square`. We can also specify `width` and `height` settings instead. Here, we have set the `size` as `square`.
- ▸ `linked`: It renders the image as a link to the user's profile. Valid values are `true` or `false`. Default is `true`.
- ▸ `width`: We can set the width of the image in pixels like we do in the `img` HTML tag.
- ▸ `height`: Similarly, we can set the height of the image in pixels.

We can use the above mentioned attributes to render the profile picture of the user appropriately.

 The `fb:profile-pic` XFBML tag is treated like an `img` HTML tag by Facebook JavaScript SDK. Hence, all `img` attributes are valid and can be used with this XFBML tag.

Adding bookmarks using XFBML

Facebook has **bookmark** functionality which enables its users to bookmark most used and necessary links on the Facebook network. We can use XFBML to provide a user with a readymade button, which can be used by him/her to bookmark your application. This is an attractive way to indulge users in your application.

Getting ready

You should have set up `index.php` as explained in the beginning of the chapter.

How to do it...

The following steps will show how to add bookmarks

1. Go to the following URL—`http://www.facebook.com/developers/apps.php`.

2. Next, choose your application from the **My Apps** section, if it is not selected by default, and then click on **Edit Settings**. This will load the settings page of your application.

3. Now, click on the **Facebook Integration** tab.

4. Here, under the **Canvas** section, there is an attribute named **Bookmark URL** as shown in the following screenshot:

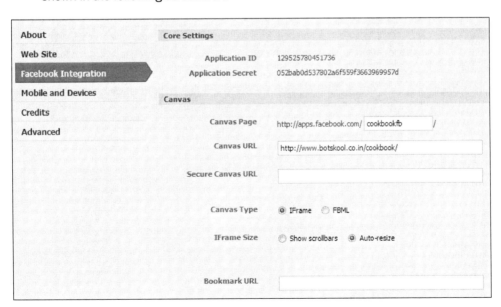

5. Enter the URL, to which the user should be redirected to when he/she clicks on your application's bookmark. If this is left blank, then the user will be redirected to your **Canvas Page**. Here, we have left this field blank as we want the user to be redirected to your main application page.

6. Open `index.php` and add the following XFBML tag inside the div `fb-root`:

    ```
    <fb:bookmark></fb:bookmark>
    ```

7. Now, if you will run `index.php`, then you will see the bookmark button. On clicking on this button, the following message is displayed inside Facebook pop-up box:

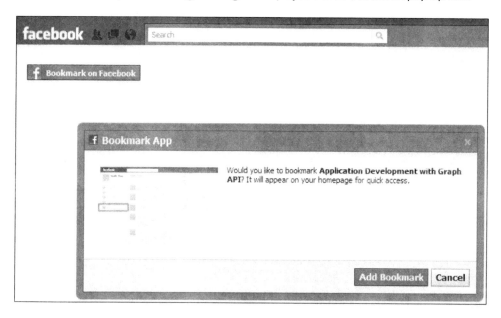

8. Once, you click on the **Add Bookmark** button, a link to your application will appear in your profile menu as shown in the following screenshot:

How it works...

The `fb:bookmark` XFBML tag renders a bookmark button for our application. If a user clicks on this button, then a pop-up box for final confirmation is displayed to the user. Once the user clicks on **Add bookmark** button, a link to our application will appear in the user's Facebook navigation menu. The bookmark link to our application can be configured on the settings page of our application as explained earlier.

A user can bookmark links to multiple applications. These links are then arranged according to the applications most frequently used by the user and this is automatically calculated and implemented by Facebook.

Authentication and setting up extended permissions using XFBML

If we use Facebook JavaScript SDK in your application, then we can harness the easy-to-use authentication functionality provided by XFBML. It is an intuitive way to get users logged in to your application and requires a limited use of coding. This XFBML authentication button can be used both on iframe-based applications which run inside Facebook as well as independent applications which run on third-party websites.

Getting ready

You should have set up `index.php`, as explained in the beginning of this chapter. Also, you should have the list of extended permissions ready which you want to request from the user.

How to do it...

The following steps will demonstrate autentication:

1. Open `index.php` and append the following XFBML tag inside the div named `fb-root`. Include the XFBML `fb:login-button` tag and set extended permissions:

    ```
    <fb:login-button show-faces="false" width="200" max-rows="1"
      autologoutlink="true" perms="read_stream,publish_stream">
    </fb:login-button>
    ```

2. Next, add the following JavaScript code snippet just after the `FB.init()` function. Use the `FB.Event.subscribe()` functions to subscribe to the login and logout events:

    ```
    FB.Event.subscribe('auth.login', function(response) {
      // do something when user logs in
      alert('You have authorized and logged in.');
    });
    FB.Event.subscribe('auth.logout', function(response) {
      // do something when user logs out
      alert('You have logged out.');
    });
    ```

3. Now, launch the application.

How it works...

Here, we have used the `fb:login-button` XFBML tag which provides end users with an option to authenticate the application and use it. It also has a provision for requesting extended permissions from the user. This XFBML tag has the following attributes:

- **show-faces**: It decides whether to display the face of friends of users already connected to this application to him/her. Valid values are `true` and `false`.

- **width**: This is the width of the login button in pixels. The default value is 200.

- **max-rows**: This the maximum number of rows of a profile picture of user's friends which are displayed below the login button. The default value is `1`.

- **perms**: It should have a list of extended permissions where each permission is separated by a comma.

- **autologoutlink**: This determines whether to display a logout button to the user in case he/she has logged in. Valid values are `true` and `false`.

We have used this XFBML tag with the following code snippet:

```
<fb:login-button show-faces="false" width="200" max-rows="1"
  autologoutlink="true" perms="read_stream,publish_stream">
</fb:login-button>
```

Here, we have set `show-faces` to `false`, `autologoutlink` to `true`, and `perms` to `read_stream` and `publish_stream` separated by a comma. We can add more extended permissions, if necessary.

Initially, when a user opens the application and if he/she has not logged onto the Facebook network, then the login button appears. On clicking on this Facebook Login dialog box, the following screen is displayed:

After this, if the user has not authorized the application and he/she is opening it for the first time, then a second dialog box is displayed requesting permissions as shown in the following screenshot:

We have used the `FB.event.subscribe()` function here to subscribe to `auth.login` and `auth.logout` events. This function takes two arguments. The first argument is the name of the event to subscribe to and the second argument is the function to call in return when the event takes place. Whenever a user logs in (`auth.login` event) or logs out (`auth.logout` event), these callback functions are executed. It displays a message box in each case. You can replace this with your own code.

When a user finally authorizes the application, the `auth.login` event is fired and the following screen is displayed:

Similarly, when a user finally logs out, the `auth.logout` event is fired and the following screen is displayed:

5
Expressing Yourself

In this chapter, we will cover:

- ▸ Prompting the user to publish a story
- ▸ Using Dialog to add someone as a friend
- ▸ Using the OAuth Dialog to request permissions for your application
- ▸ Prompting the user to send a request to friends
- ▸ Processing the requests sent to the user by friends

Introduction

Facebook incorporates many features to make social interactions over the web seamless and easy for its users. One such feature is the concept of **Facebook Dialogs**. Dialogs are a way to help users see and interact with the Facebook environment. Be it a Facebook third-party or mobile application all developers can use Facebook Dialogs to provide a consistent interface to end users for performing various tasks on Facebook. These do not require any special permission and can be easily used and integrated with our application. In this chapter we will learn how to integrate Facebook Dialogs in our application using Facebook JavaScript SDK

Prerequisites

This section will show how to perform a basic configuration before starting with the recipes discussed in this chapter:

1. Create a new file and name it as `index.php`. Copy the following code:

```html
<html xmlns="http://www.w3.org/1999/xhtml" xmlns:fb="http://www.
facebook.com/2008/fbml">

    <body>
```

2. All the application content will be inside this `div`:

```html
<div id="fb-root">
  <!-- Your application content here -->
</div>
```

3. Include jQuery library from Google CDN:

```html
<script type="text/javascript"
  src="https://ajax.googleapis.com/ajax/libs/jquery/1.5.2/
  jquery.min.js"></script>
```

4. Initialize the application by calling `FB.init()`:

```html
<script type="text/javascript">
  window.fbAsyncInit = function() {
    FB.init({
      appId  : 'your_app_id',
      status : true,
      cookie : true,
      xfbml  : true
    });

    /* Your FB JavaScript code here.
       It will be loaded asynchronously. */
  };
```

5. This code loads Facebook JavaScript SDK asynchronously:

```javascript
(function() {
  var e = document.createElement('script');
  e.type = 'text/javascript';
  e.src = document.location.protocol +
      '//connect.facebook.net/en_US/all.js';
  e.async = true;
  document.getElementById('fb-root').appendChild(e);
}());
</script>
```

```
        </body>
      </html>
```

6. Here, replace `your_app_id` in the `FB.init()` function with your own application ID.

If we want to use XFBML in our application consistently across all web browsers, we need to add an XML namespace attribute to the root `<html>` element of `index.php`. This is necessary to render XFBML tags in Internet Explorer.

```
<html xmlns="http://www.w3.org/1999/xhtml"
      xmlns:fb="http://www.facebook.com/2008/fbml">
```

We have used the standard `<script>` element to load the Facebook JavaScript SDK. We load it asynchronously to ensure fast page loads for the users as this doesn't block the loading of other elements in the page. Moreover, we need to specify the `fb-root` div, otherwise the JavaScript SDK will not load and report an error.

After JavaScript SDK loads itself asynchronously, we initialize our Facebook application by calling the `FB.init()` function. It takes the following parameters:

▸ `appId`: the application ID we get after registering our application with Facebook

▸ `status`: a `true` value implies that we can perform a user login status check if required

▸ `cookie`: it enables the cookies to allow the server to access the session

▸ `xfbml`: allows us to access and parse XFBML tags, if `true`

Another important thing to note is that the `FB.init()` function should be inside the function assigned to `window.fbAsyncInit`. This function, which is assigned to `window.fbAsyncInit`, is executed as soon as the JavaScript SDK is loaded asynchronously. Thus, any code which we want to run after the SDK is loaded should be placed within this function after the `FB.init()` function.

Additionally, we have also included jQuery by using this `<script>` code:

```
<script type="text/javascript"
src="https://ajax.googleapis.com/ajax/libs/jquery/1.5.2/jquery.min.
js"></script>
```

Now we are ready to begin with Facebook Dialogs.

Prompting the user to publish a story

If we want to publish a story or news piece on the wall of the current user by using an already built interface, we can do so with the help of Facebook Dialogs. It provides us with a ready to use interface which can be displayed to the user and finally used to publish any post.

Getting ready

You should have created `index.php` as mentioned in the beginning of this chapter.

How to do it...

The following steps will demonstrate how to publish a story:

1. Open `index.php` and add the following highlighted code inside the div named `fb-root` as shown:

   ```
   <div id="fb-root">
     <input type="button" id="launch" value="Launch" /><br />
   </div>
   ```

2. Next, add the following highlighted code to the function assigned to `window.fbAsyncInit`, just after the `FB.init()` function:

   ```
   window.fbAsyncInit = function() {
       FB.init({appId: 'your_app_id', status: true,
             cookie: true, xfbml: true});

       $(document).ready(function() {
   ```

3. Use the callback function of the `click()` method for the button launch to display the Facebook Feed Dialog:

   ```
   $("#launch").click(function() {
   ```

4. Use the `FB.ui()` function to render the dialog box along with a set of parameters:

   ```
   FB.ui({
       method: 'feed',
       name: 'Facebook Feed Dialog',
       link: 'http://developers.facebook.com/docs/
          reference/dialogs/',
       picture: 'http://www.packtpub.com/sites/all/
          themes/pixture_reloaded/images/pp/
          packt-logo.jpg',
       caption: 'Application Development with Graph API',
       description: 'This is Facebook Feed Dialog box and
          is used to post to the wall.',
   ```

```
                      message: 'This message will be posted to your
                         wall!'
                   },
```

5. Use the callback function of `FB.ui()` to determine the status of the post and alert the user:

```
            function(response) {
                if (response && response.post_id) {
                    alert('Post was published.');
                } else {
                    alert('Post was not published.');
                }
            });
        });
    });
    }
```

6. Now save and run `index.php`.

How it works...

In the preceding code, after initializing our Facebook application, we use the jQuery `click` event of the button with ID `launch` to make a call to the `FB.ui()` function. For publishing a story on the current user's wall, we make use of the inbuilt Facebook Feed Dialog. This is done by `FB.ui()` which takes a JavaScript object as a parameter. We set the `method` attribute as `feed`, which determines that we want to render the Facebook Feed Dialog box. We can configure our Facebook Feed Dialog box with the help of the following attributes:

*   `app_id`: This is an optional field. It refers to your application ID.
*   `link`: It is the URL of the link attached to this post. This is also an optional field and may or may not be mentioned.
*   `picture`: It is the URL of the picture attached to this post. This is also an optional field.
*   `name`: It is the name of a link. Again, it is an optional field.
*   `caption`: It is the caption of the link name and appears beneath it. It is also an optional field.
*   `description`: It is the description of the link. Also an optional field.
*   `message`: It is the message which has to be posted.
*   `redirect_uri`: It is the URL to which we want to redirect to after the user clicks on the dialog button.

We can even invoke the Facebook Feed Dialog box by directing the user to the following URL—`http://www.facebook.com/dialog/feed`. Also, we can specify the attributes by adding them as query parameters to the URL. The equivalent URL for the dialog is as shown:

```
http://www.facebook.com/dialog/feed?app_id=your_app_id&link=http://
developers.facebook.com/docs/reference/dialogs/&picture=http://www.
packtpub.com/sites/all/themes/pixture_reloaded/images/pp/packt-
logo.jpg&name=Facebook%20%Feed%20%Dialog&caption=%20Application%20
Development%20with%20Graph%20API&description=This%20is%20Facebook%20
Feed%20Dialog%20box%20and%20is%20used%20to%20post%20to%20the%20
wall.&message=This%20message%20will%20be%20posted%20to%20your%20
wall!&redirect_uri=http://apps.facebook.com/your_app_canvas_name/
```

 Note: We don't need to have any extended permission while using Facebook Dialogs because, for taking an action the user has to interact with them.

Also, we have an optional callback function to handle the response from the server. We check if `response` and `response.post_id` have valid values and if it's so then our post request has been processed and we display a message to the user, otherwise we have encountered an error and we inform the user that the request was not processed.

When a user clicks the **Launch** button, the Facebook Feed Dialog box appears as shown:

After the user has interacted with the dialog box, the control is returned to the callback function. If the user clicks the **Publish** button, then a unique post ID is generated and the browser is redirected to the URL of the form `http://redirect_uri?post_id=your_generated_post_id`. Additionally, the post is published on the user's wall as shown:

In the code, after interacting with the dialog box, a message is shown to the user indicating whether the post has been published or not. This may vary depending on how we define the callback function. In the code we have defined the callback function as follows:

```
function(response) {
    if (response && response.post_id) {
      alert('Post was published.');
    } else {
      alert('Post was not published.');
    }
}
```

Here, we check whether `response` and `response.post_id` exist and if they do then we display a message confirming that the post has been published.

There's more...

In the Feeds Dialog there are some additional parameters. These are **source, action, to, from, properties,** and so on. These may be used to add additional information in the post that has been made. More about them can be seen at this link: `http://developers.facebook. com/docs/reference/dialogs/feed/`

Using Dialog to add someone as a friend

One of the amazing features of Facebook is to search for people and make them friends. We can directly use Facebook Friends Dialog, if we want to add someone as a friend. It provides us with an elegant interface where we can send a friend request to someone just with a mouse click.

Getting ready

You should have setup `index.php`, as explained in the beginning of the chapter.

How to do it...

The following steps will demonstrate how to use Dialog to add friends:

1. Open `index.php` and add the following highlighted code inside the div `fb-root` as shown:

```
<div id="fb-root">
  <input type="button" id="launch" value="Launch" /><br />
</div>
```

2. Next, add the following highlighted code to the function assigned to `window.fbAsyncInit`, just after the `FB.init()` function:

```
window.fbAsyncInit = function() {
    FB.init({ appId: 'your_app_id', status: true,
            cookie: true, xfbml: true });
    $(document).ready(function() {
```

3. Use the callback function of the `click()` method for button launch to display the Facebook Feed Dialog:

```
$("#launch").click(function() {
```

4. Use the `FB.ui()` function to render the Facebook Friends Dialog box:

```
FB.ui({
    method: 'friends',
    id: 'person_id'
},
```

5. Use the callback function to process the response from Facebook:

```
function(response) {
    if (response && response.action) {
        alert('Friend request has been sent.');
    }
    else {
        alert('Friend request has not been sent.');
    }
});
});
});
};
```

6. In `FB.ui()`, you need to replace `person_id` with the ID of the person whom you want to add as a friend. Now save and run `index.php`. A dialog box similar to the one shown will appear with the profile picture and name of the person whose ID you have mentioned in the code:

7. Now if the user clicks on the **Add Friend** button, then a friend request will be sent to the respective person and we display a confirmatory message in an alert box to the current user notifying him/her about this. Otherwise, we inform the user that the friend request was not sent.

How it works...

In the code, we have made use of the Facebook Friends Dialog to send a friend request. For sending a friend request we need to direct the browser to the following URL—`http:// www.facebook.com/dialog/friends/?id=friend_id&app_id=your_app_ id&redirect_uri=your_redirect_uri`.

To display this dialog box inline within our application we make use of the `FB.ui()` function of the Facebook JavaScript SDK. In this function, we have set the `method` attribute as `friends` which indicates that we want to use the Friend Dialog. Also, we can add some more parameters to configure the Friends Dialog as listed:

*   `redirect_uri`: This is basically the URL where we have to redirect the user once he/she clicks any button inside the dialog box. It is, however, not mandatory.

*   `app_id`: This specifies the application ID. It is required but is automatically specified by most of the SDKs. For example, in our case we have made use of the `FB.init()` function. Thus, we did not define it here explicitly.

- ▸ `display`: This is used to set the display mode. Valid values are `page`, `popup`, `iframe`, `wap`, and `touch`. The default is `page` on the www subdomain and `wap` on the m subdomain. Some of the important display modes are listed as follows:

  - ❏ `page`: In this display mode, the dialogs load in full-page mode with a Facebook header and footer.

  - ❏ `popup`: This is usually used by external sites and here dialogs are displayed as browser popups which are limited to 400 px by 580 px.

  - ❏ `iframe`: This display mode renders a dialog over the current page inside a lightbox iFrame. This mode is not available for all dialogs.

  - ❏ `touch`: This display mode is for smartphones such as iPhone and Android.

  - ❏ `wap`: This display mode loads dialog in plain HTML (without JavaScript) on a small screen.

- ▸ `id`: This is the ID or username of the person to whom we want to send the friend request and thus, is mandatory.

For the `FB.ui()` method we have passed only the essential parameters as shown:

```
FB.ui(
    {
      method: 'friends',
      id: 'person_id'
    },
//more code
```

Next, we use a callback function to analyze the response and notify the user. The returned data is the `action` parameter which is set to `1` if the friend request has been sent and the user is redirected to `http://www.example.com/response/?action=1`. Otherwise it is set to `0` and directs the user to `http://www.example.com/response/?action=0`. This has been done in the following lines of code:

```
function(response) {
      if (response && response.action) {
        alert('Friend has been added.');
      } else {
        alert('Friend has not been added.');
      }
    }
```

Upon successful execution a friend request gets sent to the person whose ID has been mentioned in the `FB.ui()` function.

Note: Dialogs are supported only for iframe applications on Facebook canvas pages.

There's more...

If the person is already a friend of the current user and the application tries to send a friend request to him/her, then a dialog box saying the user is already a friend will pop up as shown:

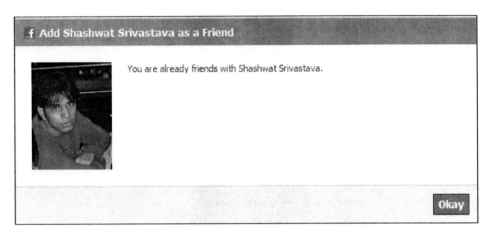

However, if the person whom we want to add has already sent us a friend request then the dialog box will appear and would ask us to either confirm or reject the friend request.

Using the OAuth Dialog to request permissions for your application

Facebook OAuth Dialog is used to request permissions from the current user for your application. The user can either accept or deny our request. We can use this dialog box to request additional extended permissions from the user after they have already used your application.

Getting ready

► You should have setup index.php as explained in the beginning of the chapter.

How to do it...

The following steps will demonstrate how to use the OAuth Dialog:

1. Open `index.php` and add the following code inside the div with `id="launch"` as shown:

```
<div id="fb-root">
  <input type="button" id="launch" value="Launch" /><br />
</div>
```

2. Add the following code just after the `FB.init()` function:

```
<script type="text/javascript">
  window.fbAsyncInit = function() {
    FB.init({appId: 'your_app_id', status: true,
          cookie: true, xfbml: true});
    $(document).ready(function() {
```

3. Use the `click()` method for the **Launch** button to display the Facebook OAuth Dialog:

```
$("#launch").click(function() {
```

4. Use the `FB.ui()` function to render the dialog box:

```
FB.ui({
    method: 'oauth',
    scope: 'email,user_birthday',
    response_type: 'token',
    client_id: 'your_app_id',
    redirect_uri: 'http://app.facebook.com/
      app_canvas_name'
});
    });
  });
};
```

5. Replace `your_app_id` and `app_canvas_name` according to your application. In the `scope` attribute mention the extended permissions which you want. Now save this file and launch the application. Upon successful execution a Permission Dialog, something like the following, will appear:

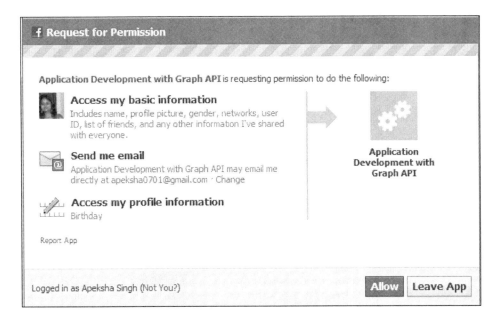

How it works...

Facebook uses the OAuth protocol for authorizing and authentication. For asking extended permissions from a user we can use the Facebook OAuth Dialog. We can directly use this Dialog by sending the user to the URL of the form—http://www.facebook.com/dialog/oauth/?scope=email,user_birthday&client_id=123050457758183&redirect_uri=http://www.example.com/response&response_type=token

Alternately, we can use the FB.ui() function to display the dialog box within the application. Here, it takes a single parameter which is a JavaScript object. In this parameter we set the method attribute as oauth which specifies that we want to use the OAuth Dialog as shown:

```
FB.ui({
    method: 'oauth',
    scope: 'email,user_birthday',
    response_type: 'token',
    client_id: 'your_app_id',
    redirect_uri: ' http://app.facebook.com/app_canvas_name'

});
```

The OAuth Dialog can have the following parameters:

Meta properties	Description
client_id	This is the ID of the application. It is mandatory, however, it is automatically specified by most of the SDKs.
redirect_uri	It is the URL to which the user will be redirected to after clicking on the button inside the Dialog.
state	An opaque string used to maintain the application state between the request and callback. When Facebook redirects the user back to your redirect_uri, this value will be included unchanged in the response.
response_type	It specifies the type of response we have requested for. It could be an access token or an authorization code or even both.
display	It is the mode in which the dialog will appear to the user, be it iframe or a popup.
scope	This contains the permissions which we want the user to grant to the application. These have to be separated by a comma. The list of permissions can be seen in the appendix. It is an optional parameter. If not specified the dialog box will ask the user for the default set of permissions. It is shown in the following screenshot:

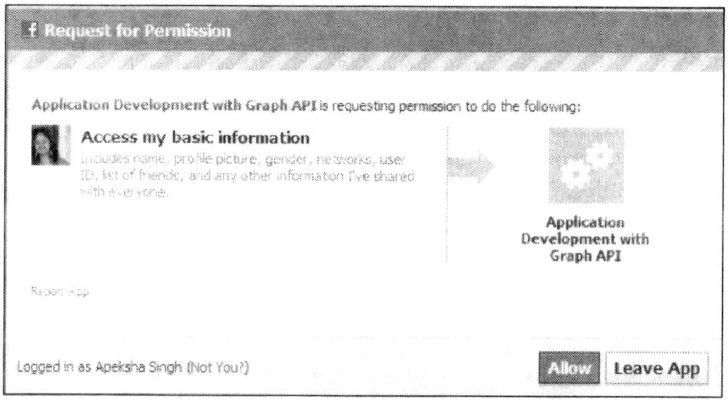

Upon execution of this a series of data gets returned. These could be the following:

Meta properties	Description
state	Same as explained earlier.
access_token	Oauth2.0 access token.
expires_in	It specifies the lifetime of the access token.
code	OAuth 2.0 authorization code.
error	It is an error string which is returned if there is an authorization error.
error_description	It is the error message which gets displayed if there is an error.

Once the code runs successfully and the Permission Dialog box gets displayed to the user, if the user accepts the permissions and clicks the **Allow** button he/she gets redirected to the URL of the form:

```
http://your_redirect_uri/response?access_token=...&expires_in=3600
```

And if the user didn't allow then the URL will be like this:

```
http://your_redirect_uri/response?error=access_denied&error_descripti
on=The+user+denied+your+request
```

Prompting the user to send a request to friends

A request in Facebook is a nice way of asking a user's friend to take some action, which involves both of them, or notify him/her about an update, which again involves both of them. For example, if the user is sending a gift to his/her friend then we can create a Facebook request and that friend will automatically be notified by Facebook.

Getting ready

You should have set up index.php as explained in the beginning of the chapter.

How to do it...

The following steps will demonstrate how to send a request:

1. Open `index.php` and add the following code to it inside the `fb-root` div as shown:

```
<div id="fb-root">
    <input type="button" id="send" value="Send a Request" /><br />
</div>
```

2. Add the following code right after the `FB.init()` function as shown:

```
window.fbAsyncInit = function() {
    FB.init({appId: 'your_app_id', status: true,
            cookie: true, xfbml: true});
    $(document).ready(function() {
```

3. Use the click event of the input type button with the ID `send` to invoke the dialog box:

```
$("#send").click(function() {
```

4. Use the `FB.ui()` function to render the dialog box:

```
FB.ui({
    method: 'apprequests',
    message: 'Try this awesome application?'},
```

5. Use the callback function to alert the user:

```
function(response) {
    if (response) {
        $.each(
            response.request_ids,
            function(index, value) {
                alert(index + ': ' + value);
            });
    }
    else {
        alert('Request was not sent');
    }
});
        });
    });
};
```

6. Now save and launch the application. Click on the **Send a Request** button. A Facebook Request Dialog box will be launched as shown:

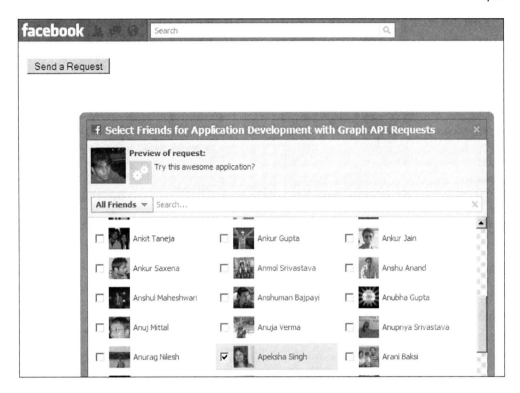

How it works...

Here, to demonstrate how to send a request we have taken an input type button with the ID send. When a user clicks on this button a call is made to the FB.ui() function. The first parameter of this function is a JavaScript object and the second parameter is a callback function.

In the first parameter we have set the value of the method attribute as apprequests, which indicates that we want to use the Facebook Request Dialog box. Additionally, we can use the following parameters to configure our dialog box:

- ▶ message: This is the request in the form of a question which is sent to the user. The maximum length is 255 characters.
- ▶ to: This is the user ID or username to whom we want to send the request. He/she must be a friend of the sender. If this is not specified then the user can choose up to 50 recipients otherwise he/she can't choose anyone.
- ▶ data: This optional attribute can be used to pass additional data which we can use for tracking purposes in our application.
- ▶ title: This is an optional attribute used to set the title of the friend selector dialog. The maximum length is 50 characters.

A request can be of any type ranging from gifts to game invitations. We can use the `data` attribute to assign each request a predefined code or tag for our application, that is we can create a code system for all types of requests that our application will be generating. When a receiving user accepts this request, we can use this code system to determine how to process the request, that is, what action should we take on behalf of the user depending upon the type of the request.

The second parameter of the `FB.ui()` function is a callback function. When a user selects multiple friends to send requests to, then each request to a specific friend is assigned to a unique ID. We can retrieve the ID of all the requests sent out by the current user by using the `response.request_ids`, a JavaScript array, which is returned by the callback function. We use the following code in the callback function:

```
function(response) {
    if (response) {
        $.each(response.request_ids, function(index, value) {
            alert('Request ' + index + ' id - ' + value);
        });
    }
    else {
        alert('Request was not sent');
    }
}
```

Here, we use the `$.each()` function to iterate over all the elements of the array and display their IDs. We can store these request IDs in our database and when they are processed (explained in the next recipe, *Processing requests sent to the user by friends*) we can delete them. If the request is not sent successfully, then we display an alert message to the user notifying him/her about this.

See also

▸ *Processing requests sent to the user by friends*

Processing requests sent to the user by friends

A Facebook user can send an application request to his/her friends. It is the responsibility of the application to check for new requests for a particular user when he/she interacts with the application. If the receiving user opens our application we should provide him/her with an appropriate interface to interact with depending on the type of request. Once the user has taken an action based on the request we should delete it.

Also, Facebook provides us with a feature known as counter which is a number right next to our application, if the application has been bookmarked, and appears in the navigation as shown:

Here, the **7** adjacent to **Application Development with Graph API** shows the total number of pending requests or invites of the application for the current user. This counter is maintained automatically by Facebook.

Getting ready

You should have created `index.php` and `config.php` as explained in the beginning of *Chapter 2, Be a part of Social Graph.*

How to do it...

The following steps will demonstrate how to process requests sent to the user by friends:

1. Open `index.php` and append the following code to it:

```html
<html>
  <head>
  </head>
  <body>
    <?php
      $requests = $facebook->api('/me/apprequests');
      foreach($requests['data'] as $request) {
        if($request['application']['id'] == $facebook->getAppId())
        {
          echo 'Request ID: ' . $request['id'] . '<br>';
          echo 'From: ' . $request['from']['name'] . '<br>';
```

```
            echo 'Message: ' . $request['message'] . '<br>';
        }
    }
  ?>
  </body>
</html>
```

2. Save and run `index.php`. If the user has received a request then the output will be something like this:

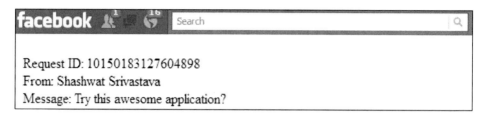

Request ID: 10150183127604898
From: Shashwat Srivastava
Message: Try this awesome application?

How it works...

To check whether a user has received any new requests we use the `$facebook->api()` function of the `Facebook` class to make a `GET` request to the following URL—`https://graph.facebook.com/me/apprequests`. If there is any request that has been sent to the current user, then the server returns it in JSON format. This is converted to a PHP array and stored in the `$requests` by `api()` function. The following is the PHP array:

```
Array
(
    [data] => Array
        (
            [0] => Array
                (
                    [id] => 10150183127604898
                    [application] => Array
                        (
                            [name] => Application Development with Graph API
                            [id] => 129525780451736
                        )

                    [to] => Array
                        (
                            [name] => Apeksha Singh
                            [id] => 637089897
                        )
```

```
              [from] => Array
                (
                    [name] => Shashwat Srivastava
                    [id] => 786017563
                )

              [message] => Try this awesome application?
              [created_time] => 2011-05-15T12:20:08+0000
            )
        )
    )
```

Next, we have used a `foreach` loop to print all the request details using this piece of code:

```
foreach($requests['data'] as $request) {
    if($request['application']['id'] == $facebook->getAppId()) {
        echo 'Request ID: ' . $request['id'] . '<br>';
        echo 'From: ' . $request['from']['name'] . '<br>';
        echo 'Message: ' . $request['message'] . '<br>';
    }
}
```

Here, first we check whether the request belongs to our application, or not, by comparing `$request['application']['id']` with `$facebook->getAppId()` and if these two are the same then we print the request ID and the request message along with the sender.

We can use these request details to display an interface to the user and prompt him/her to take action based upon this. For example, if someone has sent the current user a challenge to beat his/her score given by your application in the form of a request, then you can show this to the user when he/she comes to your application and then ask him/her to try to score more than the sender by using your application.

See also

  ▶ Refer to *Chapter 2, Be a part of Social Graph*

6
Bringing Facebook to your Website

In this chapter, we will cover:

- ▶ Setting up the Like button on your web page
- ▶ Adding a Like box
- ▶ Setting up the Activity Feed plugin
- ▶ Setting up the Facepile plugin on your web page
- ▶ Integrating the Live Stream plugin using XFBML
- ▶ Integrating the Comment box using XFBML
- ▶ Integrating the Send Button using XFBML
- ▶ Login with faces

Introduction

One of the most sought after features of Facebook that has made its popularity increase to million folds is Facebook's **Social Plugins**. With the concept of social plugins, Facebook has made it possible for people to connect with each other, no matter where they are and what they do. Sharing of comments, data, messages, likes, dislikes, and contents has all become possible with the concept of social plugins.

The most interesting thing about these plugins is the ease with which they can be installed, even on a third-party application.

In this chapter, we will learn how to integrate and use the various social plugins made available by Facebook to us.

Setting up the Like button on your web page

One of the most frequently used and famous social plugins of Facebook is the **Like** button. With the Like button, Facebook helps the third-party application developers and websites to interact with the Facebook platform, share content, and get the advantage of its large user base. Here, we will learn how to integrate the Like button with our website.

How to do it...

The following steps will demonstrate how to set up a Like button on your web page:

1. Open the page of your website, where you want the Like button to be placed, and copy the following code:

    ```
    <iframe src="http://www.facebook.com/plugins/like.php?
      href=http%3A%2F%2Fpacktpub.com&amp;
      layout=standard&amp;width=450&amp;show_faces=true&amp;
      action=like&amp;colorscheme=light&amp;font&amp;
      height=80" scrolling="no" frameborder="0"
      style="border:none; overflow:hidden;
      width:450px;height:80px;"allowTransparency="true">
    </iframe>
    ```

2. In this code, replace the `href` attribute with the URL of the page for which you want to activate the Like button.

3. Now, refresh the page. A Like button will instantly appear on the page at the place where you have posted the code. It will appear as shown in the following screenshot:

4. If a user clicks on the Like button, it will appear as shown in the following screenshot:

5. This feed will automatically be posted on the user's profile, who has liked the particular page. The following screenshot shows you how it will appear:

Apeksha Singh likes a link.

Home | Packt Publishing Technical & IT Book and eBook Store
www.packtpub.com

Packt is a modern publishing company, producing cutting-edge books, eBooks, and articles for communities of developers, administrators, and newbies alike.

 15 seconds ago · Like · Comment · Share

How it works...

The above code is an `iframe` source code, which integrates the Like button to our page. Here, we can set its properties by specifying the following attributes:

- `href`: This points to the URL of the page, which we want the user to like and whose update will be posted on the profile of the user as feeds.

- `layout`: It sets the layout of the Like button. The following are three different modes in which a layout can be set:

  - `standard`: This is the default Facebook Like button layout in which all the text appears on the right hand side and the user's profile picture at the bottom. Its minimum width is 225 pixels and by default is set to 450 pixels. The default value of the height is 35 pixels without photos and 80 pixels with photos.

  - `button_count`: This displays the total number of likes made, to the right of the button. Its default width and height is 90 and 20 pixels respectively:

  - `box_count`: This displays the total number of likes above the button. Its default width and height is 55 and 65 pixels respectively:

- `show_faces`: It allows us to display the profile pictures of the users who like the particular page. If set to `true`, it will make profile pictures of the users appear at the bottom of the Like button when they click on it. Otherwise, when `false`, it disables this feature. However, this attribute is valid only for the `standard` layout. Without the `show_faces` enabled the Like button will appear, as shown in the following screenshot:

- `width`: It specifies the width of the Like button.

- `action`: It specifies the text or verb that will appear with the Like button. It can be equal to `like` or `recommend`. You can set this attribute to the latter if you want the users to "recommend" your content to others. In a way, the Like button then transforms into the **Recommend** button and will appear, as shown in the following screenshot:

- `font`: It decides the font in which the text will appear on the button. Facebook provides us with the following options: `arial`, `lucida grande`, `segoe ui`, `tahoma`, `trebuchet ms`, and `verdana`.

- `colorscheme`: It decides the color scheme of the Like button. There are two options for this—`light` and `dark`.

- `ref`: This attribute is used for for tracking referrals and its value must be less than 50 characters. The value can only consist of alphanumeric characters and the following punctuation: +, /, =, -, ., :, and _. When we set this `ref` attribute, it causes two parameters to be added to the referrer URL, when a user clicks a link from a stream story about a Like action:

  - `fb_ref`: This contains our `ref` parameter which we can use to track how many users are coming from Facebook.

  - `fb_source`: This tells us the stream type ('**home**', '**profile**', '**search**', '**other**') in which the click occurred and the story type ('**oneline**' or '**multiline**'), concatenated with an underscore.

- `send`: It specifies whether to include a Send button with the Like button and works only with the XFBML version.

Using these attributes, we can customize the Like button as per our choice.

There's more...

Often it becomes cumbersome to hard code and put the value of the `href` parameter in every page. This problem can be solved by dynamically generating the URL of the current page and setting it as the value of the `href` parameter of the Like button. For doing this, we need to replace the value of the `href` parameter with the following code snippet:

```
<?php echo rawurlencode('http://' . $_SERVER['HTTP_HOST'] .
  $_SERVER['REQUEST_URI']); ?>
```

The following would be the complete code:

```
<iframe src="http://www.facebook.com/plugins/like.php?
  href=<?php echo rawurlencode('http://' .
  $_SERVER['HTTP_HOST'] . $_SERVER['REQUEST_URI']);
  ?>&amp;send=true&amp;layout=standard&amp;
  width=450&amp;show_faces=true&amp;action=like&amp;
  colorscheme=light&amp;font&amp;height=80" scrolling="no"
  frameborder="0" style="border:none; overflow:hidden;
  width:450px; height:80px;" allowTransparency="true">
</iframe>
```

Notice how we have used PHP code to get the URL of the current page and then assign it to the `href` parameter. This is a more generic implementation of the Like button.

Also, the Like button gives the users the ability to comment on Facebook through it. For this, they simply need to hover over the Like button and they will get a comment box as shown in the following screenshot:

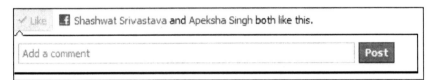

Adding a Like box

Facebook provides another interesting plugin known as the **Like box**. With the Like box, we can have many features in one. For example, we can get the recent posts of our page displayed in it; we can display the list and number of users who have liked that particular page. Also, we can display the profile pictures of the users who have liked our page and can even give them the provision to like it.

How to do it...

The following steps will show how to add a Like button:

1. Open your web page, where you want this Like box to be to be placed, and copy the following code:

```
<iframe src="http://www.facebook.com/plugins/likebox.php?
    href=http%3A%2F%2Fwww.facebook.com%2FPacktPub&amp;
    width=292&amp;colorscheme=light&amp;show_faces=true&amp;
    stream=true&amp;header=true&amp;height=427"
    scrolling="no" frameborder="0" style="border:none;
    overflow:hidden; width:292px; height:427px;"
    allowTransparency="true">
</iframe>
```

2. Replace the `href` attribute value in the code with the URL of the Facebook page for which you want the Like box to appear.

3. Now, refresh and launch the application. A Like box will appear, just at the place in your web page where you had pasted this code. It will be similar to the following screenshot:

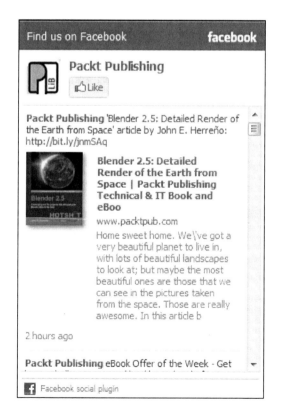

4. We can use this Like box to directly like the page, as well as read the latest posts on the website.

How it works...

In the code, we just saw, we have used the `iframe` source code to integrate the Like box. Here, we simply need to set the URL of the iframe as `http://www.facebook.com/plugins/likebox.php` along with some GET attributes. We can customize the Like button using the following attributes:

- ► `href`: This is used to specify the URL of the Facebook page for the Like button. This needs to be taken care of as the URL should only be that of a Facebook page and not any other URL.

- ► `width`: This is used to specify the width of the Like box. By default, it is set to 300 pixels.

- ► `colorscheme`: The color in which we want the Like box to appear. There are two options for this—`light` and `dark`.

- ► `show_faces`: This is used to specify whether we want to display the profile pictures of the users who have liked our page or not. By default, it is set to `true`.

- ► `stream`: This is used to specify if we want to have the latest posts taken from the page's wall or not.

- ► `header`: This is used to specify if we want to display the Facebook header at the top of the box or not.

When the `header` and `stream` is set to `false` and `show_faces` is set to `true`, the box may appear, as shown in the following screenshot:

There's more...

We can also make the generation of the Like box dynamic for every page. In that case, we will not have to hard code the `href` value on every page in the `iframe` source code of the Like box. All we need to do is to simply replace the value of the `href` parameter with the following code snippet:

```
<?php echo rawurlencode('http://' . $_SERVER['HTTP_HOST'] .
   $_SERVER['REQUEST_URI']); ?>
```

The following would be the complete code:

```
<iframe src="http://www.facebook.com/plugins/likebox.php?
   href=<?php echo rawurlencode('http://' .
   $_SERVER['HTTP_HOST'] . $_SERVER['REQUEST_URI']); ?>
   &amp;width=292&amp;colorscheme=light&amp;
   show_faces=true&amp;stream=true&amp;header=true&amp;
   height=427" scrolling="no" frameborder="0"
   style="border:none; overflow:hidden; width:292px;
   height:427px;" allowTransparency="true">
</iframe>
```

Here, the PHP code actually generates the URL of the current page and assigns it to the href parameter.

Setting up the Activity Feed plugin

Facebook also supports an **Activity Feed** plugin on which we can get the latest activities that happen on our page. These can be the shared content of our site by the users on Facebook, the comments made, likes, and so on. This plugin can be easily integrated using an iframe source code.

How to do it...

The following steps will demonstrate how to set up the Activity Feed plugin:

1. Open the page of your website, where you want this Activity Feed plugin to be, and copy the following code. Here, we set up the Activity Feed plugin:

   ```
   <iframe src="http://www.facebook.com/plugins/activity.php?
     site=http%3A%2F%2Fpacktpub.com&amp;width=300&amp;
     height=300&amp;header=true&amp;colorscheme=light&amp;
     font&amp;border_color&amp;recommendations=false"
     scrolling="no" frameborder="0" style="border:none;
     overflow:hidden; width:300px; height:300px;"
     allowTransparency="true">
   </iframe>
   ```

2. In this code, replace the value of site with the domain for which you want the activities to get displayed for.

3. Now, launch the application.

4. An Activity Feed dialog box will appear, as shown in the following screenshot:

How it works...

The code, we just saw, for the Activity Feed Plugin is a simple `iframe` source code. We can get this by making the `iframe src` equal to `http://www.facebook.com/plugins/activity.php`. Also, this plugin can be customized by changing the following attributes:

- `site`: This is the URL of the domain for which we want the activities to get displayed for.

- `width` and `height`: This is used to specify the `width` and `height` of the plugin with the default value being 300 pixels.

- `header`: The `true` value will make the Facebook header appear at the top, while `false` will render it invisible.

- `colorscheme`: This is used to specify in which color scheme we want the plugin to get displayed. There are two options for this—`light` and `dark`.

- `font` and `border_color`: This is used to specify the font in which the text will appear, as well as the border color of the plugin.

- `recommendations`: This, if set to `true`, will display the recommendations in the bottom half of the plugin.

- `filter`: This is used to specify the URLs for which we want the plugin to get displayed. For example, if the site parameter is set to `www.my_site.com` and the filter parameter was set to `/page1/page2`, then the activity feed plugin will only display the activities for `www.my_site.com/page1/page2`.

- `ref`: This attribute is used for tracking referrals. Its value must be less than 50 characters and can only consist of alphanumeric characters, along with the following punctuation— +, /, =, -, ., :, and _. If we use this `ref` attribute, it causes two parameters to be added to the referrer URL when a user clicks a link from a stream story about a Like action:

    - `fb_ref`: This contains our `ref` parameter, which we can use to track how many users are coming from Facebook.

    - `fb_source`: This tells us the stream type (**'home'**, **'profile'**, **'search'**, **'other'**) in which the click occurred and the story type (**'oneline'** or **'multiline'**), concatenated with an underscore.

There's more...

There is an alternate way of configuring and customizing the Activity Feed plugin.

1. Go to the following URL—`http://developers.facebook.com/docs/reference/plugins/activity/`.

2. At the center of this page, you will see an Activity Feed plugin widget generator, as shown in the following screenshot:

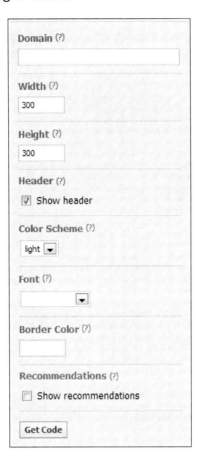

3. Fill in the attributes details and click on **Get Code**. Facebook will automatically generate a code depending on the values you have specified and it will appear, as shown in the following screenshot:

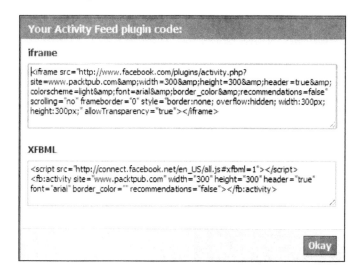

4. Copy the `iframe` code and paste it in an appropriate place on your web page, where you want the plugin to be rendered. Now, if you open your web page in a web browser, then the Activity Feed plugin will be displayed showing recent activities related to your web page.

Also, if we want to integrate the `recommendations` plugin too, along with the Activity plugin, then all we need to do is to check in the **Show Recommendations** checkbox in the GUI. This will set the `recommendations` attribute to `true` and allow the activity plugin to display the recommendations too.

Setting up the Facepile plugin on your web page

The Facebook **Facepile** plugin allows us to display the profile pictures of the users who have liked, or signed up for, a particular page. We can easily set this up for our website by performing a few basic steps.

How to do it...

The following steps will demonstrate how to set up the Facepile plugin:

1. Open your web page, where you want the Facepile plugin to be placed, and copy the following code:

```
<iframe src="http://www.facebook.com/plugins/facepile.php?
  href=http%3A%2F%2Fwww.facebook.com%2FbOtskOOl&amp;
  width=200&amp;max_rows=5" scrolling="no"
  frameborder="0" style="border:none; overflow:hidden;
  width:200px;" allowTransparency="true">
</iframe>
```

2. Replace the `href` value in this code with the URL of the page for which you want to display the profile pictures.

3. Save the file and launch the application. A series of profile pictures of the users, who have liked the page will appear, as shown in the following screenshot:

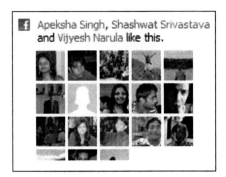

4. Facepile also allows us to display the users who have signed up for a particular page or application. To do this, copy the following code:

```
<iframe src="http://www.facebook.com/plugins/facepile.php?
  app_id=your_app_id&amp;width=200&amp;max_rows=3"
  scrolling="no" frameborder="0" style="border:none;
  overflow:hidden; width:200px;" allowTransparency="true">
</iframe>
```

5. In this code, replace the `your_app_id` with the ID of the your application.

6. Now save the file and launch the application. A list of users, who have signed up for that particular page or application will appear, as shown in the following screenshot:

How it works...

The Facebook Facepile plugin allows us to display the profile pictures of the users who have liked, or signed up for, a particular page or application. For this, we have used the `iframe` source code. Here, we mention the URL of iframe as `http://www.facebook.com/plugins/facepile.php` along with some URL GET parameters. We can set the properties of Facepile by modifying its following attributes:

▶ `href`: This is used to specify the URL of the page for which we want to display the profile pictures of the users who have liked it.

▶ `app_id`: If we want to to display the profile pictures of the users who have signed up for our application, we need to use `app_id` instead of `href` and put the application ID there.

▶ `max_rows`: This is used to specify the maximum rows of faces that can be displayed. By default, it is set to `1`.

▶ `width`: This is used to specify the width of the Facepile plugin. By default, it is set to 200 pixels.

 The Facepile plugin only displays the photos of the user's friends who have liked or signed up for your application or page. So if there are no friends of the user who have either liked or signed up for the page, nothing will get displayed.

Integrating the Live Stream plugin using XFBML

The Facebook **Live Stream** plugin allows the users to share comments and activities in real time on your application or site. It even provides us with the option to share it and post it to Facebook. We can easily integrate it using XFBML in our application. This recipe tells you how to do it.

Getting ready

You should have set up `index.php`, as explained in the beginning of Chapter 4.

How to do it...

The following steps will demonstrate the integration of Live Stream plugin:

1. Go to the following URL—`http://developers.facebook.com/docs/reference/plugins/live-stream/`.

2. At the center of the page, you will see a Live Stream plugin widget, which will appear as shown in the following screenshot:

3. In the widget, replace the already existing **App ID** with the ID of the application for which you want the Live Stream plugin.

4. Also, mention the **Width** and **Height**. You might leave the other parameters for the time being.

5. Now, click on the **Get Code** button.

6. A box having an XFBML code will get generated and will appear, as shown in the following screenshot:

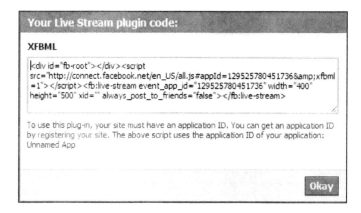

7. Now, copy the following line from the displayed code—<fb:live-stream event_ app_id="your_app_id" width="400" height="500" xid="" always_post_ to_friends="false"></fb:live-stream> and paste it inside the fb-root division in index.php.

8. Now, run the application. A Live Stream box for the users will appear, as shown in the following screenshot:

9. Here, the user can type in the text area and share the content and even post it to Facebook.

10. When posted to Facebook, the comment will appear on the user's profile, as shown in the following screenshot:

Apeksha Singh
this is through the Live stream plugin
2 minutes ago via Application Development with Graph API · 🔒 · Like · Comment

How it works...

Here, to display the Live Stream plugin, we have used the XFBML `fb:live-stream` tag, which provides the end users with an option to share live contents. We have set its properties through the Facebook Live Stream widget generator. It has the following attributes:

- ► **App ID**: In this we need to specify the application ID for which we want this Live Stream plugin to work.

- ► **Width**: This is used to specify the width of the plugin.

- ► **Height**: This is used to specify the height of the plugin.

- ► **XID**: It is a unique ID, which we associate with the Live Stream plugin incase we are using multiples of live stream boxes on the same page.

- ► **Via Attribution URL**: It is the URL to which the users are redirected when they click on the application name on a status. By default, it is set to the application's ConnectURL.

- ► **Always post to friends**: This, when set to `true`, makes all the posts go to the corresponding user's profile.

Thus, based on these properties, an XFBML code is generated, which can be easily used in our application to render the Live Stream box.

Integrating the Comment box using XFBML

The Facebook **Comment** plugin allow users to comment on our site or application. The advantage of this plugin is that users can comment from anywhere, our site, or through Facebook. The comments will remain in sync.

Getting ready

You should have set up `index.php`, as explained in the beginning of *Chapter 4*.

How to do it...

The following steps will demonstrate how to integrate a Comment box:

1. Go to the following URL—`http://developers.facebook.com/docs/reference/plugins/comments/`.

2. There, at the center of the page, you will see a Comment plugin widget, as shown in the following screenshot:

3. In the widget, in the **URL to comment on** field, enter the URL of the site or application for which you want to have the Comment box.

4. Also, mention the **Number of posts**, **Width**, and **Color Scheme** parameters.

5. Now, click on the **Get Code** button.

6. A box having an XFBML code will get generated and will appear, as shown in the following screenshot:

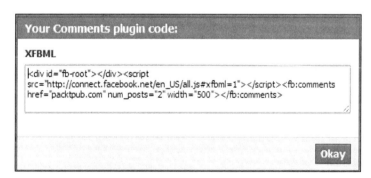

7. Now copy the following line from the displayed code—`<fb:comments href="yoursite.com" num_rows="2" width="500"></fb:comments>` and paste it inside the `fb-root` division in `index.php`.

8. Now run the application. A Comment box for the users will appear, as shown in the following screenshot:

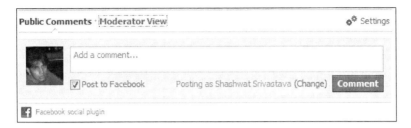

9. Here, the user can type in the Comment box, share the content, and even post it to Facebook.

How it works...

We use Facebook's in-built XFBML `<fb:comments>` tag to add the Comment plugin. The Comment plugin is added through the following line that is added in the `fb-root` division ID:

```
<fb:comments href="yoursite.com" num_rows="2"
   width="500"></fb:comments>
```

The attributes of the `<fb:comments>` tag are as follows:

- `href`: It is used to specify the URL for the Comments plugin. All news feeds or stories on Facebook will link to this URL.

- `width`: It is used to specify the width of this plugin.

- `num_rows`: It is used to specify the number of comments, which have to shown. By default, it is set to `10`.

- `colorscheme`: It is used to specify the color in which the plugin has to be displayed. There are two options—`light` and `dark`.

We can use these attributes to render the Comment plugin for our web page.

Integrating the Send button using XFBML

Facebook has recently launched the **Send** button for its users. This allows them to send messages and information to a few selected friends of theirs. The messages and feed, along with the URL, are directly sent to their friend's inbox. There are two ways to render a Send button. One is along with the Like button, and the other is to have a stand-alone Send button. Let us see how to integrate the Send button to our web page.

Getting ready

You should have set up `index.php`, as explained in the beginning of Chapter 4.

How to do it...

We will first look at integrating the Send button with a Like button.

Integrating the Send button with the Like button

1. Go to the following URL—`http://developers.facebook.com/docs/reference/plugins/like/`.

2. Now, at the center of the page, you will see a Like button widget, as shown in the following screenshot:

3. In this widget, you will see the **Send Button (XFBML Only)** option. Check in the box to enable the **Send Button** option.

4. Now, fill in the required information as per your requirement.

5. Click on the **Get Code** button.

6. A box displaying an XFBML code will appear, as shown in the following screenshot:

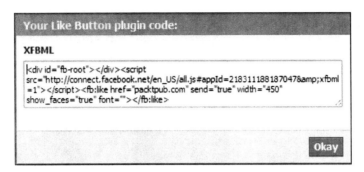

7. Now, copy the following line from the displayed code—`<fb:like href="yoursite.com" send="true" width="450" show_faces="true" font=""></fb:like>` and paste it inside the `fb-root` division in `index.php`.

8. Replace the `href` value with the URL you want to send, along with the messages. Now run the application. A Send button along with the Like button will appear, as shown in the following screenshot:

9. Now, if the user clicks on the Send button, a message box will appear:

10. A user can use this message box to send personalized messages to his/her friend.

11. The following screenshot shows how a message will appear in the inbox of a user's friend:

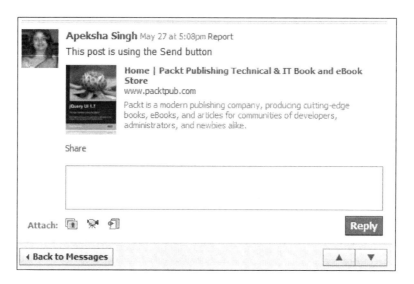

Now, we look at the stand-alone Send button integration.

Integrating a stand-alone Send button

1. Go to the following URL—`http://developers.facebook.com/docs/reference/plugins/send/`.

2. Under the **Get a Send button** section, you will see a Send button widget, as shown in the following screenshot:

3. Enter the required information in this widget and click on the **Get Code** button. A box having an XFBML code will get generated, as shown in the following screenshot:

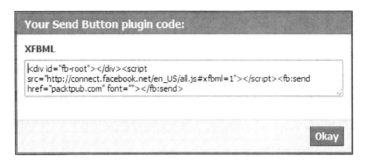

4. Now, copy the following text from the displayed code—`<fb:send href="yoursite.com" font=""></fb:send>` and paste it in the `fb-root` division of `index.php`.

5. Replace the `href` value with the URL, which you want to send, along with the message. Now run the application. A Send button will appear, as shown in the following screenshot:

6. This Send button can be used in the same way as described earlier. The message will be sent to the inbox of the user's friend and will have the URL content as mentioned in the **URL to Send** text box.

How it works...

For integrating the Send button along with the Like button, we use the `<fb:like>` XFBML tag and set the value of `send` attribute as `true`. This has been done in the following piece of code:

```
<fb:like href="yoursite.com" send="true" width="450"
    show_faces="true" font=""></fb:like>
```

We render the stand-alone Send button by using the following piece of code:

```
<fb:send href="yoursite.com" font=""></fb:send>
```

It can be customized using the following attributes:

▶ `href`: It refers to the URL that is to be sent in the messages

▶ `font`: It is to set the font in which text is to displayed in the plugin

▶ `colorscheme`: This is to set the color scheme of the plugin

Login with Faces

Facebook provides us with a **Login** plugin in order to make it easy for its users to log in to a particular application or third-party website. It also shows the user his/her friends who have already used this plugin for a particular application or website.

Getting ready

You should have setup `index.php`, as explained in the beginning of Chapter 4.

How to do it...

The following steps will demonstrate how to login using Faces:

1. Go to the following URL—`http://developers.facebook.com/docs/reference/plugins/login/`.

2. Now, at the center of the page, you will see a Login button widget, as shown in the following screenshot:

3. In this widget, you will see the **Show faces** option. Check in the box to enable the **Show faces** option.

4. Now, fill up the required information as per your choices.

5. Click on the **Get Code** button.

6. A box displaying an XFBML code will appear, as shown in the following screenshot:

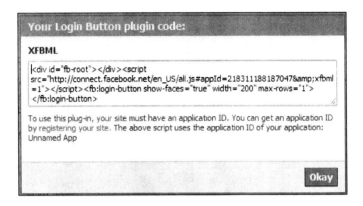

7. Now copy the following line from the displayed code—`<fb:login-button show-faces="true" width="200" max-rows="1"></fb:login-button>` and paste it inside the `fb-root` division in `index.php`.

8. Now, run the application. If the user has not already logged into your application a Login button will appear, displaying the faces of the user's friends who have already connected to the application, as shown in the following screenshot:

9. If the user now logs in, the button will display the profile pictures of the user, as well as of his/her friends who have connected to the application.

How it works...

For integrating the Login button, along with the faces, we use the `<fb:login-button>` XFBML tag and add to it the `show-faces` attribute, which we set as `true`. When set to `true`, the `show-faces` attribute displays the profile pictures of all the user's friends who have connected to the particular application for which we are integrating this plugin. Other attributes are as follows:

  ▶   `width`: It specifies the width of the plugin
  ▶   `max-rows`: It specifies the maximum number of rows of faces to be displayed

7
Connecting Websites to the Social Graph

In this chapter, we will cover:

- ▶ Integrating web pages into the social graph
- ▶ Integrating audio and video data
- ▶ Administering your page
- ▶ Publishing stream updates to the users

Introduction

Facebook has organised its huge database of 800 million users as a social graph. This graph consists of unique entities (such as people, photos, and so on) known as objects and these objects are interrelated to each other by *connections* such as friends, photo tags, and so on.

We can connect our website(s) to this infinite social graph by using the Facebook Open Graph protocol. We can do so by converting our web pages into graph objects. This is done by adding the `<meta>` tags and a **Like** button to these pages. After this modification, whenever a user likes our web page by clicking on the Facebook **Like** button, a connection is established between that user and our page just like any other Facebook page. We can even publish updates to the users who have liked our pages. So these tags, along with the **Like** button, allow us to specify structured information about the web page which, in turn, determines how the web page will be put up on Facebook.

In this chapter, we will learn how, using the **Like** button, we can make our webpage appear in the **Likes and Interests** section of the users' profile.

Now, let's move on and see how we can unify our web pages into the Facebook social graph.

Integrating web pages into the social graph

The Facebook Open Graph protocol allows us to specify how to represent our web page on its network when a user likes our page. This is done with help of the `<meta>` tags present in our web page. We can configure them to make our web page appear in relevant **Likes and Interests** sections of a Facebook users' profile so that they are able to relate to our web page in a better manner. Here, we will show you how to do this:

How to do it...

The following steps will demonstrate how to integrate web pages:

1. Open your web page, say `content.php`, and add the following code to it:

```
<html xmlns="http://www.w3.org/1999/xhtml"
      xmlns:og="http://ogp.me/ns#"
      xmlns:fb="http://www.facebook.com/2008/fbml">
  <head>
    <title>Packt Publishing</title>
```

2. Add the following `<meta>` tags which are related to the Facebook Open Graph protocol:

```
    <!-- Open graph meta tags will be placed here -->
    <meta property="og:title" content="Chess"/>
    <meta property="og:type" content="sport"/>
    <meta property="og:url"
          content="http://www.yoursite.com/content.php"/>
    <meta property="og:image"
          content="http://www.yoursite.com/chess.jpg"/>
    <meta property="og:site_name" content="Chess"/>
    <meta property="fb:admins" content="786017563,637089897"/>
    <meta property="og:description"
          content="Chess is the gymnasium of the mind."/>
  </head>
  <body>
```

3. Place your web page content here:

```
    <!-- Your webpage content here -->
```

4. Also, add the code for the **Like** button, as explained in the previous chapter, at an appropriate location in your web page:

```
<iframe src="http://www.facebook.com/plugins/like.
php?href=<?php echo rawurlencode('http://' . $_SERVER
['HTTP_HOST'] . $_SERVER['REQUEST_URI']); ?>&amp;
send=true&amp;layout=standard&amp;width=450&amp;
show_faces=true&amp;action=like&amp;colorscheme=ligh
t&amp;font&amp;height=80" scrolling="no" frameborder="0"
style="border:none; overflow:hidden; width:450px;
height:80px;" allowTransparency="true"></iframe>
   </body>
</html>
```

Now, if a user likes this page, it will be displayed on Facebook as shown in the following screenshot:

How it works...

Here, we have created a web page that is related to a Chess game. We have accordingly set the <meta> tags (such as thumbnail image, description, title, and so on), as defined by the Facebook Open Graph protocol. If any Facebook social plugin is present on a web page, primarily a **Like** button, and when a user interacts with that plugin, Facebook uses these <meta> tags to interpret and classify the current page and render it properly on the user's and his or her friends' feed. In this way, the Facebook Open Graph protocol, with the help of the <meta> tags, allows us to configure and control how our web pages are classified and rendered inside Facebook. The Open Graph protocol defines four required properties:

▶ og:title: This defines the title of the graph object; for example, Chess.

▶ og:type: This specifies the category of the graph object; for example, sport. The various object types are listed as follows:

  ❑ **Activities**: This object type group is for the objects related to some sport or activity in general. The object type can be activity or sport.

  ❑ **Businesses**: This group corresponds to different types of businesses. It can take the following values—bar, company, cafe, hotel, and restaurant.

- ❑ **Groups**: Valid values for this are `cause`, `sports_league`, and `sports_team`.

- ❑ **Organizations**: This category contains the objects related to different types of organization. Valid values are `band`, `government`, `non_profit`, `school`, and `university`.

- ❑ **People**: If the graph object describes a person, the value for the object type can be `actor`, `athlete`, `author`, `director`, `musician`, `politician`, or `public_figure`.

- ❑ **Places**: If the web page, to be represented as a graph object, describes a place, the value for object type can be `city`, `country`, `landmark`, or `state_province`.

- ❑ **Products and Entertainment**: This contains the objects corresponding to entertainment and product industry. The object type can be `album`, `book`, `drink`, `food`, `game`, `product`, `song`, `movie`, or `tv_show`.

- ❑ **Website**: If your web page represents a website as a whole, the object type can be `blog`, `website`, or `article`.

- ▸ `og:image`: This specifies the URL of the image, which we want to attach with the graph object. The image must be at least 50 by 50 pixels and have a maximum aspect ratio of 3:1. PNG, JPEG, and GIF formats are supported. Multiple `og:image` tags are allowed in order to associate multiple images to your page.

- ▸ `og:url`: This specifies the canonical URL of the graph object, which is used as its permanent ID in the graph; for example, `http://www.yoursite.com/sports/chess/`.

Apart from the preceding `<meta>` tags, Facebook requires two additional fields in order to establish a successful connection, as a graph object, when a user likes your web page:

- ▸ `og:site_name`: This is a human-readable name of your website which will be used by Facebook.

- ▸ `fb:admins` or `fb:app_id`: It is a comma-separated list of either Facebook user IDs or a Facebook Platform application ID that administers this page. It is valid to include both `fb:admins` and `fb:app_id` on your page.

Facebook recommends using the following property as well:

- ▸ `og:description`: It is a one or two line description of your current web page.

When a user likes your web page, a **News Feed** story, as shown on preceding page, is published to Facebook. In this story, og:title links to og:url and og:site_name points to the website domain. Also, og:image gives the URL of the thumbnail used in the story. The og:type is used by Facebook to decide the category in which to place your web page and it appears accordingly on the user's profile page. Here, as we have listed og:type for our web page as sport, it is listed in the **Activities and Interests** section of the users' profile, as shown in the following screenshot:

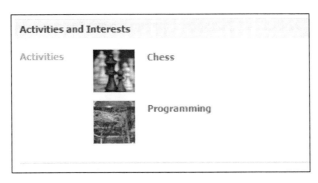

In this way, the Facebook Open Graph protocol helps us to integrate our web pages in a better manner to the Facebook network and associate ourselves in a more defined manner to its millions of users.

There's more...

Usually, web pages have location and contact information associated with them. Here, we will show you how to define them appropriately with the help of the Facebook Open Graph protocol.

Defining location information

We can use the Open Graph protocol to define location information for our object. Here, object can be business, school, organization, and so on. We can provide latitude and longitude information for our location with the help of the following set of metadata:

```
<meta property="og:latitude" content="52.4667"/>
<meta property="og:longitude" content="1.9167"/>
```

We can also represent the same location information in human-readable format with the following set of metadata:

```
<meta property="og:street-address" content="32 Lincoln Road"/>
<meta property="og:locality" content=" Birmingham "/>
<meta property="og:region" content="Birmingham"/>
<meta property="og:postal-code" content="B27 6PA"/>
<meta property="og:country-name" content="UK"/>
```

We can modify the properties according to our location in the preceding code.

Defining contact information

If your web page contains contact information, it can be defined with the help of the following metadata set:

```
<meta property="og:email" content="contact@packtpub.com"/>
<meta property="og:phone_number" content="+44 121 683 1170"/>
<meta property="og:fax_number" content="+44 121 535 7039"/>
```

Similarly, we can set our e-mail ID, telephone number, and fax number as shown in the preceding code.

Defining a custom object type

If you are unable to find a suitable object type, defined by using og:type property, you can define your own custom object type. Facebook recommends using your own namespace when defining a custom object type. An example is shown as follows:

```
<html xmlns:college="http://www.college.edu/ns#" >
  <head>
    <meta property="og:type" content="college:faculty"/>
  </head>
```

Here, we have used the college namespace for our site, www.college.edu, and the current page represents the college faculty. Facebook will categorize this object type as other.

See also

▶ Refer to the *Integrating audio and video data* recipe that follows.

Integrating audio and video data

Many a time, our web page contains audio and video data, which we will want to share on Facebook when a user likes our page. We can do so with the help of the Facebook Open Graph protocol. It has a specific set of metadata for this purpose. In this recipe, we will show you how to integrate audio/video data of your web page into the social graph.

Getting ready

Read the *Integrating web pages into the social graph* recipe.

How to do it...

The following steps will demonstrate how to integrate audio and video:

1. Open your web page, say `content.php`, and add the following code to it:

    ```
    <html xmlns="http://www.w3.org/1999/xhtml"
          xmlns:og="http://ogp.me/ns#"
          xmlns:fb="http://www.facebook.com/2008/fbml">
      <head>
    ```

2. Add the metadata for the web page:

    ```
        <!-- Open graph meta tags will be placed here -->
        <title>Sleep Away</title>
        <meta property="og:title" content="Sleep Away"/>
        <meta property="og:type" content="song"/>
        <meta property="og:url"
              content="http://www.yoursite.com/content.php"/>
        <meta property="og:image"
              content="http://www.yoursite.com/sleep_away.jpg"/>
        <meta property="og:site_name" content="Sleep Away"/>
        <meta property="fb:admins" content="786017563,637089897"/>
        <meta property="og:description"
              content="Watch the video & listen to Bob Acri - Sleep
    Away for free."/>
    ```

3. Next, add the metadata for the audio file present on the web page:

    ```
        <meta property="og:audio"
              content="http://www.yoursite.com/sleep_away.mp3" />
        <meta property="og:audio:title" content="Sleep Away" />
        <meta property="og:audio:artist" content="Bob Acri" />
        <meta property="og:audio:album" content="Bob Acri" />
        <meta property="og:audio:type" content="application/mp3" />
      </head>
    <body>
    ```

4. Add your web page content here:

    ```
        <!-- Your webpage content here -->
    ```

5. Also, add the code for the **Like** button, as explained in *Chapter 6, Bring Facebook to your website*, at an appropriate location in your web page:

```
<iframe src="http://www.facebook.com/plugins/like.
php?href=<?php echo rawurlencode('http://' . $_SERVER
['HTTP_HOST'] . $_SERVER['REQUEST_URI']); ?>&amp;send=
true&amp;layout=standard&amp;width=450&amp;sh
ow_faces=true&amp;action=like&amp;colorscheme=light
&amp;font&amp;height=80" scrolling="no" frameborder="0"
style="border:none; overflow:hidden; width:450px;
height:80px;" allowTransparency="true"></iframe>
</body>
</html>
```

When a user likes this page, he or she will get a feed story on his or her wall, as shown in the following screenshot:

As you can see in the preceding screenshot, the song (audio data) is directly embedded on the user's wall and music can be directly played from there itself.

How it works...

Here, first we set the metadata for the page as explained in the first recipe of this chapter. Now, we want to attach metadata for an audio file present on this web page. We have an audio file named `sleep_away.mp3`, which we want to post on the user's wall when he or she likes this page. For this, we need to set the following meta properties:

Meta properties	Description
`og:audio`	This contains the path to the audio file which, in this case, is `http://www.yoursite.com/sleep_away.mp3`.
`og:audio:title`	This specifies the title of the audio track which, in this case, is `Sleep Away`.
`og:audio:artist`	This specifies the name of the artist who, in this case, is Bob Acri.
`og:audio:album`	This specifies the name of the album of the audio track which, in this case, is `Bob Acri`.
`og:audio:type`	This specifies the type of the audio content which, in this case, is `application/mp3`.

Now, if a user likes this page, Facebook will use the metadata for the audio given and post it to his or her wall. The audio track gets embedded on the user's wall and now will be directly played from there, as shown in the preceding screenshot.

There's more...

Similar to the audio file, we can attach the video file as a graph object to the social graph as well.

Attaching the video to the social graph

Here, we will show you how to attach the video to the social graph. Add the following code to the web page:

```
<meta property="og:video" content="http://www.yoursite.com/my_video.
swf" />
<meta property="og:video:height" content="500" />
<meta property="og:video:width" content="400" />
<meta property="og:video:type"
content="application/x-shockwave-flash" />
```

In order to enable the video content to be automatically shown on a user's wall when he/she likes our page, we need to set the following meta properties for our video data:

Meta properties	Description
og:video	This contains the path to our video file which, in this case, is `http://www.yoursite.com/my_video.swf`.
og:video:height	This specifies the height of our video file which, in this case, is `500` pixels.
og:video:width	Similarly, this specifies the width of our video.
og:video:type	This specifies the type of the video content which, in this case, is `application/x-shockwave-flash`.

Currently, Facebook supports embedding of video in SWF format only. Also, you should have a `og:image` meta tag for the video to be displayed on the user's wall.

See also

  ▸ Refer to the *Integrating web pages into the social graph* recipe seen earlier in this chapter.

Administering your page

When we convert a web page to a graph object and attach it to the Facebook social graph, Facebook creates a unique ID for this graph object and provides us with an administration interface to configure its settings.

How to do it...

The following steps will demonstrate working with the administration interface:

1. Open the web page, which you have converted to a graph object and locate the **Like** button.

2. Beside the **Like** button, you will see a link titled as **Admin Page** as shown in the following screenshot. Click on it:

3. Next, you will be redirected to the administrative interface for your current web page on Facebook as shown in the following screenshot. By default, you will be taken to the **Get Started** section, where you can take various actions:

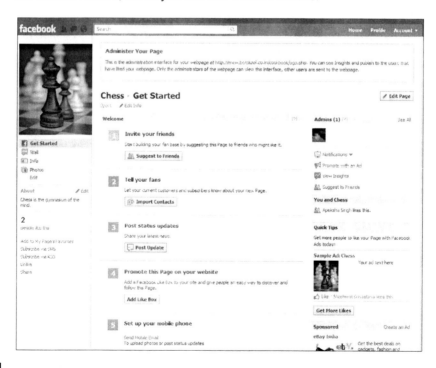

4. Additionally, you can click on the **Edit Page** button, present on the right-hand side, to further configure different settings such as permissions, administrators, applications, insights, and so on.

5. For changing permissions, click on the **Manage Permissions** link present in the sidebar, as shown in the following screenshot:

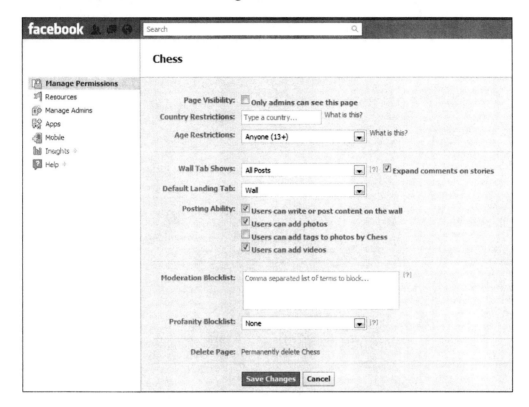

6. Here, we can apply various restrictions based on age, country, and so on. Also, we can decide whether to show posts made by all users or administrators on the page wall. We can decide the **Default Landing Tab**, too. It can be set to **Wall**, **Info**, **Photos**, and so on.

7. Apart from this, we can control the posting ability of the page users and moderate the keywords entered by the users. Additionally, there is a **Profanity Blocklist** field which can be set to **None, Medium,** or **Strong**. One such configuration is shown in the following screenshot:

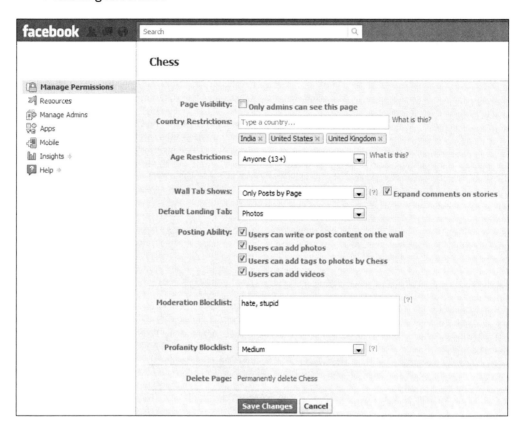

How it works...

Facebook treats the web page-based graph object like any other page and its administrative interface is similar to that of a Facebook page. With the help of this administrative interface, you can configure this Facebook page (graph object) which represents your web page on Facebook. In this way, you can interact with and send updates to the people who have liked your web page.

Connecting your websites to the social graph brings in more traffic and user interactions to your website, as there is a high probability of users' friends also getting involved in your web page based Facebook page.

You can also go to the Facebook based administration interface of your web page by going to your Facebook profile. Search for the Facebook page which represents this page and click on it, as shown in the following screenshot:

Also, we can use the Facebook URL Linter (`http://developers.facebook.com/tools/lint/`) for this. Enter your web page URL on this page and it will show you the **Admin URL**, along with other useful information, as shown in the following screenshot:

Publishing stream updates to the users

We can publish updates to the users who have liked our web page. This helps us to notify the users about the updates related to the topic discussed on the web page and hence, this opens doors for more traffic.

How to do it...

The following steps will demonstrate how to publish stream updates:

1. Open your web page and locate the **Like** button. Click on the **Admin Page** link.

2. Next, in the administrative interface, click on the **Wall** section present on the left-hand side of the page and enter the update as a status message, as shown in the following screenshot:

3. Now, click on the **Share** button. The update will automatically appear in the **News Feed** of all the users who have liked your web page as shown in the following screenshot:

How it works...

Facebook treats a web page, which is represented as a graph object, like a page and allows us to publish updates to the users who have liked the web page. The interface provided is similar to a regular Facebook page; in fact it's identical.

Apart from updates, we can publish links, photos, and videos to the web page. We can even integrate Facebook applications to this page, thereby increasing flexibility. Hence, Facebook allows us to connect to our users in various intuitive ways.

8
Fiddling with Virtual Currency

In this chapter, we will cover:

- ▸ Setting up the application for Facebook Credits
- ▸ Setting up an application callback for Facebook Credits
- ▸ Creating Facebook Credits frontend using JavaScript SDK
- ▸ Getting the order details
- ▸ Implementing custom offers
- ▸ Refunding the order
- ▸ Developing a "Send a gift" application and integrating with Facebook Credits

Introduction

Facebook has recently introduced its virtual currency known as **Facebook Credits**. It can be used to buy digital and virtual goods made available by millions of Facebook applications. This has taken the concept of social networking to a complete new level. For instance, now you can gift your friend virtual or real goods right through Facebook on any occasion, say his or her birthday. Similarly, now you can purchase premium items of your favorite games present as Facebook applications. All this has been made possible by Facebook Credits. So, now users don't need to bother about their credit information being stolen by some insecure Facebook application. They can simply buy some Facebook Credits by using their credit card and then this virtual currency can be used to purchase items from any Facebook application. This is good for developers too. Facebook itself handles the tough part, which is the transaction of real money, and the developers can charge users the virtual currency by using the Facebook Credits API. The real money equivalence of the virtual money earned by a Facebook application is then credited back to a fixed account, set up by developers, at regular intervals.

Also, this greatly reduces the time spent by users on purchasing items as there is a uniform interface across all Facebook applications and once users have set up their credit information in Facebook, they can easily recharge their credits when they run out of their virtual currency.

Setting up the application for Facebook Credits

With the Facebook Credits API, we can enable users to use credits as a method of purchasing digital and virtual goods inside our Facebook application. Also, we don't need to concern ourselves with transaction handling, which is automatically done by Facebook. So, let's get our application ready for Facebook Credits.

How to do it...

The following steps will demonstrate how to set up the application:

1. Go to the **Developer App** section (`https://developers.facebook.com/apps/`). Click on your application name inside the **Recently Viewed** block present on the left hand side.

2. Next, click on **Edit Settings** and then click on the **On Facebook** tab, present on the left rail. Finally, click on the **Credits** sub tab, as shown in the following screenshot:

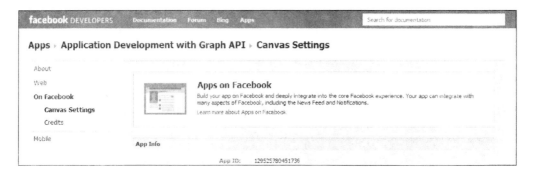

3. Before we can start using Facebook Credits, we need to register our company. Choose your **Company Country** and click on **Register a company now**, as shown in the following screenshot:

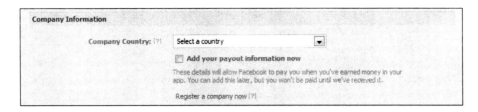

4. You will be presented with a form to sign up your company for **Facebook Credits**, as shown in the following screenshot. Fill in the relevant details:

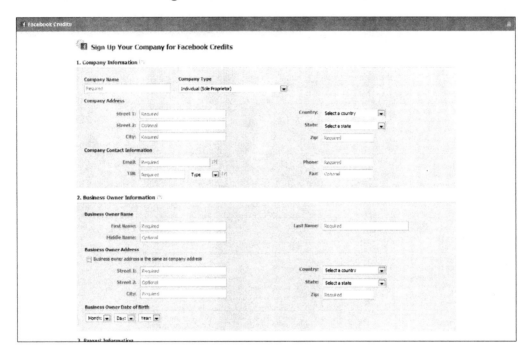

5. Once you have registered your company, you will be redirected back to the Facebook application Credits settings page. Enter your **Credits Callback URL** as `http://www.yoursite.com/callback.php`. This will be used by Facebook while updating an order, and has been explained in the recipe *Setting up an Application Callback for Facebook Credits* of this chapter. Also, set your test users, as shown in the following screenshot:

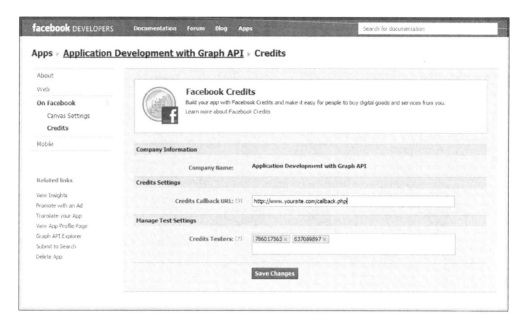

How it works...

Here, we have shown how to set up your application for using Facebook Credits. **Credits Callback URL** is the URL where Facebook pings to inform us after a user has opted for an order. We then process the order for the user with the help of Facebook Credits API, as explained in the recipe *Creating Facebook Credits frontend using JavaScript SDK* of this chapter.

Also, we can set up a few test users, which are dummy users, for testing Facebook Credits. This lets us check, and debug, our online purchasing system, discussed in the *Developing "Send a gift" application and integrating with Facebook Credits* recipe, developed with the help of Facebook Credits.

- ▸ *Setting up an Application Callback for Facebook Credits*
- ▸ *Creating Facebook Credits frontend using JavaScript SDK*
- ▸ *Developing a "Send a gift" application and integrating with Facebook Credits*

Setting up an application callback for Facebook Credits

Whenever a user does any transaction through Facebook credits, Facebook makes a call to the callback URL that has been set in the application's Credits settings, as described in the recipe—*Setting up the application for Facebook Credits*. Facebook communicates with this callback URL of your server multiple times, guiding the user through various stages in a buying process. Thus, configuration of this callback URL is the initial step, which we have to do if we want to implement credits functionality in our application. Here, we will show you how to set up your application callback for credits.

Getting ready

You should have enabled your application for Facebook credits as described in the preceding recipe.

How to do it...

The following steps demonstrate how to set up an application callback:

1. Create a new file named `callback.php` and copy the following code to it.
2. First, set your application API key (not application API ID) and application secret as shown below:

```php
<?php
    $api_key = 'YOUR_APP_API_KEY_HERE';
    $secret = 'YOUR_APP_SECRET_HERE';
```

3. Now, include the main file `facebook.php` and prepare the array `$data` for the return data:

```php
include_once 'facebook.php';

$data = array('content' => array());
```

4. Next, pass `signed_request` and secret key to the `parse_signed_request()` function to authenticate, and make sure that the request is coming from Facebook:

```
$request = parse_signed_request($_REQUEST['signed_request'],
    $secret);
```

5. If the request is not from Facebook we quit:

```
if ($request == null) {
    exit();
}

$payload = $request['credits'];
```

6. Then, retrieve `method` and `order_id`, which have been passed from Facebook:

```
$func = $_REQUEST['method'];
$order_id = $payload['order_id'];
```

7. Next, check for the callback method named `payment_status_update` and if it is so, then accordingly change the order status to `settled`:

```
if ($func == 'payments_status_update') {
    $status = $payload['status'];

    if ($status == 'placed') {
        $next_state = 'settled';
        $data['content']['status'] = $next_state;
    }

    $data['content']['order_id'] = $order_id;

}
```

8. If the callback method is `payment_get_items`, set the item details depending upon the value of `order_info`:

```
else if ($func == 'payments_get_items') {

    $order_info = stripcslashes($payload['order_info']);
```

9. If `order_info` is set to 1:

```
if ($order_info==1) {

    $item['title'] = 'Rose';
    $item['price'] = 1;
    $item['description'] = 'This is a rose';
    $item['image_url'] = 'http://www.yoursite.com/images/
        rose.png';
```

```php
    $item['product_url'] = 'http://www.yoursite.com/images/rose.
      png';

  }
```

10. If `order_info` is equal to 2:

```php
    else if ($order_info==2) {

      $item['title'] = 'Teddy Bear';
      $item['price'] = 2;
      $item['description'] = 'This is a Teddy Bear';
      $item['image_url'] = 'http://www.yoursite.com/images/teddy.
        png';
      $item['product_url'] = 'http://www.yoursite.com/images/
        teddy.png';

    }
```

11. Next, return the item details in the `content` key of the array `$data`:

```php
    $data['content'] = array($item);
  }
  $data['method'] = $func;
  echo json_encode($data);
```

12. Now, define the `parse_signed_request()` function, which authenticates the incoming request:

```php
  function parse_signed_request($signed_request, $secret) {
    list($encoded_sig, $payload) = explode('.', $signed_request, 2);
```

13. Next, verify `signed_request` and the algorithm, which is used to sign the request:

```php
    $sig = base64_url_decode($encoded_sig);
    $data = json_decode(base64_url_decode($payload), true);

    if (strtoupper($data['algorithm']) !== 'HMAC-SHA256') {
      error_log('Unknown algorithm. Expected HMAC-SHA256');
      return null;
    }

    $expected_sig = hash_hmac('sha256', $payload, $secret,
      $raw = true);
    if ($sig !== $expected_sig) {
      error_log('Bad Signed JSON signature!');
      return null;
    }
```

```
        return $data;
    }


    function base64_url_decode($input) {
        return base64_decode(strtr($input, '-_', '+/'));
    }
```

14. In the preceding code, you may want to write your own logic for the items you want to have in your application. Save this file.

 We have used `https://github.com/facebook/credits-api-sample/blob/master/callback.php` as a reference for the preceding code.

How it works...

Whenever any Facebook Credits transaction happens, Facebook communicates and makes certain requests to this callback URL. The initial step is to verify that the request comes from Facebook. For this, we verify the value of the `signed_request` key of the `$_REQUEST` array, which contains a base64 and a URL encoded JSON object sent by Facebook whenever a user accesses our application. We verify by using the `parse_signed_request()` function, as shown in the following code snippet:

```
function parse_signed_request($signed_request, $secret) {
    list($encoded_sig, $payload) = explode('.', $signed_request, 2);
    $sig = base64_url_decode($encoded_sig);
    $data = json_decode(base64_url_decode($payload), true);
    if (strtoupper($data['algorithm']) !== 'HMAC-SHA256') {
        error_log('Unknown algorithm. Expected HMAC-SHA256');
        return null;
    }
    $expected_sig = hash_hmac('sha256', $payload, $secret,
      $raw = true);
    if ($sig !== $expected_sig) {
        error_log('Bad Signed JSON signature!');
        return null;
        }
    return $data;
}
```

We use the `list()` function for separating `$signed_request` into sub arrays named `$sig` and `$data`, which contain signature and data respectively. Next, we decode them by using `base64_url_decode()`, a custom function, and `json_decode()`. Upon decoding, we check whether `$data['algorithm'])` is equal to `HMAC-SHA256`, a type of algorithm, which is used by Facebook. Next, we calculate the expected signature, `$expected_sig`, by using the `hash_hmac()` function and check if it is equal to the decoded signature, `$sig`. Once this is verified, we are ready to communicate back to Facebook.

As soon as a new order request is made to Facebook, it pings this callback URL and sends a request with the `payment_get_items` method along with `order_info` and `order_id`. The following table gives a detailed description of `order_id` and `order_info`:

Meta properties	Description
`order_id`	It is the 64-bit ID of the order. It is uniquely generated by Facebook every time an order is made.
`order_info`	It is the order information which is provided to Facebook by the application from the frontend. It is used to uniquely identify the item which has been ordered.

Once this is passed to the callback URL, we then need to return the requested item information based on the value of `order_info` to Facebook. The item information should be a JSON encoded array and should consist of these seven parameters, as shown in the following table:

Meta properties	Description
`item_id`	It is used to identify each item uniquely. It is not used by Facebook.
`title`	It is the name of the item. It can have a maximum of 50 characters.
`description`	It is the description of the item. It should be less than, or equal, to 175 characters.
`image_url`	It is the URL of the image of the item specified.
`product_url`	It is a permalink to the URL where we display the product to the user.
`price`	It is the price of the item. It must always be more than 0 credits.
`data`	It is an optional field and may or may not be specified. It can be used to store additional information about the product.

This has been done in the following lines of code. Here, we have shown the item information for two different `order_info` values:

```
else if ($func == 'payments_get_items') {
    $order_info = stripcslashes($payload['order info']);
```

```
if ($order_info==1) {
    $item['title'] = 'Rose';
    $item['price'] = 1;
    $item['description'] = 'This is a Rose';
    $item['image_url'] = 'http://www.yoursite.com/images/rose.png';
    $item['product_url'] = ' http://www.yoursite.com/images/rose.
png';
}

else if ($order_info==2) {
    $item['title'] = 'Teddy Bear';
    $item['price'] = 1;
    $item['description'] = 'This is a Teddy Bear';
    $item['image_url'] = 'http://www.yoursite.com/images/teddy.png';
    $item['product_url'] = ''http://www.yoursite.com/images/teddy.
png';
}
    $data['content'] = array($item);
}
$data['method'] = $func;
echo json_encode($data);
```

Once this is done, the user gets prompted with the option to pay. When the user clicks on it and confirms the payment, Facebook makes a request with the `payment_status_update` method to the callback URL and passes `status` as `placed`, along with `order_info` and the ordered item's information. If the method is `payment_status_update` and `status` is `placed`, we can next change the status to any of the states mentioned in the following table:

Meta properties	Description
settled	If the transaction is authorized and can be done. In this case, the required credit gets deducted from the user's account.
canceled	In this case, if the user does not have enough balance, then the required amount gets added to the user's balance. However, it can't be spent in the game.
refunded	This state can only be initiated by the developer or Facebook, in which case the entire amount gets refunded to the user, with no additional charge.

We set `status` to `settled` and pass it back to Facebook along with `order_id`. It has been done in these lines of code:

```
if ($func == 'payments_status_update') {
  $status = $payload['status'];
    if ($status == 'placed') {
```

```
        $next_state = 'settled';
        $data['content']['status'] = $next_state;
    }
    $data['content']['order_id'] = $order_id;

}
```

When Facebook receives this updated data, it completes the transaction deducting the amount from the user's account and moving the balance to our account. After this, Facebook once again calls the callback URL with the method as `payment_status_update` and `status` set to `settled`. It is then that we get to know that the transaction has been completed successfully and we can the store order details such as `order_id` in our database or perform some other operation.

See also

▸   *Calling Facebook Credits API using JavaScript SDK*

Creating Facebook Credits frontend using JavaScript SDK

We can make Facebook Credits frontend by directly using the JavaScript SDK. In this recipe, we will use the Facebook Pay Dialog box to handle credits and call it through Facebook's JavaScript SDK.

Getting ready

You should have created `index.php`, as mentioned in the *Getting ready* section given at the beginning of *Chapter 5*.

How to do it...

The following steps will demonstrate how to create a Facebook Credits frontend:

1. Open `index.php` and add the following highlighted code inside the div `fb-root`, as shown:

    ```
    <div id="fb-root">
        PURCHASE FROM THE LIST GIVEN BELOW <br /><br />
        <br />
        <ol>
            <li><a href="#" id="bdaygift">Rose</a></li>
            <li><a href="#" id="teddybear">Teddy Bear</a></li>
    ```

```
     </ol>
   </div>
```

2. Next, add the following highlighted code to the function assigned to `window.`
   `fbAsyncInit`, just after the `FB.init()` function:

   ```
   window.fbAsyncInit = function() {
           FB.init({appId: 'your_app_id', status: true, cookie: true,
   xfbml: true});
           $(document).ready(function() {
   ```

3. Use the callback function of the `click()` method for the above links to display the
   Facebook Pay dialog box:

   ```
   $("#bdaygift").click(function() {
   ```

4. Use the `FB.ui()` function to render the pay dialog box along with a set of
   parameters:

   ```
   FB.ui(
     {
     method: 'pay',
     credits_purchase: false,
     redirect_uri: 'http://apps.facebook.com/your_app/',
     order_info: 1,
     purchase_type:'item'

     },
   ```

5. Use the callback function of `FB.ui()` to determine the status of the order and alert
   the user:

   ```
   function(response) {
     if (response['order_id']) {
       alert('Your order id is ' + response['order_id']);
     } else {
       alert('Some error occurred.');
     }
   });


   });
   ```

6. For the item with `order_info` equal to 2:

   ```
   $("#teddybear").click(function() {
   FB.ui(
   {
   method: 'pay',
   ```

```
        credits_purchase: false,
        redirect_uri: 'http://apps.facebook.com/your_app/',
        order_info: 2,
        purchase_type:'item'


    },

    function(response) {
      if (response['order_id']) {
        alert('order made');
      } else {
        alert('error');
      }
    });
  });
});
};
```

7. In the preceding code, replace `your_app_id` with your own application ID. Now, save and run `index.php`.

How it works...

In the above code, after initializing our Facebook application, we use the jQuery `click` event for links with ID `rose` and `teddybear` to make a call to the `FB.ui()` function. For handling transactions through Facebook Credits, we make use of the inbuilt Facebook Pay Dialog. This is done by the `FB.ui()` function, which takes a JavaScript object as its first parameter. We set the `method` attribute as `pay`, which determines that we want to render the Facebook Pay Dialog box. We can configure our Facebook Pay Dialog box with the help of the following attributes:

Meta properties	Description
`app_id`	It is an optional field. It refers to your application ID.
`redirect_uri`	It is the URL to which we want to redirect to after the user clicks on the dialog button.
`credits_purchase`	It can be set to either `true` or `false`. It determines whether it is a credit purchase dialog or not.
`order_info`	This is an internal key and is related to our products' information.
`dev_purchase_params`	These are developer parameters used at different times such as earning credits, using offers, and so on.
`purchase_type`	This is used to decide which type of purchase is being done. Over here we have set it to `item`.

After making these configurations, we are all set to use Facebook Credits. Now, if we run `index.php`, we will be asked to choose an item to purchase as shown in the following screenshot:

When the user clicks on any of these items' names, Facebook pings the callback URL, which we have defined in our application's Credits settings, with the method set as `payment_get_items`. Now, corresponding to the `order_info` value of the clicked item, the callback file retrieves the item's fields, such as its description, price, and so on, and returns it back to Facebook. This information is then displayed in the Pay dialog box and it will appear as shown in the following screenshot:

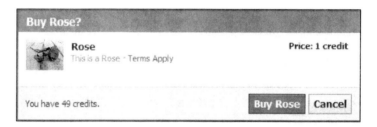

Along with this, it also displays the available credits in the user's account at the bottom-left corner. If the user has a sufficient balance and clicks on the buy button, a screen confirming the purchase appears, and the item's price gets deducted from the available credits of the user, as shown in the following screenshot:

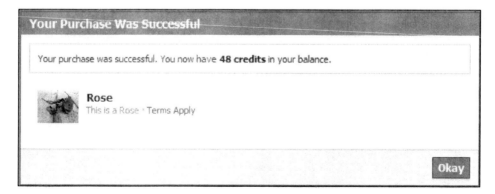

When the user clicks on **Okay**, the callback function of the FB.ui() function is called along with **order ID** that has been generated by Facebook for this order. If the order is successful, an alert box is displayed, as shown in the following screenshot:

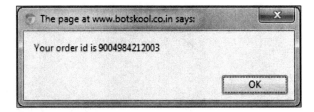

Also, when the user clicks the **OK** button, then Facebook again pings our callback URL with the method as payment_status_update and status as settled. It is then that we know the transaction has been completed successfully.

There's more...

If the user does not have sufficient credits in his account, then Facebook automatically acknowledges this and provides the user with a series of payment options, as shown in the following screenshot:

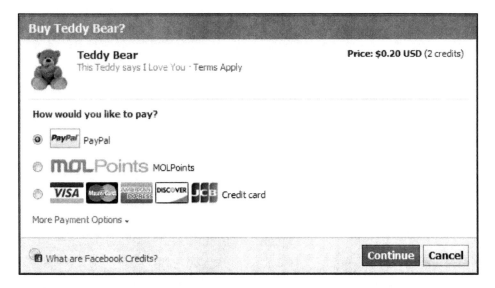

The user can now enter his/her credentials, buy the credits, and can then make the purchase as desired.

Getting credits without purchase

If the user does not want to purchase any item, and rather only wants to buy some credits, then this can be done simply by making `credit_purchase`, inside the `FB.ui()` function, as `false`. Also, we need not mention any other attribute such as `order_info`. The code for this is as follows:

```
FB.ui(
    {
      method: 'pay',
      credits_purchase: true,
    });
```

Upon running this code, a pay dialog box with the following options for payment will appear:

Now, the user can select from any of these options and buy the credits as desired.

Getting the order details

Facebook allows us to retrieve the order details of credit purchased by a user. We can use Facebook Graph API for this purpose and retrieve the details, such as the person who has purchased the particular item, the time, and so on.

Getting ready

You should know the order ID of whose information you want to retrieve. Also, you should have registered your application and should have created `config.php`, as explained in the *Getting ready* section in the beginning of *Chapter 2*.

How to do it...

The following steps will demonstrate how to retrieve the order details:

1. Create a file named `action_get_order.php` and add the following code to it:

   ```php
   <?php
   ```

2. Include the configuration file:

   ```php
   require_once 'config.php';
   ```

3. Specify the arguments that need to be posted to the authorization URL in the `$args` array:

   ```php
   $args = array('grant_type' => 'client_credentials',
                 'client_id' => $facebook->getAppId(),
                 'client_secret' =>  $facebook->getApiSecret());
   ```

4. Initialize cURL using the `curl_init()` function:

   ```php
   $ch = curl_init();
   ```

5. Set the authorization URL by using the `curl_setopt()` function:

   ```php
   $url = 'https://graph.facebook.com/oauth/access_token';
   curl_setopt($ch, CURLOPT_URL, $url);
   ```

6. Set the POST and RETURNTRANSFER method and POSTFIELDS using the `curl_setopt()` function:

   ```php
   curl_setopt($ch, CURLOPT_HEADER, false);
   curl_setopt($ch, CURLOPT_RETURNTRANSFER, true);
   curl_setopt($ch, CURLOPT_POST, true);
   curl_setopt($ch, CURLOPT_POSTFIELDS, $args);
   ```

7. Use the `curl_exec()` function to execute the POST request and the `explode()` function to extract the access token:

   ```php
   $access_token = explode("=", curl_exec($ch));
   curl_close($ch);

   $access_token = $access_token[1];
   ```

8. GET the order details using the `api()` function:

```
$order_id='your_order_id';
$orderinfo = $facebook->api('/'.$order_id,'GET',array
   ('access_token' => $access_token,));
print_r($orderinfo);
?>
```

9. Enter your order ID in place of `your_order_id` and save the file. Now run it.

How it works...

For retrieving details of an order made using Facebook Credits, we first need to get an `OAuth` access token on behalf of the application. This is necessary, as an order made is an application's connection and it does not correspond to any particular user. To get the application's access token, we need to make a `POST` request to the following URL – `https://graph.facebook.com/oauth/access_token`. We use the functions of the PHP `cURL` library to assist us. We first use `curl_init()`, which initializes and returns a cURL handle.

Next, we set certain options for configuring the request before executing it. We have configured the following attributes by using the `curl_setopt()` function:

Meta properties	Description
`CURLOPT_HEADER`	It determines whether or not to include the header in the output.
`CURLOPT_RETURNTRANSFER`	It determines whether or not to return the transfer as a string of the return value of `curl_exec()`, instead of outputting it directly.
`CURLOPT_POST`	It determines whether or not to make a normal HTTP POST request.
`CURLOPT_POSTFIELDS`	It contains the data to post when making a POST request.

After this, we use `curl_exec()` to finally make the `POST` request and we store the result in `$access_token`, after using the `explode()` function on the returned result. We have used the `explode()` function because the data returned is something like this—`access_token=XXXXXXX`, and we have to extract the value of the access token.

Once we have the access token, we make a GET request to the URL of the form—`https://graph.facebook.com/[order_id]` by using the `api()` function, as follows:

```
$orderinfo = $facebook->api('/'.$order_id, 'GET', array('access_token'
=> $access_token,));
```

After we have successfully made our request, Facebook will return the order details, such as the order ID, buyer, sender, price, status, application name, country, and purchase time. It will look as shown in the following screenshot:

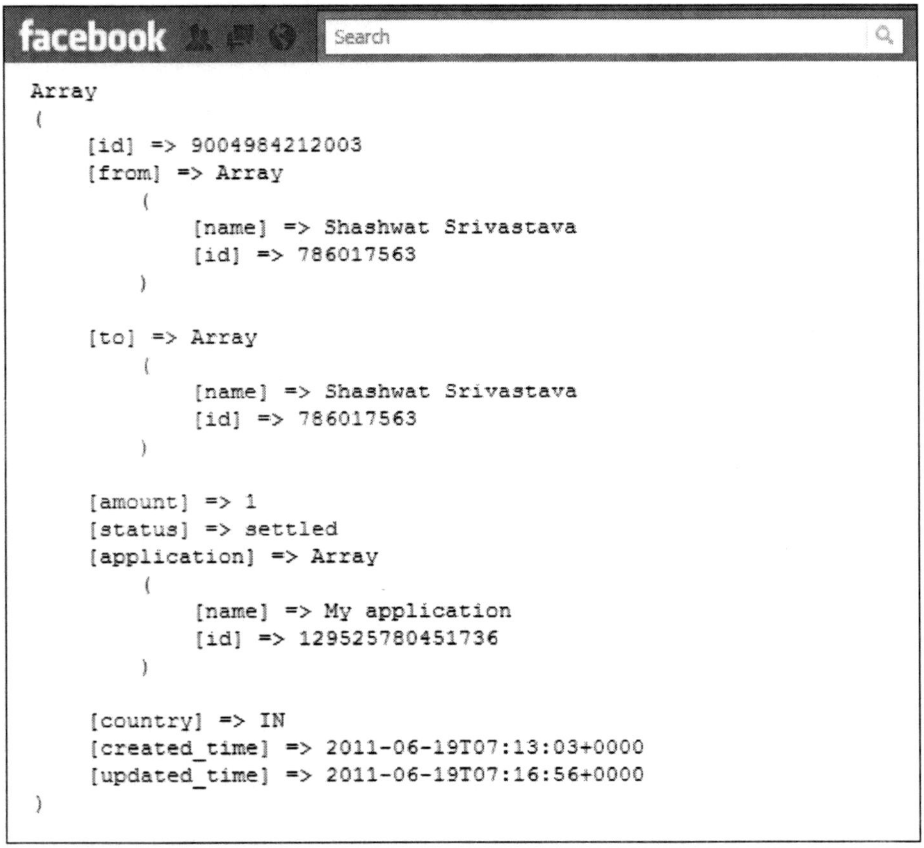

```
facebook              Search                                          Q

   Array
   (
        [id] => 9004984212003
        [from] => Array
            (
                    [name] => Shashwat Srivastava
                    [id] => 786017563
            )

        [to] => Array
            (
                    [name] => Shashwat Srivastava
                    [id] => 786017563
            )

        [amount] => 1
        [status] => settled
        [application] => Array
            (
                    [name] => My application
                    [id] => 129525780451736
            )

        [country] => IN
        [created_time] => 2011-06-19T07:13:03+0000
        [updated_time] => 2011-06-19T07:16:56+0000
   )
```

See also

▶ The *Getting ready* section in the beginning of *Chapter 2*

Implementing custom offers

Facebook allows us to earn credits by completing certain offers. This is most beneficial when we do not want to pay from our own account.

Getting ready

You should have created `index.php` as mentioned in the beginning of *Chapter 5*.

How to do it...

The following steps will demonstrate the implementation of custom orders:

1. Open `index.php` and add the following highlighted code inside the div named `fb-root` as shown:

```
<div id="fb-root">
  <ol>
  <li><a href="#" id="earncredit">Earn Credits through
    Offers</a></li>
  </ol>
</div>
```

2. Next, add the following highlighted code to the function assigned to `window.fbAsyncInit`, just after the `FB.init()` function:

```
window.fbAsyncInit = function() {
    FB.init({appId: 'your_app_id', status: true, cookie: true,
        xfbml: true});

    $(document).ready(function() {
```

3. Use the callback function of the `click()` method for the previous links to display the Facebook Pay Dialog:

```
$("#earncredit").click(function() {
```

4. Use the `FB.ui()` function to render the pay dialog box, along with a set of parameters :

```
FB.ui(
    {
        method: 'pay',
        credits_purchase: true,
        dev_purchase_params: {"shortcut":"offer"}
    });


    });
  });
};
```

5. Replace `your_app_id` in the previous code with your application ID. Now run the code. A screen will appear, as shown in the following screenshot:

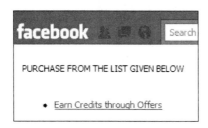

6. Now, if you will click on the option **Earn Credits through offers**, a screen displaying the list of offers by TrialPay will appear and would be similar to the following screenshot:

The user can now click on any of these offers, complete them, and the corresponding credits will get added to his/her account.

Here, first of all we initialize our Facebook application using the `FB.init()` function of the Facebook JS SDK. Next, we use the jQuery `click` event of div with ID `earncredit` to make a call to the `FB.ui()` function. We make use of the Facebook Pay Dialog box to render the offers. This is done by the `FB.ui()` function, which takes a JavaScript object as a parameter. We set the `method` attribute as `pay`, which determines that we want to render the Facebook Pay Dialog box.

To render offers for earning credits, the main attribute that needs to be set is `dev_purchase_params`. It requires a JSON object and we make it equal to `{"shortcut":"offer"}` in order to tell Facebook to render the TrialPay offers, which will help us earn credits. This has been done in the following lines of code:

```
FB.ui(
    {
        method: 'pay',
        credits_purchase: true,
        dev_purchase_params: {"shortcut":"offer"}
    });
```

Once we have set these attributes, we simply need to run the code and complete the offers available to earn Facebook Credits.

There's more...

The method just mentioned allows us to earn the credits by completing certain offers. There is another way by which we can get credits. This is done by integrating DealSpot in our application.

Integrating DealSpot

DealSpot offers the customers credits in exchange for completing certain advertisement offers. DealSpot relies on a set of in-game icons that rotate, based on offers, and automatically hides from the customers if no offers are available.

To integrate DealSpot, copy the code given next, in your application:

```php
<?php
    require_once 'config.php';
    $info = $facebook->api('/me?fields=third_party_id');
?>
```

```
<span id="trialpay_dealspot"></span>
<script type="text/javascript" src="http://assets.tp-cdn.com/static3/
js/api/payment_overlay.js"></script>
<script type="text/javascript">

  TRIALPAY.social.render_dealspot_swf({
    "id" : "trialpay_dealspot",
    "app_id" : "<?php print $facebook->getAppId()?>",
    "onOfferUnavailable" : "TRIALPAY.social.delete_dealspot_swf",
    "mode" : "fbpayments",
    "sid" : "<?php print $info['third_party_id']?>"
  });
</script>
```

For integrating DealSpot into your application, we require the following parameters:

- `app_id`: It is your Facebook application ID. We have retrieved it in the previous code using `<?php print $facebook->getAppId()?>` and assigned it to `app_id`.

- `sid`: It is the customer's unique third party ID. Facebook has associated a unique third party identifier with every user. This is when developers have to share information with some legitimate third party. It had been retrieved by making a call to the Facebook Graph API in `$info = $facebook->api('/me?fields=third_party_id');`.

- `onOfferUnavailable`: It collapses the DealSpot swf if no offers are available. You can call your own function when no offers are available by replacing `TRIALPAY.social.delete_dealspot_swf` with your own function's name.

Refunding the order

Sometimes, it may happen that a user has placed an order, but we are unable to process the order due to some problem that might have occurred unexpectedly. In such a case, the developer needs to refund the money to the user. In this recipe, we will learn how to refund an order.

Getting ready

You should know the ID of the order whose payment you want to refund. Also, you should have registered your application and should have created `config.php`, as explained in the *Getting ready* section in the beginning of *Chapter 2*.

How to do it...

The following steps will demonstrate how to refund the order:

1. Create a file named `action_update_order.php` and add the following code to it:

   ```php
   <?php
   ```

2. Include the configuration file:

   ```php
   require_once 'config.php';
   ```

3. Specify the arguments needed to post to the authorization URL in the `$args` array:

   ```php
   $args = array('grant_type' => 'client_credentials',
                 'client_id' => $facebook->getAppId(),
                 'client_secret' =>  $facebook->getApiSecret());
   ```

4. Initialize cURL using the `curl_init()` function:

   ```php
   $ch = curl_init();
   ```

5. Set the authorization URL by using the `curl_setopt()` function:

   ```php
   $url = 'https://graph.facebook.com/oauth/access_token';
   curl_setopt($ch, CURLOPT_URL, $url);
   ```

6. Set the `POST` and `RETURNTRANSFER` method and `POSTFIELDS` using the `curl_setopt()` function:

   ```php
   curl_setopt($ch, CURLOPT_HEADER, false);
   curl_setopt($ch, CURLOPT_RETURNTRANSFER, true);
   curl_setopt($ch, CURLOPT_POST, true);
   curl_setopt($ch, CURLOPT_POSTFIELDS, $args);
   ```

7. Use the `curl_exec()` function to execute the `POST` request and the `explode()` function to extract the access token:

   ```php
   $access_token = explode("=", curl_exec($ch));
   curl_close($ch);

   $access_token = $access_token[1];
   ```

8. POST the order refund request using the api() function:

   ```php
   $order_id='your_order_id';
   $info = $facebook->api('/'.$order_id,'POST',array('access_token'
      => $access_token,'status'=> 'refunded','message'=> ' We are
      refunding the order due to delivery failure',));
   print_r($info);
   ?>
   ```

8. Enter `order id`, whose payment you want to refund, in place of `your_order_id` and save the file. Now run it. Upon successful execution, it returns 1, which gets stored in `$info`, and refunds the credits charged from the user for that particular order ID.

How it works...

For refund of the payment, related to an order made using Facebook Credits, we first need to get an `OAuth` access token on behalf of the application. This is necessary, as an order made is an application's connection. To get the application's access token, we need to make a POST request to the following URL (`https://graph.facebook.com/oauth/access_token`). We use PHP cURL library functions to assist us. We first use `curl_init()`, which initializes and returns a cURL handle.

Next, we set certain options for configuring the request before executing it. We have configured the following attributes by using the `curl_setopt()` function:

Meta properties	Description
CURLOPT_HEADER	It determines whether or not to include the header in the output.
CURLOPT_RETURNTRANSFER	It determines whether or not to return the transfer as a string of the return value of `curl_exec()`, instead of outputting it directly.
CURLOPT_POST	It determines whether or not to make a normal HTTP POST request.
CURLOPT_POSTFIELDS	It contains the data to post when making a POST request.

After this, we use `curl_exec()` to finally make a POST request and we store the result in `$access_token`, after using the `explode()` function on the returned result. We have used the `explode()` function because the data returned is – `access_token=XXXXXXX` and we have to extract the value of the access token and store it in `$access_token`.

```
$access_token = explode("=", curl_exec($ch));
curl_close($ch);
$access_token = $access_token[1];
```

Once we have the access token, we make a POST request to the URL of the form (`https://graph.facebook.com/[order_id]`) using the `api()` function, as shown in the following code snippet:

```
$order_id='your_order_id';
$info = $facebook->api('/'.$order_id,'POST',array('access_token' =>
$access_token,'status'=> 'refunded','message'=> ' We are refunding the
order due to delivery failure',));
```

While updating the status of an order, we need to mention certain parameters. These are listed in the following table:

Meta properties	Description
order_id	It is the ID of the order whose status we want to update. This should be known to the developer beforehand.
access_token	This is the application's access token as status change requires application control.
status	The status of the order to which we want to move it from its present status. This could be settled, refunded or canceled.
message	This will contain the message which we pass along with the update.
refund_funding_source	It is a Boolean value. Its value is true if we want to refund the source of payment such as credit card, Paypal, and so on or false if we refund credits.
refund_reason	This is an optional field where we might specify the reason for the refund or status change.
params	It is an optional JSON-encoded dictionary {'comment' => }.

Once we have successfully executed this code, the payment made, with respect to the order ID, will get refunded to the user's account.

Developing a "Send a Gift" application and integrating with Facebook Credits

Facebook credit provides a safe and easy payment method to pay for digital and virtual goods. It helps developers maximize their revenue and improves their operational efficiency as they do not have to worry about the payment method anymore. Here, we will develop a Facebook application and integrate it with Facebook Credits.

Getting ready

You should have created callback.php as mentioned in the recipe *Setting up an Application Callback for Facebook Credits* of this chapter. Also, you should have created config.php as mentioned in the *Getting ready* section in the beginning of *Chapter 2*. We will use the MySQL database to store gifts and order details. So, you need to create a database, named db_gifts, and a corresponding username and password for it.

How to do it...

The following steps will demonstrate how to develop a "Send a Gift" application:

1. Create a table `gifts` inside the `db_gifts` database using the SQL code given next:

```
CREATE TABLE IF NOT EXISTS `gifts` (
  `serial` int(11) NOT NULL auto_increment,
  `name` text NOT NULL,
  `image_url` text NOT NULL,
  `price` int(11) NOT NULL,
  `description` text NOT NULL,
  PRIMARY KEY  (`serial`)
) ENGINE=MyISAM  DEFAULT CHARSET=latin1 AUTO_INCREMENT=11 ;
```

2. Now insert the values inside the `gifts` table using the following SQL insert statement:

```
INSERT INTO `gifts` (`serial`, `name`, `image_url`, `price`,
`description`) VALUES
(1, 'Chocolates', 'http://www.url_for_gift1.com/gift1.jpg',
1, 'Delicious pack of Cadbury chocolates having more than 10
different varieties'),
(2, 'Teddies', 'http://www.url_for_gift2.com/gift2.jpg', 3, 'Gift
a pair of cute teddy bears wishing happy birthday'),
(3, 'Cake', 'http://www.url_for_gift3.com/gift3.jpg', 5,
'Delicious home-made cake available in all the flavours'),
(4, 'Mug', 'https://www.url_for_gift4.com/gift4.jpg', 1, 'Gift a
Coffee Mug saying happy birthday'),
(5, 'Ring', 'http://www.url_for_gift5.info/gift5.jpg', 10, 'Gift a
platinum ring to your loved one'),
(6, 'Card', 'http://www.url_for_gift6.com/gift6.jpg', 2, 'Wish
happy birthday through cards'),
(7, 'Balloons', 'http://www.url_for_gift7.com/gift7.jpg', 1,
'Birthday Balloons'),
(8, 'Clock', 'http://www.url_for_gift8.com/gift8.jpg', 5, 'Gift a
Wall Clock'),
(9, 'bouquet', 'http://www.url_for_gift9.com/gift9.jpg', 3, 'Send
flowers with good wishes');
```

3. Create a new `index.php` file.

4. Include the file `config.php`. Now, using Facebook Graph API, extract the user's friend list into an array and change its `name` attribute to `label`:

```
<?php
  require_once 'config.php';
  $friends = $facebook->api('/me/friends');
  foreach($friends['data'] as &$friend) {
```

```
      $friend['label'] = $friend['name'];
      unset($friend['name']);
    }
  ?>
```

5. Now, add the external JavaScript files and the CSS stylesheet needed for using jQuery and jQuery UI widgets and themes:

```
<html xmlns="http://www.w3.org/1999/xhtml" xmlns:fb="http://www.
facebook.com/2008/fbml">
<head>
  <script type="text/javascript" src="https://ajax.googleapis.com/
    ajax/libs/jquery/1.5.2/jquery.min.js"></script>
  <script type="text/javascript" src="https://ajax.googleapis.com/
    ajax/libs/jqueryui/1.8.13/jquery-ui.min.js"></script>
  <link href="http://ajax.googleapis.com/ajax/libs/jqueryui/1.8.3/
    themes/u
  i-lightness/jquery-ui.css" rel="stylesheet" type="text/css" />
</head>
<body>
```

6. Add the following divs:

```
<div id="fb-root">
  <div class="ui-widget">
```

7. Now, define the div tabs as shown:

```
<div id="tabs">
  <ul>
    <li><a href="#tabs-1">Choose a Friend</a></li>
    <li><a href="#tabs-2">Choose a Gift</a></li>
  </ul>
```

8. Inside the div tabs, define a div tabs-1, as shown next:

```
<div id="tabs-1">
  <p><label for="friend">Choose a friend: </label>
    input id="friend" />
    <input type="hidden" id="selected_friend" /></p>
</div>
```

9. Next, define another div tabs-2, as shown:

```
<div id="tabs-2">
  <p><table width="100%" border="0">
    <tr>
    <?php
```

10. Connect to the MySQL database and select all the gifts from the database table named `gifts`:

```
$con = mysql_connect("localhost",
  "your_username","your_password");
if (!$con)
{
  die('Could not connect: ' . mysql_error());
}

mysql_select_db("botskoco_order", $con);

$result = mysql_query("SELECT * FROM gifts");
$i=0;
while($row = mysql_fetch_array($result))
{
```

11. Display the gifts in a tabular format, as shown next:

```
echo '<td width="33%" align="center"><img src="'
  . $row['image_url'] . '" id="gift_' .
  $row['serial'] . '" height="100" width="100"
  class="gifts"/><br>' . $row['name'] . '</td>';
$i++;
if($i%3==0)
echo '</tr><tr>';
}
mysql_close($con);
?>
</tr>
</table>
</div>
</div>
</div>
</div>
```

12. Load Facebook JavaScript SDK to define the functionalities:

```
<script type="text/javascript">
window.fbAsyncInit = function() {
```

13. Initialize the application using JavaScript's `FB.init()` function:

```
FB.init({appId: 'your_app_id', status: true, cookie: true,
  xfbml: true});
```

14. Inside the `document.ready` function, define the `callCredit()` function:

```
$(document).ready(function() {
  var callCredit = function(id) {
```

15. Use `FB.ui()` for displaying the Facebook Pay Dialog box:

```
FB.ui(
{
  method: 'pay',
  credits_purchase: false,
  redirect_uri: 'http://apps.facebook.com/your_app/',
  order_info:id,
  purchase_type:'item'
},
```

16. Define the callback function for `FB.ui()`:

```
function(response) {
  if (response['order_id']) {

    $("#tabs").append('<div id="tabs-3">Your order id is
      - ' + response['order_id'] + '.<br>Your gift will
      be delivered to your friend, ' + $('#friend').val()
      + ', within 2 days.<br>Thanks for using our
      service.</div>');
    $("#tabs").tabs('add', '#tabs-3', 'Order Details');
    $( "#tabs" ).tabs('select',2);
    } else {
      alert('Sorry, some error occurred. Please try
        placing order again.');
    }
  });
};
```

17. Define the user interface using jQuery UI:

```
$("#selected_friend").val(0);
$( "#tabs" ).tabs();
$("[id^='gift']").click(function() {
  if($("#selected_friend").val()!=0)
    callCredit($(this).attr('id').split('_')[1]);
  else
    alert('Please choose a friend first');
});
var friends = <?php echo json_encode($friends['data']); ?>;
$("#friend").autocomplete({
  source: friends
});
```

```
    $("#friend").bind("autocompleteselect",
        function(event, ui) {
      $("#selected_friend").val(ui.item.id);
      $( "#tabs" ).tabs('select',1);
    });
  });
};
```

18. Add the code to load **FB-JS SDK** asynchronously:

```
(function() {
  var e = document.createElement('script');
  e.type = 'text/javascript';
  e.src = document.location.protocol +
  '//connect.facebook.net/en_US/all.js';
  e.async = true;
  document.getElementById('fb-root').appendChild(e);
}());
</script>
</body>
</html>
```

19. Save this file.

20. Now we will make certain changes to the `callback.php` file, which we had created in the second recipe. Open it and make the changes that are highlighted next. Here, we have replaced the `if ($func == 'payments_get_items')` condition block with the following code:

```
else if ($func == 'payments_get_items') {
  $order_info = stripcslashes($payload['order_info']);

  $con = mysql_connect("localhost","botskoco_order","order");
  if (!$con)
  {
    die('Could not connect: ' . mysql_error());
  }

  mysql_select_db("botskoco_order", $con);
```

21. Retrieve the items' information dynamically from the database:

```
$row = mysql_fetch_array(mysql_query("SELECT * FROM gifts
    WHERE serial=" . $order_info));
$item['title'] = $row['name'];
$item['price'] = $row['price'];
```

```
$item['description'] = $row['description'];
$item['image_url'] = $row['image_url'];
$item['product_url'] = 'http://apps.facebook.com/your_app/';
mysql_close($con);
$data['content'] = array($item);
}
```

22. Save the edited `callback.php` file and now run `index.php`. A sample screenshot is shown next:

23. Type the name of a friend to whom you want to send the gift, in the **Choose a friend** textbox. A drop down list will appear from which you can select the name of your friend. As soon as you select the friend, you will be redirected to the second tab, where you will see a list of the available gifts, as shown next:

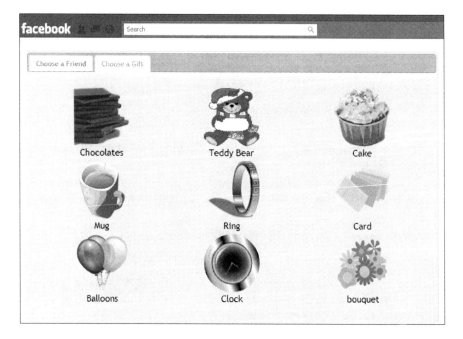

24. Next, click on the gift which you want to send. A pay dialog box, showing you the price of the item, will appear as shown next:

25. Click on the buy button if you want to send the gift. A dialog box confirming that the purchase was successful will appear and the equivalent credits will get deducted from your account:

26. As soon as you click on the **Okay** button, another tab will appear right next to the **Choose a Gift** tab, providing you the order details, as shown in the next screenshot:

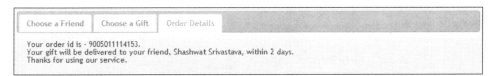

How it works...

Here, we have created a database table named `gifts` for storing the details of the gifts. It contains the following fields:

- ▶ `serial`: This is our unique ID for every gift.
- ▶ `name`: This is the name of the gift displayed to the user.
- ▶ `image_url`: This contains the URL of the gift image.
- ▶ `price`: This is the gift price expressed in Facebook credits.
- ▶ `description`: This contains a relevant description for the gift.

We store all our gift details in this table by executing SQL queries given in the previous section.

The frontend of our application contains three sections as listed next:

- ▶ Friend selection
- ▶ Gift selection
- ▶ Order details

For designing the frontend interface, we have used jQuery UI library and jQuery UI theme named UI Lightness. We have used jQuery UI widget – **Tabs** to render our three sections. Additionally, we have used a jQuery UI widget named **AutoComplete** to ease and automate the process of friend selection. Let's discuss the HTML and PHP code now.

First we need to provide the user with an interface to select his/her friends to whom a gift shall be sent. For this we make a `GET` request by using Facebook Graph API to the URL – `http://www.graph.facebook.com/me/friends` and store the names and IDs of the current user in the array named `$friends`. This has been done in this line of code:

```
$friends = $facebook->api('/me/friends');
```

The `$friends` array will be similar to this, having two attributes (`name` and `id`):

```
{
    "data": [
        {
            "name": "Apeksha Singh",
            "id": "32553"
        },
        {
            ..
        },
    ..
    ]
}
```

Next, we need to set this list of friends as an input to the jQuery UI AutoComplete widget. However, the jQuery UI AutoComplete widget needs an attribute named label or a value in the input data for rendering the friend selector. Thus, we change the name attribute of the previous friends' array and rename it as label. This has been done in the following lines:

```
foreach($friends['data'] as &$friend) {
    $friend['label'] = $friend['name'];
    unset($friend['name']);
```

The unset() function deletes the array key, which is passed to it. Next, we have used the Tabs widget to render the different sections on the page. For this, we have used the following HTML structure to define the various tabs:

```
<div id="tabs">
    <ul>
        <li><a href="#tabs-1">Choose a Friend</a></li>
        <li><a href="#tabs-2">Choose a Gift</a></li>
    </ul>
    <div id="tabs-1">
        <!-- Content of first section here -->
    </div>
    <div id="tabs-2">
        <!-- Content of second section here -->
    </div>
</div>
```

The <li> elements here will be used as the name of the different tabs, and when a user clicks on these tabs, then the relevant content will be displayed, as defined by various sub div tags, tabs-1 and tabs-2, inside the div named tabs. The third tab is generated dynamically. We will discuss it later.

The div tabs-1 contains the following code:

```
<label for="friend">Choose a friend: </label>
<input id="friend" />
<input type="hidden" id="selected_friend" />
```

Here, the input field with ID friend will be used to load the selector, as discussed later, and input field with id selected_friend, which is also a hidden type input field will contain the uid of the selected Facebook friend of the current user.

The div `tabs-2` contains the following code:

```
<table width="100%" border="0">
  <tr>
    <?php
      $con = mysql_connect("localhost","username","password");
      if (!$con) {
        die('Could not connect: ' . mysql_error());
      }
      mysql_select_db("db_gifts", $con);
      $result = mysql_query("SELECT * FROM gifts");
      $i=0;
      while($row = mysql_fetch_array($result)) {
        echo '<td width="33%" align="center">'
        <img src="' . $row['image_url'] . '" id="gift_'
        . $row['serial'] . '" height="100" width="100"
        class = "gifts"/><br>' . $row['name'] . '</td>';
        $i++;
        if($i%3==0)
          echo '</tr><tr>';
      }
      mysql_close($con);
    ?>
  </tr>
</table>
```

Here, we have dynamically generated an HTML table for displaying the gifts stored in the database. First, we establish a connection to the MySQL database by using the `mysql_connect()` function. Next, we connect to a database named `db_gifts` by using the `mysql_select_db()` function. After this we use `mysql_query()` along with the `mysql_fetch_array()` function and print the results, row by row, in the form of an HTML table.

Now, let's discuss the JavaScript code. First we have initialized our Facebook application by using the `FB.init()` function:

```
<script type="text/javascript">
window.fbAsyncInit = function() {
  FB.init({
  appId: 'your_app_id',
  status: true,
  cookie: true,
  xfbml: true
});
```

Next, we define the `callCredit()` function, which is called whenever a user clicks on a gift, in the following code:

```
$(document).ready(function() {
  var callCredit = function(id) {
    FB.ui(
      {
      method: 'pay',
      credits_purchase: false,
      redirect_uri: 'http://apps.facebook.com/your_app/',
      order_info: id,
      purchase_type: 'item'
      },
```

It takes a single parameter named ID, which is the gift ID. This function, in turn, loads the Facebook Pay Dialog box by calling the `FB.ui()` function with the following parameters:

Meta properties	Description
`method`	We set it equal to `pay`. This is used to render the Facebook Pay Dialog.
`credits_purchase`	It takes in a Boolean value. It can be set to either `true` or `false`. It determines whether it is a credit purchase dialog or not.
`redirect_uri`	It is the URL to which we want to redirect to after the user clicks on the dialog button.
`order_info`	This is an internal key and is related to our products' information.
`purchase_type`	This is used to decide which type of purchase is being done. Over here we have set it to `item`.

Next, we have shown the callback function of `FB.ui()`, which is inside the `callCredit()` function:

```
function(response) {
  if (response['order_id']) {
    $("#tabs").append('<div id="tabs-3">Your order id is - ' +
    response['order_id'] + '.<br>Your gift will be delivered to your
    friend, ' + $('#friend').val() + ', within 2 days.<br>Thanks for
    using our service.</div>');
    $("#tabs").tabs('add', '#tabs-3', 'Order Details');
    $("#tabs").tabs('select',2);
  } else {
    alert('Sorry, some error occurred. Please try placing
          order again.');
  }
});
                    };
```

When `callCredit()` is called and the purchase turns out to be successful, then the if condition in the callback function will be executed. Here, we use the `append()` function of jQuery to dynamically add a new tab, which will display the information of the newly created order. The div `tabs-3` is appended inside div `tabs`. Next, we call the `tabs()` function of jQuery UI to add a new tab with the content of the div `tabs-3` and the name of the tab is `Order Details`. After this, we again call the `tabs()` function with the first parameter as `select` and second parameter as 2. This brings the tab with index 2, which is the (newly added) third tab, in focus. In the else condition, we display an error message to the user requesting him/her to again place the order.

```
$("#selected_friend").val(0);
$("#tabs").tabs();
```

Here, we have set the value of div `selected_friend` as 0 and the `tabs()` function renders all the tabs based on the div `tabs`.

```
$("[id^='gift']").click(function() {
if($("#selected_friend").val()!=0)
    callCredit($(this).attr('id').split('_')[1]);
  else
    alert('Please choose a friend first');
});
```

All the images of the gifts have their ID in the form of `gift_id`, where id is the gift id. In the previous code, we have selected all the divs whose id start with `gift` and are registered to their click event:

```
var friends = <?php echo json_encode($friends['data']); ?>;
$("#friend").autocomplete({
  source: friends
});
```

Here, we first convert the `$friends['data']` array, as explained earlier, to the JSON format by using the `json_encode()` function. And then we store this JSON data into the JavaScript variable friends. Next, we call the `autocomplete()` function of jQuery UI and specify the source to be `friends`, which contains the JSON data of the Facebook friends of the current user. Hence, the jQuery UI's AutoComplete widget is loaded in the div `friend`.

```
$("#friend").bind("autocompleteselect", function(event, ui) {
    $("#selected_friend").val(ui.item.id);
    $("#tabs").tabs('select',1);
  });
  });
};
</script>
```

Finally, we have registered to the `autocompleteselect` event, which happens when a user chooses a friend and then we store the corresponding `id` of the selected friend in the div `selected_friend` by using the `val()` function. Next, we switch to the second tab by using the `tabs()` function, where the gifts get displayed as previously described.

9
Creating Advertisements and Analyzing Metric Data

In this chapter, we will cover:

- ▸ Retrieving impressions of the Like Box plugin
- ▸ Retrieving a page's stream views and wall posts using Batch Request
- ▸ Getting the number of installations of an application using FQL
- ▸ Getting statistics about visitors using FQL multiquery
- ▸ Creating a new advertisement for your Facebook application

Introduction

Facebook Insights is a free service by Facebook which provides its page owners, platform developers, and third-party website administrators with analytics and statistics about their pages, applications, and websites respectively. This enables the developers to understand how users are interacting with their content, and helps them to keep up with the latest changing trends. So, with the help of Facebook Insights we can get in-depth information about traffic and user data. This helps developers to formulate their business strategy in a more efficient and productive manner.

Facebook records various statistics for our application, such as daily impressions, number of active users, number of likes received, and so on. These metrics can be retrieved from either the Facebook table named **insights** or the Facebook Graph objects having an **insights** type connection. The **insights** table and connection contains statistics about applications, pages, and domains. Facebook application developers can export this metric data with the help of Facebook Graph API or Facebook Query Language, as will be discussed in this chapter. These metrics are collected and updated over a certain period which can vary from day, week, and month to year.

Additionally, Facebook also provides us with an **Insight Dashboard** where a developer can view and export some of the most common metrics related to his/her application, page, or domain. The Insight Dashboard can be accessed at `http://www.facebook.com/insights/`.

Also, Facebook provides us with an option to display an advertisement on our application by which we can increase its popularity. In this chapter, we will show you how to retrieve the details of the various metrics for your application or third-party website. Additionally, we will also show you how to create custom advertisements.

Prerequisites

First, we will create a basic layout. The recipes discussed in this chapter will contain code based on this. We need to create two files as will be illustrated. Follow these steps:

1. Create a `config.php` file and add the following code to it:

   ```php
   <?php
       require_once 'facebook.php';
       /** Create our Application instance. */
   ```

2. Initialize the Facebook application:

   ```php
   $facebook = new Facebook(array(
       'appId' => 'your_application_id',
       'secret' => 'your_application_secret_key',
       'cookie' => true,
   ));
   ```

   Here, a **Facebook** class is defined in `facebook.php` and can be downloaded from GitHub. `$facebook` is an object of this class and we will use it in `index.php`. You need to provide your application ID and secret key here. For more information, read the first chapter.

3. Next, create a file named `index.php` and add the following code to it:

   ```php
   <?php
   ```

4. Include the configuration file we just defined:

   ```php
   require_once 'config.php';
   ```

5. Get the current user's session information by using the `getSession()` function and then perform session validation:

```
$session = $facebook->getSession();
$me = null;
if ($session) {
  try {
    $me = $facebook->api('/me');
    /* Check whether the current session is valid by
       retrieving user information.*/
  }
  catch (Exception $e) {
  }
}
/* If the current session is invalid or user has not
   authorized the application then redirect to a
   authorization URL.*/
```

6. If the session is invalid redirect the application to the authorization URL:

```
if(!($me)) {
  echo '<script>
    top.location.href="'
    . $facebook->getLoginUrl(
        array(
          'req_perms' => 'read_insights',
          'next' =>
            'http://apps.facebook.com/[your_app_url]/',
        )
      )
    . '";
    </script>';
  exit;
}
?>
```

Here, we first retrieve a valid session for the user by calling `$facebook->getSession()` and storing the response in a `$session` variable. Next, we try to retrieve the basic information of the current user by posting a GET request to `https://graph.facebook.com/me`, we use the `$facebook->api()` function to do so. `https://graph.facebook.com` is automatically prefixed by an `api()` function to its first argument, that's why we have passed/me as its first argument. The returned data is stored in the `$me` variable.

Finally, we check whether the $me variable is null or not. If it's null, then we need to redirect the user to the authorization URL in order to get appropriate permission(s) from, and a valid session token for, the user. To redirect the user, we use JavaScript code. We set `top.location.href` to the URL where we want to re-direct the user. This URL is given by the function `$facebook->getLoginUrl()`. Also, this function takes array as its argument. The index `req_perms` is used to request from the user-specific permissions. Multiple permissions can be requested by separating them with a comma. Additionally, the index `next` specifies where the user will be redirected after successful authorization and session generation.

Once you have created these two files, you can use them directly in the subsequent recipes.

Retrieving impressions of the Like Box plugin

Facebook allows us to retrieve information about our various Social Plugins programmatically. We can retrieve the impressions of our Like Box by using the Facebook Graph API. Here, we will see how to do so.

Getting ready

You should have created `index.php` and `config.php` as mentioned in the beginning of this chapter. Also, you should have provided `read_insights` extended permission to the application.

How to do it...

The following steps will demonstrate how to retrieve impressions of the Like Box plugin:

1. Open `index.php` and append the following code to create an output table:

    ```
    <table border='1'>
      <tr>
        <th>metric</th>
        <th>end_time</th>
        <th>period</th>
        <th>value</th>
      </tr>
    ```

2. Next, add your application ID here:

    ```php
    <?php

        $app_id = 'your_app_id_here';
    ```

3. Now, use the `api()` function to make a GET request:

```
$insights = $facebook->api('/' . $app_id . '/insights/
   application_widget_fan_views');
```

4. Format the output in tabular form:

```
foreach ($insights['data'] as $metric) {
   foreach ($metric['values'] as $row) {
      $date = new DateTime($row['end_time']);
      echo "
        <tr>
          <td>{$metric['name']}</td>
          <td>{$date->format('Y-m-d')}</td>
          <td>{$metric['period']}</td>
          <td>{$row['value']}</td>
        </tr>";
    }
   }
  ?>
  </table>
```

5. Now save the file and run it. Upon running it you will get an output displaying the daily impressions of your application Like Box, as shown below:

How it works...

The analytical details of all applications corresponding to a Facebook developer are stored in the **insights** table and can be extracted, or exported, from it. Facebook has defined various metrics for different types of analytical data. For example, the number of impressions of the Like Box is given by the metric named `application_widget_fan_views`. Here, we have used the Facebook Graph API to get this information. In order to extract the details we need to make a GET request to the URL of the form `https://graph.facebook.com/ [application_id]/insights/[metric_name]` where `[application_id]` and `[metric_name]` are configurable.

To make the GET request via the Facebook Graph API, we use the `api()` function of **Facebook** class as shown:

```
$insights = $facebook->api('/' . $app_id . '/insights/application_
widget_fan_views');
```

The `api()` function defaults to a GET request when only a single argument is passed to it. This argument contains a portion of the URL, to which the GET request is made, and is automatically appended to `https://graph.facebook.com`. `$insights` and stores the response from the server in the form of a PHP array. Next, we use nested the `foreach` loops to print the received data in tabular format, as shown:

```
foreach ($insights['data'] as $metric) {
    foreach ($metric['values'] as $row) {
        $date = new DateTime($row['end_time']);
        echo "
            <tr>
                <td>{$metric['name']}</td>
                <td>{$date->format('Y-m-d')}</td>
                <td>{$metric['period']}</td>
                <td>{$row['value']}</td>
            </tr>";
    }
}
```

We use the `DateTime` PHP class to format the `end_time` dates in `'Y-m-d'` format before displaying them. The final output is a table which contains the metric name, `end_time` date, metric period, and metric value. Here, metric period refers to the length of the period during which the metric was collected and can take values such as `day`, `week`, `month`, or `lifetime`.

 All periods may not be available for every metric.

Similarly, metric value contains the value of the desired metric.

 The response from Facebook, which is stored in `$insights`, contains paging URLs `previous` and `next` which allows us to page through the whole data set for a particular metric.

There's more...

We can also create a chart to represent the metric.

Using the Google Chart API to create a chart for a given metric

Here, we will use the Google Chart API to do so. We will dynamically generate a bar chart to show the impressions of the Like Box on a daily basis with the help of the following code:

```php
<?php
require_once 'config.php';
$app_id = 'your_app_id';
$insights = $facebook->api('/' . $app_id . '/insights/
  application_widget_fan_views');
foreach ($insights['data'] as $metric) {
  foreach ($metric['values'] as $row) {
    $date = new DateTime($row['end_time']);
    $y_axis_data[] = urlencode($row['value']);
    $x_axis_data[] = urlencode($date->format('Y-m-d'));
  }
}
$y_axis_data  = implode(",", $y_axis_data);
$x_axis_data  = implode("|", $x_axis_data);
?>
<img src='<?php echo 'http://chart.apis.google.com/chart?chxl=1:|' .
  $x_axis_data . '&chxt=y,x&chbh=a&chs=300x225&cht=bvg&chco=A2C180&chd
  =t:' . $y_axis_data . '&chtt=Like+box+impressions'; ?>' />
```

The output of the code will be like this:

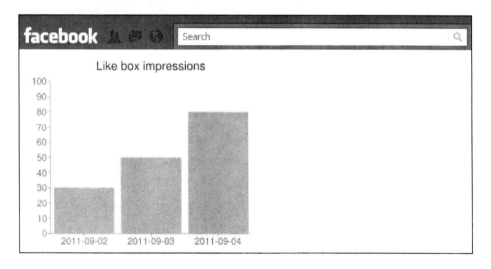

Here, we have used the Google Chart API which returns a chart image in response to a URL GET request. All the information regarding the bar chart has been passed as part of the URL to the Google server. The base URL is `http://chart.apis.google.com/chart` and we have added the following GET parameters to it:

- `chxl`: This is used to define custom labels on any axis. Here, we defined custom labels on the X-axis to print the date.
- `chxt`: This represents the axes to show on the chart.
- `chbh`: This decides the width of the bars in the chart. The value `a` means that the bars will be resized in such a manner that all the bars fit in the specified chart dimension.
- `chs`: This represents the dimension of the chart.
- `cht`: This represents the type of the chart.
- `chd`: This represents the chart data.
- `chco`: This decides the color for the individual bars.
- `chtt`: This represents the title of the chart.

Finally, we use the `img` tag to embed the chart in our webpage.

Retrieving a page's stream views and wall posts using batch request

If we want to extract significant data from the Facebook API, we can batch together all the queries and then make a single request, instead of making multiple HTTP requests. Here, we will show you how to extract daily stream views and wall posts of a Facebook page using this batch API.

Getting ready

You should know the ID of your Facebook page whose information you want to retrieve. Also, you should have created `config.php` and `index.php` as explained in the beginning of this chapter.

How to do it...

The following steps will demonstrate a batch request:

1. Open `index.php` and add the following code to it:

```php
<?php
```

2. Define the page ID:

```
$page_id = 'your_page_id';
```

3. Define an array in which we will store all the requests:

```
$batch = array();
```

4. Store your request in the form of the array as shown:

```
$batch[] = array(

   'method' => 'GET',
   'relative_url' => "/$page_id/insights/page_stream_views",
);
```

5. Similarly, store the second request:

```
$batch[] = array(
   'method' => 'GET',
   'relative_url' => "/$page_id/insights/page_wall_posts",
);
```

6. Make a batched request by using the `api()` function as shown:

```
$insights = $facebook->api('/', 'POST',
   array(
      'batch' => json_encode($batch),
   ));
```

7. Decode and display the data received:

```
foreach ($insights as $insight) {
   print_r(json_decode($insight['body']));
}
?>
```

How it works...

Usually, when we use the Facebook Graph API, we make a request to an object of the Facebook Graph on a specific URL and this is accomplished with a single HTTP request. But, if we want to collect multiple data in the Facebook Graph then instead of making multiple HTTP requests again and again we can use the batch API. Here, we define all our requests collectively and then make a batched request. It is more efficient and saves time.

Batching allows us to pass instructions for several operations in a single HTTP request. These operations are then processed in parallel by Facebook if the operations are independent, otherwise they are processed sequentially. After the processing is complete, Facebook returns the collective response back to the user in a single HTTP request.

For batching, Facebook expects a JSON encoded array of HTTP requests. In our code we have declared a PHP array `$batch`. Next, we append our requests to this array one by one as its elements. Each request is an array and contains the following parameters:

- `method`: This defines the type of HTTP method; for example GET, PUT, POST, DELETE, and so on.

- `relative_url`: This is the portion of the URL which is appended to `https://graph.facebook.com`.

- `body`: It is used in POST and PUT requests and should be formatted as a raw body string. This is an optional field.

We prepare the PHP array for the batched request using the following code:

```
$batch[] = array(
  'method' => 'GET',
  'relative_url' => "/$page_id/insights/page_stream_views",
);

$batch[] = array(
  'method' => 'GET',
  'relative_url' => "/$page_id/insights/page_wall_posts",
);
```

Here, we have defined two separate GET requests for metrics—`page_stream_views` and `page_wall_posts`. These two metrics provide us with the daily impressions of page stream and wall posts respectively.

Next, to make a batched request, we convert this PHP array to a JSON array by using the `json_encode()` function. And finally we use the `api()` function to make a POST request to the Facebook Graph API endpoint at `https://graph.facebook.com` with a parameter key `batch` which contains this JSON encoded PHP array as its value. This is done with the following code:

```
$insights = $facebook->api('/', 'POST',
  array(
    'batch' => json_encode($batch),
  ));
```

The data returned by Facebook is in JSON format and we decode the body portion of all requests by using `json_decode()`. Then we display the body, as a PHP array, of each request by using the `print_r()` function with the following code:

```
foreach ($insights as $insight) {
  print_r(json_decode($insight['body']));
}
```

The output array will look like this:

```
stdClass Object
(
    [data] => Array
        (
            [0] => stdClass Object
                (
                    [id] => 148389099542/insights/page_stream_views/day
                    [name] => page_stream_views
                    [period] => day
                    [values] => Array
                        (
                            [0] => stdClass Object
                                (
                                    [value] => 15
                                    [end_time] => 2011-07-05T07:00:00+0000
                                )

                            [1] => stdClass Object
                                (
                                    [value] => 0
                                    [end_time] => 2011-07-04T07:00:00+0000
                                )

                            [2] => stdClass Object
                                (
                                    [value] => 50
                                    [end_time] => 2011-07-05T07:00:00+0000
                                )

                        )

                    [description] => Daily The number of times people (Fans and non-Fans) have viewed a News Feed story posted by your Page. (Total
Count)
                )

        )

    [paging] => stdClass Object
        (
            [previous] => http://graph.facebook.com/graph/server.php?
    fb_url=%2Fbotskool%2Finsights%2Fpage_stream_views&access_token=129525780451736%7C2.AQA26o8AniSYB7Mk.3600.1310029200.1-
78601756397CIv01GbQiZhrwlhyxIc6MGEIyIvQ&_fb_batch_child_request=1&since=1309934438&until=1309593658
```

Developers can store this locally or export the array for data analysis and mining.

Getting the number of installations of an application using FQL

We can use the Facebook `insights` table to query for the number of installations of our application up to a specified date. Here, we will show you how to do it.

Getting ready

You should have created `index.php` and `config.php` as mentioned in the beginning of this chapter. Also, you should have provided `read_insights` extended permission to the application.

How to do it...

The following steps will demonstrate how to get the number of installations of an application:

1. Open `index.php` and append the following code to it:

   ```php
   <?php
   ```

2. Write a query to retrieve the number of installations of the application:

```
$results = $facebook->api(
  array(
    'method' => 'fql.query',
    'query' =>"SELECT metric,value FROM insights WHERE
      object_id = [object_id] AND
      metric = 'application_installed_users' AND
      end_time = end_time_date('2011-05-26') AND
      period = period('lifetime')",
  )
);
```

3. Display the result:

```
foreach($results as $result) {
  echo $result[metric] .'='.$result[value];
}

?>
```

4. Replace the `[object_id]` in the previous code with your application ID. Now save the file. Upon running we will get an output showing us the number of users who have installed our application. It will be something like this:

How it works...

To find out the number of installations of our application we query the `insights` Facebook table for the `application_installed_users` metric. Here, we have done this by using FQL. We use the `api()` function of the `Facebook` class in order to execute our FQL query. In the `api()` function, we pass an array as an argument. It has two indexes—`method` and `query`. We set the method to `fql.query` and this indicates that we want to execute an FQL query by making a GET request to the URL of the form `https://api.facebook.com/method/fql.query?query=QUERY` where the FQL query to be executed is given by the value of the index named `query`. In the FQL query, we simply select the number of users who have installed our application by selecting the `application_installed_users` from the `insights` table. It has been done using the following FQL query:

```
SELECT metric,value FROM insights WHERE
     object_id = [object_id] AND
```

```
        metric = 'application_installed_users' AND
        end_time = end_time_date('2011-05-26') AND
        period = period('lifetime')
```

So, the complete code for calling the `api()` function looks like this:

```
$results = $facebook->api(
  array(
    'method' => 'fql.query',
    'query' =>"SELECT metric,value FROM insights WHERE
      object_id = [object_id] AND
      metric = 'application_installed_users' AND
      end_time = end_time_date('2011-05-26') AND
      period = period('lifetime')",
  )
);
```

The retrieved result is stored in the `$results` array. Its structure will look like this:

```
Array
(
    [0] => Array
        (
            [metric] => application_installed_users
            [value] => 116
        )

)
```

Next, we use a `foreach` loop to extract the value of the number of installed users and display it accordingly.

Getting statistics about visitors using FQL multiquery

We can retrieve statistical information corresponding to the visitors who use our application such as their cities, countries, age, gender, and so on. Here, we will do so by using the FQL multiquery method.

Getting ready

You should have created `index.php` and `config.php` as mentioned in the beginning of *Chapter 3, Querying Facebook*. Also, you should have provided `read_insights` extended permission to the application.

How to do it...

The following steps will demonstrate how to acquire visitor statistics:

1. Open `index.php` and append the following code to it:

```php
<?php
    $app_id = "your_app_id";
```

2. Declare the array for executing multiple queries:

```php
$multi_queries = array();
```

3. Select the user related metric from the `insights` table:

```php
$multi_queries[] = "SELECT metric,value FROM insights
    WHERE object_id=$app_id
    AND metric='application_active_users_gender'
    AND end_time=end_time_date('2011-05-26')
    AND period=period('day')";

$multi_queries[] = "SELECT metric,value FROM insights
    WHERE object_id=$app_id
    AND metric='application_active_users_age'
    AND end_time=end_time_date('2011-05-26')
    AND period=period('day')";

$multi_queries[] = "SELECT metric,value FROM insights
    WHERE object_id=$app_id
    AND metric='application_active_users_country'
    AND end_time=end_time_date('2011-05-26')
    AND period=period('day')";

$multi_queries[] = "SELECT metric,value FROM insights
    WHERE object_id=$app_id
    AND metric='application_active_users_city'
    AND end_time=end_time_date('2011-05-26')
    AND period=period('day')";

$multi_queries[] = "SELECT metric,value FROM insights
    WHERE object_id=$app_id
    AND metric='application_active_users_locale'
    AND end_time=end_time_date('2011-05-26')
    AND period=period('day')";
```

4. Convert the `$multi_queries` array to a JSON data type:

```
$multi_queries = json_encode($multi_queries);
```

5. Execute the multiquery by using the `api()` function and display the results:

```
$results = $facebook->api(array('method' => 'fql.multiquery',
    'queries' => $multi_queries));

foreach($results as $result) {
  echo '<br>Table for metric - <strong>' . $result
    [fql_result_set][0][metric] . '</strong><br><br><table
    width="100%" border="1">';
  foreach($result[fql_result_set][0][value] as $key => $value) {
    echo "<tr><td width='50%'>$key</td><td width='50%'>$value
      </td></tr>";
  }
  echo '</table><br>';
}

?>
```

In the code replace `your_app_id` with the ID of your Facebook application.

6. Now, save the file and run. An output screen, something like the following, will appear showing you the metrics mentioned in the code:

The active users arranged country-wise are listed:

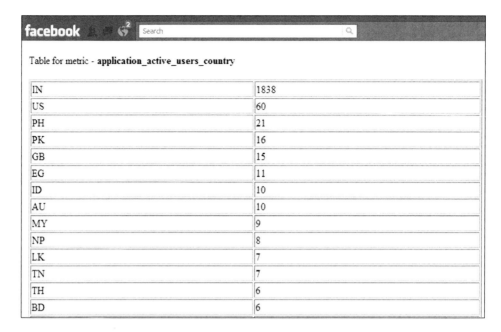

Table for metric - **application_active_users_country**

IN	1838
US	60
PH	21
PK	16
GB	15
EG	11
ID	10
AU	10
MY	9
NP	8
LK	7
TN	7
TH	6
BD	6

Similarly, the metric `application_active_users_city` lists the active users city-wise as shown:

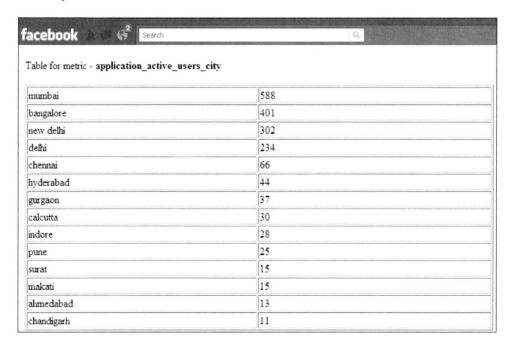

Table for metric - **application_active_users_city**

mumbai	588
bangalore	401
new delhi	302
delhi	234
chennai	66
hyderabad	44
gurgaon	37
calcutta	30
indore	28
pune	25
surat	15
makati	15
ahmedabad	13
chandigarh	11

Division of the application's active users based on locale is as shown:

facebook 🔍 Search

Table for metric - **application_active_users_locale**

en_US	1738
en_GB	295
en_IN	16
fr_FR	6
ar_AR	6
ru_RU	5
en_PI	4
id_ID	3
pt_BR	3
tr_TR	2
es_LA	2
ro_RO	2
lv_LV	1
nl_NL	1

How it works...

In the previously mentioned code, we have retrieved the visitor statistics of the application such as the country to which the active users of the application belong, their gender, locale, and so on. For extracting this information, we used the `insights` table of FQL. Here, five different queries have been run simultaneously in a single HTTP request and thus, we have made use of FQL multiquery. `$multi_queries` is a PHP array with five indexes which contain one query each. Thus, we have these five set of queries:

- `SELECT metric,value FROM insights WHERE object_id=$app_id AND metric='application_active_users_gender' AND end_time=end_time_date('2011-05-26') AND period=period('day')`: retrieves the gender information of all the active users of the application.

- `SELECT metric,value FROM insights WHERE object_id=$app_id AND metric='application_active_users_age' AND end_time=end_time_date('2011-05-26') AND period=period('day')`: retrieves the age range of all the active users of the application.

- ▶ `SELECT metric,value FROM insights WHERE object_id=$app_id AND metric='application_active_users_country' AND end_time=end_time_date('2011-05-26') AND period=period('day')`: gives the country of the active users of the application.

- ▶ `SELECT metric,value FROM insights WHERE object_id=$app_id AND metric='application_active_users_city' AND end_time=end_time_date('2011-05-26') AND period=period('day')`: gives the cities of the active users of the application.

- ▶ `SELECT metric,value FROM insights WHERE object_id=$app_id AND metric='application_active_users_locale' AND end_time=end_time_date('2011-05-26') AND period=period('day')`: retrieves the locale of all the active users.

Each of the mentioned queries has been formulated using the `insights` table of FQL. The `insights` table contains the following parameters:

- ▶ `object_id`: refers to the ID of the object for which we want to retrieve the information. It is an indexable field.

> These objects can be the IDs of pages, applications, as well as domains with 30 or more connections.

- ▶ `metric`: refers to the information which we want to retrieve. For example, in the code we have used the metrics `application_active_users_gender`, `application_active_users_country`, and so on. It is an indexable field.

- ▶ `end_time`: refers to the end of the period during which the metrics were collected. It is expressed as Unix time. It is also an indexable field.

> All values for the `end_time` should be specified as midnight, Pacific Daylight Time. Also, we can use another function, `end_time_date()` for the `end_time` field. It takes a date string in `YYYY-MM-DD` format and returns the appropriate value for `end_time`.

- ▶ `period`: It refers to the length of the period during which the metrics were collected, in seconds. It is also an indexable field.

> The `period` value is different for different metrics. To specify these we need to look up the `insights` table given in the appendix. Also, we can use the `period()` function for the period field. It takes one of the four strings as a parameter, `day`, `week`, `month`, `lifetime`.

▶   `value`: It refers to the value of the respective metric.

Thus, to formulate a single query we simply need to select the metric, its value, and specify the name of the metric, end time, the ID of the object for which we want to select it, and period from the **insights** table. It will be something like this:

```
SELECT metric, value FROM insights
   WHERE object_id = your_object_id
   AND metric = your_metric_name
   AND end_time = your_end_time
   AND period = period_value
```

Thus, after forming the queries by using this format we make use of multiquery to execute all of them in the same call.

We use the `json_encode()` function to convert the array named `$multi_queries` to a JSON data type and we store this in `$multi_queries`. For executing the multiquery, we use the `api()` function. It takes an array as its argument parameter. In the array, we set `fql.multiquery` as the `method` to indicate that we want to execute multiple queries in the same call. The `queries` index contains the FQL queries in JSON format which we want to execute. This is achieved by the following block of code:

```
$multi_queries = json_encode($multi_queries);
$results = $facebook->api(array('method' => 'fql.multiquery',
                                'queries' => $multi_queries));
```

After execution of the multiquery, the returned information gets stored in the `$results` variable. We use `foreach()` PHP loops to print the retrieved data from all the queries in a table.

 You can use `print_r($results)` to understand the structure of the returned data array.

Creating a new ad for your Facebook application

Facebook provides us with the opportunity to publicize our Facebook application once it is ready. We can reach a targeted user base by creating relevant advertisements. Here, we will show you how to create an ad for your Facebook application.

How to do it...

The following steps will demonstrate how to create an ad:

1. Go to `http://www.facebook.com/advertising/`. Now, click on the **Create an Ad** button at the top-right corner, as shown:

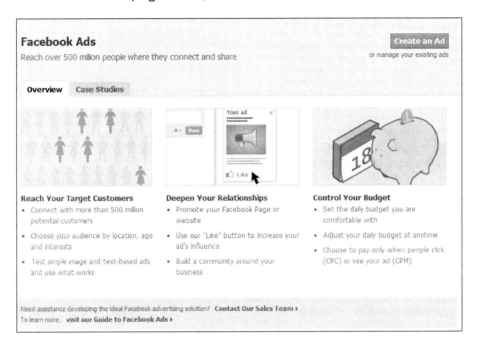

2. Another screen titled as **Design Your Ad** will pop up which will look like the following screenshot:

3. Fill in the required information (such as **Destination**, **Type**, **URL**, **Body**, **Image**, and so on), as shown in the previous screenshot. A preview will be generated simultaneously to show what your ad will look like. Next, click on the **Continue** button.

4. Another screen will appear which is titled as **Targeting** where you can choose whom to serve the advertisement for your application based on **Location, Demographics, Interests**, and **Connections on Facebook**. You will also be shown an estimated user base based upon particular criteria. It will look like the following screenshot:

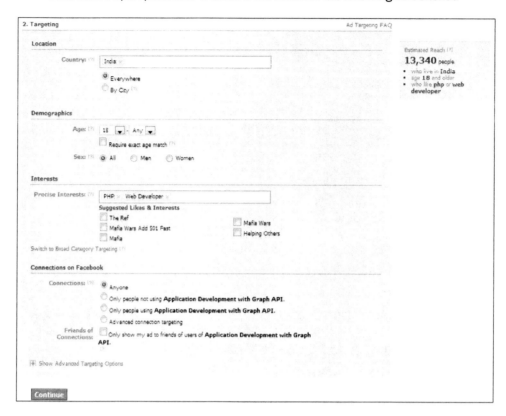

5. Now fill in the **Targeting** details according to your preferences and click on **Continue**. You will see a third screen like the following:

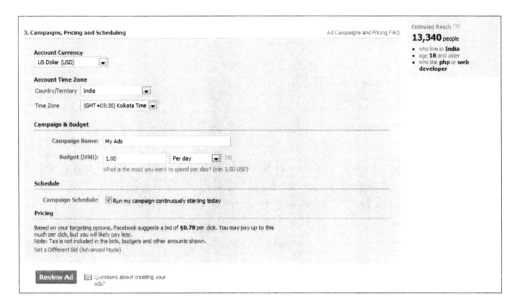

6. Here, you can specify your pricing scheme and budget. Once you have filled in all the necessary details, you can see your advertisement by clicking on the **Review Ad** button. A screenshot is shown:

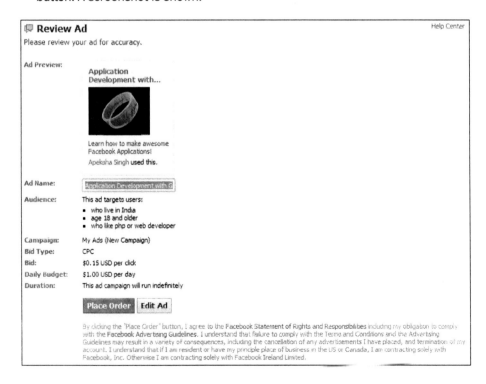

7. You can edit your ad by clicking on the **Edit Ad** button. If everything is fine you may place your order by clicking on the **Place Order** button and your advertisement will get deployed.

How it works...

We created a Facebook advertisement for an application by completing a few basic steps. First we need to design the advertisement. In this we need to mention parameters like:

- `Destination`: In this you need to choose from the drop down menu the application for which you need to create an advertisement
- `Type`: It has to be **Facebook Ads** for creating an advertisement
- `URL`: Is the URL to which the users should get directed to when they click on your advertisement
- `Title`: Is the title which will appear in your Facebook ad
- `Body`: It will contain the description which you want to put in your ad

After completion of the design phase we next enter the **Targeting** section of the advertisement. Here, we need to specify our target audience such as their **Age**, **Demographics**, **Country**, and so on. Apart from this, a box showing us the **Estimated Reach** which is the approximate number of people this ad will reach, depending on our values entered, is also shown on the top-right corner.

Then, comes the **Campaign, Pricing and Scheduling** section where we specify the **Currency**, **Budget**, **Click per Ads** value, and so on.

On completion of these three sections we get to review our ad. If everything seems fine we can place the order and get our advertisement running.

10
Creating Instant Applications

In this chapter, we will cover:

- ► Creating a "Your Good Luck Charm of the Day" Facebook application
- ► Designing a "My Fast Friends" Facebook application
- ► Setting up a photo collage
- ► Building a birthday calendar
- ► Developing an application to classify friends according to the cities they live in

Introduction

In this chapter, we will show how to create Facebook applications from scratch.

Getting ready

First, we will create a basic layout. The applications discussed in this chapter will contain code based on this layout. We need to create two files as shown in the following steps:

1. Create a `config.php` file and add the following code to it:

```
<?php
  require_once 'facebook.php';
  /** Create our Application instance. */
```

2. Initialize the Facebook application:

```
$facebook = new Facebook(array(
  'appId' => 'your_application_id',
```

```
        'secret' => 'your_application_secret_key',
        'cookie' => true,
));
```

Here, we have included `facebook.php`, which contains the `Facebook` class and can be downloaded from GitHub. `$facebook` is an object of this class and we will use it in `index.php`. You need to provide your application ID and secret key here. For more information, read the first chapter.

3. Create a file named `index.php` and add the following code to it:

```
<?php
```

4. Include the configuration file `config.php` that we defined earlier:

```
require_once 'config.php';
```

5. Get the current user's session information by using the `getSession()` function and then perform session validation:

```
$session = $facebook->getSession();
$me = null;
if ($session) {
  try {
    $me = $facebook->api('/me');
    /*Check whether the current session is valid by
      retrieving user information.*/
  }
  catch (Exception $e) {
  }
}
/* If the current session is invalid or user has not authorized
   the application then redirect to a authorization URL.*/
```

6. If the session is invalid, redirect the application to the authorization URL:

```
if(!($me)) {
  echo '<script>
    top.location.href="'
    . $facebook->getLoginUrl(
        array(
          'req_perms' => 'publish_stream',
          'next' =>
            'http://apps.facebook.com/[your_app_url]/',
        )
      )
    . '";
  </script>';
  exit;
```

```
      }
    ?>
```

7. Load jQuery from Google CDN:

```html
<html xmlns="http://www.w3.org/1999/xhtml"
      xmlns:fb="http://www.facebook.com/2008/fbml">
  <head>
    <script type="text/javascript" src=
"https://ajax.googleapis.com/ajax/libs/jquery/1.5.2/jquery.min.
js">
    </script>
  </head>
```

8. Create `div` with `fb-root` set as `id` for displaying the application content:

```html
<body>
  <div id="fb-root">
    <!-- Your application content here -->

  </div>
```

9. Initialize the application by calling `FB.init()`:

```html
<script type="text/javascript">
  window.fbAsyncInit = function() {
    FB.init({
      appId  : '<?php echo $facebook->getAppId(); ?>',
      status : true,
      cookie : true,
      xfbml  : true
    });
    $(document).ready(function() {

    });
  };
```

10. Load the Facebook JavaScript SDK asynchronously:

```javascript
(function() {
  var e = document.createElement('script');
  e.type = 'text/javascript';
  e.src = document.location.protocol +
    '//connect.facebook.net/en_US/all.js';
  e.async = true;
  document.getElementById('fb-root').appendChild(e);
}());
</script>

</body>
</html>
```

Here, we first retrieve a valid session for the user by calling `$facebook->getSession()` and storing the response in the `$session` variable. Next, we try to retrieve the basic information of the current user by making a GET request to `https://graph.facebook.com/me`. We use the `$facebook->api()` function to do so. `https://graph.facebook.com` is automatically prefixed by the `api()` function to its first argument, that's why we have passed `/me` as its first argument. The returned data is stored in the `$me` variable.

Finally, we check whether `$me` is null and if it is so we redirect the user to the authorization URL in order to get appropriate permission(s) from, and a valid session token, for the user. We use JavaScript code to redirect the user and set `top.location.href` to the desired URL. This URL is given by the function `$facebook->getLoginUrl()`, which takes an array as its argument. The index `req_perms` is used to request specific permissions from the user. Multiple permissions can be requested by separating them with commas. Additionally, the index `next` specifies where the user will be redirected after successful authorization and session generation.

In order to use XFBML in your application consistently across all web browsers, we need to add an XML namespace attribute to the root `<html>` element of `index.php`. This is necessary to render the XFBML tags in Internet Explorer.

```
<html xmlns="http://www.w3.org/1999/xhtml"
      xmlns:fb="http://www.facebook.com/2008/fbml">
```

To load the Facebook JavaScript SDK, we use the standard `<script>` element. We load it asynchronously so that it does not hinder the loading of other elements in our application and this ensures fast page loads. Also, we have specified a `<div>` element named `fb-root` within the document. It is important to include `div` with this name, otherwise the JavaScript SDK will not load and reports an error. The code for this is shown next:

```
<div id="fb-root">
  <!-- Your application content here -->
</div>
<script type="text/javascript">
  window.fbAsyncInit = function() {
    FB.init({
       appId  : 'your_app_id',
       status : true,
       cookie : true,
       xfbml  : true
    });
/* Your FB JavaScript code here. It will be loaded asynchronously. */
  };
  (function() {
    var e = document.createElement('script');
    e.type = 'text/javascript';
```

```
    e.src = document.location.protocol +
      '//connect.facebook.net/en_US/all.js';
    e.async = true;
    document.getElementById('fb-root').appendChild(e);
  }());
</script>
```

As soon as the JavaScript SDK is loaded asynchronously and is ready to use, we initialize our Facebook application by calling the `FB.init()` function. Here we pass four parameters:

Meta properties	Description
appId	This is the application ID which we get after registering our application with Facebook.
status	A true value implies that we can perform a user login status check if required.
cookie	It enables the cookies to allow the server to access the session.
xfbml	It allows us to access and parse XFBML tags, if set to true.

The `FB.init()` function is called inside the function assigned to `window.fbAsyncInit`. This function, which is assigned to `window.fbAsyncInit`, is executed as soon as the JavaScript SDK is loaded asynchronously. Thus, any code that we want to run after the SDK is loaded should be placed within this function after the `FB.init()` function.

Additionally, we have loaded jQuery by using the `<script>` code:

```
<script type="text/javascript"
src="https://ajax.googleapis.com/ajax/libs/jquery/1.5.2/jquery.min.
js"></script>
```

Creating a "Your Good Luck Charm of the Day" Facebook application

In this recipe, we will create a Facebook application called "Your Good Luck Charm of the Day". It will forecast the name of the user's friend who will bring him/her good luck. The friend will be selected randomly. Let's begin creating this application.

Getting ready

You should have created `config.php` and `index.php` as mentioned in the beginning of this chapter.

How to do it...

The following steps will describe the creation of the application:

1. Open `index.php` and add the following code before the `<html>` tag. Get the user's friends' details by using the `api()` function:

```php
<?php
    $friends = $facebook->api('/me/friends');
```

2. Choose a friend as a *Good Luck Charm of the Day* randomly:

```php
    $rand_key = array_rand($friends['data']);
    $random_friend = $friends['data'][$rand_key];
?>
```

3. Add the following highlighted code inside `fb-root`. This will display the name and profile picture of the randomly selected friend:

```html
<div id="fb-root">
    <h2>Your Good Luck Charm for today is
        <?php echo $random_friend['name']; ?>
    </h2>
    <br />
    <img src='https://graph.facebook.com/<?php echo $random_friend['id']; ?>/picture?type=large' />
</div>
```

4. Now, use the `FB.ui()` function, inside `$(document).ready()`, to prompt the user to post this on his/her friend's wall:

```javascript
$(document).ready(function() {
  FB.ui({
    method: 'feed',
    name: 'Good Luck Charm of the day',
    link: 'http://apps.facebook.com/[your_app_url]/',
    picture: 'http://yourwebsite.com/images/app.PNG',
    caption: 'Find who brings Good Luck to you today',
    description: 'Today\'s Lucky Charm for you is
       <?php echo $random_friend['name']; ?>.',
    message: 'My Good Luck Charm of the day is
       <?php echo $random_friend['name']; ?>.',
    to: '<?php echo $random_friend['id']; ?>'
  },
```

5. Define the response function:

```javascript
function(response) {
    if (response && response.post_id) {
```

```
            alert('Post was published.');
        } else {
            alert('Post was not published.');
        }
    });
});
```

6. Now, save the file and run it. A screen showing the **Good Luck Charm** for you will be displayed and will look like this:

7. Along with it, a **Feed Dialog Box** will pop up asking you to publish or skip the feed. It will look like this:

Now you can share the post or skip it according to your choice.

How it works...

Here, for finding the Good Luck Charm of a user, we first extract all the friends of the user and then choose one friend randomly. This we do by making a GET request to the `https://graph.facebook.com/me/friends` by using the Facebook Graph API via the `api()` function. The response is stored in `$friends`. The following line of code accomplishes this task:

```
$friends = $facebook->api('/me/friends');
```

Next, we randomly choose a friend of the user. We use the `array_rand()` function which picks up a random key from the `$friends` array. Corresponding to this random key, there is a sub-array which contains the `name` and `id` parameters of a user who is a friend of the current user. We store this sub-array, which contains the details of our randomly selected user, in `$random_friend`. This is done by the following code:

```
$rand_key = array_rand($friends['data']);
$random_friend = $friends['data'][$rand_key];
```

We display the name of the user's friend and also his/her picture inside a div named `fb-root`. The profile picture of the user can be retrieved from the following URL `https://graph.facebook.com/[user_id]/picture?type=large`. Here, we set the query parameter type to large in order to get a big profile picture of the user's friend.

```
<div id="fb-root">
    <h2>Your Good Luck Charm for today is
        <?php echo $random_friend['name']; ?>.
    </h2>
    <br />
    <img src='https://graph.facebook.com/<?php echo $random_
friend['id']; ?>/picture?type=large' />
</div>
```

Also, we prompt the user to post on his/her friend wall. For this we make use of the Facebook **Feed Dialog Box**. This is done by the `FB.ui()` function which takes a JavaScript object as a parameter. We set the `method` attribute as `feed`, which determines that we want to render the **Feed Dialog Box**. We can configure our Facebook **Feed Dialog Box** with the help of the following attributes:

Meta properties	Description
picture	The URL of the picture attached to this post. This is also an optional field.
link	The link attached to this post. Here we have linked it to our application.
name	The name of the link. This is an optional field.
caption	The caption of the link name and it appears beneath it. This is an optional field.
description	The description of the link. Also an optional field.
message	The message which has to be posted.
to	This contains the ID, or username, of the person on whose wall we want to post this feed.

We have rendered the Facebook **Feed Dialog Box** by using the following code:

```
FB.ui({
    method: 'feed',
    name: 'Good Luck Charm of the day',
    link: 'http://apps.facebook.com/[your_app_url]/',
    picture: 'http://yoursite.com/images/app.PNG',
    caption: 'Find who brings Good Luck to you today',
    description: 'Today\'s Lucky Charm for you is
        <?php echo $random_friend['name']; ?>.',
    message: 'My Good Luck Charm of the day is
        <?php echo $random_friend['name']; ?>.',
    to: '<?php echo $random_friend['id']; ?>'
},
```

Additionally, we define the response function to handle the response of the post inside the FB.ui() function as shown:

```
function(response) {
    if (response && response.post_id) {
        alert('Post was published.');
    } else {
        alert('Post was not published.');
    }
});
```

Designing a "My Fast Friends" Facebook application

Here, we will create a Facebook application which will list the top five fast friends of the current user. This application will dynamically create a photo which will contain a profile picture of all top five friends. It will tag these friends in the newly created photo and publish the photo in the user's album.

Getting ready

You should have already created `config.php` and `index.php` as explained in the beginning of this chapter. Additionally you need to have the `publish_stream` and `user_photos` extended permission.

Also, we have used a TrueType font named **Turn Tablz** in this application. Download any such font from the internet. There are several sites which give TrueType fonts for free. Download a font of your choice from such a website. The TrueType font file will have a `.ttf` extension. Place this `.ttf` file in the same folder in which `index.php` and `config.php` are present.

How to do it...

The following steps will demonstrate how to create this application:

1. Open `index.php` and add the following PHP code before the `<html>` code. First, we define a function named `cmp()` to compare the number of mutual friends of the user:

```php
<?php
  function cmp($a, $b) {
    if ($a['no'] == $b['no']) {
      return 0;
    }
    return ($a['no'] > $b['no']) ? -1 : 1;
  }
}
```

2. Next, retrieve the friends of the user by using the `api()` function:

```php
$friends = $facebook->api('/me/friends');
```

3. Now, we loop through all the friends of the user, one at a time, and retrieve the array containing the list of their mutual friends by using FQL:

```php
foreach ($friends['data'] as $friend) {
  $result = $facebook->api(array(
    'method' => 'fql.query',
    'query' => "SELECT uid1 FROM friend
```

```
        WHERE uid2={$friend['id']}
        AND uid1 IN (SELECT uid2 FROM friend
           WHERE uid1=me())"
   ));
```

4. Count the number of mutual friends and store the result in the `$mutual_friends` array:

    ```
    $mutual_friends[] = array('id' => $friend['id'],
       'no' => count($result), 'name' => $friend['name']);
    }
    ```

5. Sort `$mutual_friends` array (in descending order):

    ```
    usort($mutual_friends, 'cmp');
    ```

6. Create a 500 x 500 px image:

    ```
    $image = imagecreatetruecolor(500, 500);
    ```

7. Create a color identifier for the orange color:

    ```
    $orange = imagecolorallocate($image, 0xFF, 0x8c, 0x00);
    ```

8. Create a new image from a JPEG file named `app2_bg.jpg` which will be used as background image:

    ```
    $bg = imagecreatefromjpeg('./app2_bg.jpg');
    ```

9. Set the image as a tile image for filling the background:

    ```
    imagesettile($image, $bg);
    ```

10. Fill the background:

    ```
    imagefilledrectangle($image, 0, 0, 499, 499, IMG_COLOR_TILED);
    ```

11. Specify the path of the TTF font file:

    ```
    $font_file = './TURNBB__.TTF';
    ```

12. Write text to the image using the TTF font:

    ```
    imagefttext($image, 20, 0, 105, 50, $orange, $font_file,
       'My Fast Friends');
    ```

13. Write the top five fast friends in a rank wise manner:

    ```
    for($i=0;$i<5;$i++) {
       imagefttext($image, 13, 0, 10, (100+($i*80)), $orange,
          $font_file, 'Rank #' . ($i+1) . ':');
    ```

14. Print their names:

```
imagefttext($image, 13, 0, 250, (100+($i*80)), $orange,
            $font_file, $mutual_friends[$i]['name']);
```

15. Retrieve and merge their profile pictures into the main image:

```
$frnd_pic = $facebook->api('/' . $mutual_friends[$i]['id'] .
    '/?fields=picture&type=square');
$frnd = imagecreatefromstring(file_get_contents
    ($frnd_pic['picture']));
imagecopymerge($image,$frnd,150,(80+($i*80)),0,0,50,50,100);
```

16. Add the friend's information to the $tags array which will be used later for tagging:

```
$tags[] = array(
    'tag_uid' => $mutual_friends[$i]['id'],
    /*Current user's id*/
    'x' => (150/5),
    'y' => ((80+($i*80))/5)
);
}
```

17. Save the main image as a PNG image:

```
imagepng($image, './img/' . $me['id'] . '.png');
```

18. Use the realpath() function to return the canonicalized absolute pathname of the location of the image:

```
$pic = realpath("/home/path/to/your/app/img/" . $me['id'] .
    '.png');
```

19. Enable the file upload to the Facebook server using setFileUploadSupport():

```
$facebook->setFileUploadSupport("http://" .
    $_SERVER['SERVER_NAME']);
```

20. Post the picture by using the api() function:

```
$pic_id = $facebook->api('/me/photos', 'POST',
    array('message' => 'My Fast Friends',
        'source' => '@' . $pic,
        'tags' => $tags));
```

21. Free the memory which is associated with the image:

```
imagedestroy($image);
?>
```

22. Place the following code given in `fb-root` and render the image:

```
<img src="./img/<?php echo $me['id']; ?>.png" />
```

23. Save the file. Also, create a folder named `img` inside the application directory and set its permission as `777`.

24. Now run the file. A screen displaying the top most friends of the user will appear and will look something like the following:

The friends of the user will automatically get tagged, as shown in the screenshot and a new album named **My Fast Friends** will get created in the user's profile.

How it works...

Here, to decide the top five fast friends of a user we have used the concept of mutual friends. We find the mutual friends between the current user and his friends, one at a time, and then we store this in an array and rank them accordingly. To find out the mutual friends of the user we make use of an FQL query:

```
SELECT uid1 FROM friend WHERE uid2={$friend['id']} AND uid1 IN (SELECT
uid2 FROM friend WHERE uid1=me())
```

We run this query for all the friends of the current user and the response contains an array of user IDs of the mutual friends of the specified two users. We run this FQL query on all user's friends with the help of the `foreach` loop as shown:

```
$friends = $facebook->api('/me/friends');
foreach ($friends['data'] as $friend) {
  $result = $facebook->api(array(
    'method' => 'fql.query',
    'query' => "SELECT uid1 FROM friend
      WHERE uid2={$friend['id']}
      AND uid1 IN (SELECT uid2 FROM friend
        WHERE uid1=me())"));
```

Here, first we retrieve all the friends of the current user by using the Facebook Graph API and making a call to `https://graph.facebook.com/me/friends`. We store the returned data in `$friends`. Then we run a loop through all the friends of the user, and run the discussed FQL query to retrieve the mutual friends by using the `api()` function. The result is stored in the `$result` array.

Next, we count the number of mutual friends between each of the user's friends and him/her using the `count()` function and store this information, using a custom defined sub-array, in an array named `$mutual_friends` as shown:

```
$mutual_friends[] = array('id' => $friend['id'], 'no' =>
count($result), 'name' => $friend['name']);
```

Our custom sub-array contains three keys:

- `id`: contains the friend ID
- `no`: contains the total number of mutual friends between the friend having a unique ID and the current user
- `name`: contains the friend's name

Now, to ascertain the top five fast friends we make use of the `usort()` function to which we pass the array `$mutual_friends` as the first argument, and a self defined function `cmp()`, to compare two elements of an array, as the second argument as shown:

```
function cmp($a, $b) {
    if ($a['no'] == $b['no']) {
        return 0;
    }
    return ($a['no'] > $b['no']) ? -1 : 1;
}
usort($mutual_friends, 'cmp');
```

The cmp() function compares the number of mutual friends for two different elements in the array $mutual_friends and the usort() function sorts the $mutual_friends array in the descending order based on the number of mutual friends.

Once we have this sorted array with us we create a photo which will display all the top five fast friends of the current user. For this we made use of the PHP GD library. It gives us the ability to create and manipulate image files in different formats in PHP. We create the image with the help of the following code:

```
$image = imagecreatetruecolor(500, 500);
$white = imagecolorallocate($image, 0xFF, 0xFF, 0xFF);
$orange = imagecolorallocate($image, 0xFF, 0x8c, 0x00);
$bg = imagecreatefromjpeg('./app2_bg.jpg');
imagesettile($image, $bg);
imagefilledrectangle($image, 0, 0, 499, 499, IMG_COLOR_TILED);
$font_file = './TURNBB__.TTF';
imagefttext($image, 20, 0, 105, 50, $orange, $font_file, 'My Fast
Friends');
```

First we create a new image of size 500 x 500 px by using the imagecreatetruecolor() function. It takes the width and height of the image as its arguments. After this we use the imagecolorallocate() function to create resource identifiers for the orange color. Also, we create an image from a file present on the server, app2_bg.jpg, with the help of imagecreatefromjpeg(). It takes the path of the JPEG file as its argument. We set this newly created image as the tile with which we will fill the background of our original image by using the imagesettile() function. We fill the background of our original image by using the imagefilledrectangle() function. This function takes the following arguments:

Meta properties	Description
image	Defines the image resource on which this function will be applied.
x1	The x-coordinate of the starting point from where the rectangle will begin.
y1	The y-coordinate of the starting point from where the rectangle will begin.
x2	The x-coordinate of the end point to where the rectangle will end.
y2	The y-coordinate of the end point to where the rectangle will end.
color	Defines the fill color to be used.

We have passed `IMG_COLOR_TILED` as the last argument of the discussed function. This tells PHP to use the tile image, as defined by `imagesettile()`, for filling up the rectangle.

We use the `imagefttext()` function to display our desired text message on the photo. This function takes the following arguments:

Meta properties	Description
image	Represents an image resource.
size	The font size in points.
angle	The angle in degrees, with 0 being left-to-right reading text. Higher values represent a counter-clockwise rotation.
x	The x-coordinate from where the basepoint of the first character (roughly the lower-left corner of the character) will start.
y	The y-coordinate which sets the position of the font's baseline, not the very bottom of the character.
color	The index of the desired color for the text.
fontfile	The path to the TrueType font you wish to use.
text	The actual text to be inserted into the image.

Next, we print the rank of all the top five fast friends, along with their profile picture and name on the photo. Here, for text we have used **Turn Tablz** font. We use a `for` loop to print this as shown:

```php
for($i=0;$i<5;$i++) {
    imagefttext($image, 13, 0, 10, (100+($i*80)), $orange,
                $font_file, 'Rank #' . ($i+1) . ':');
    imagefttext($image, 13, 0, 250, (100+($i*80)), $orange,
                $font_file, $mutual_friends[$i]['name']);
    $frnd_pic = $facebook->api('/' . $mutual_friends[$i]['id'] . '/?fiel
ds=picture&type=square');
    $frnd = imagecreatefromstring(file_get_contents($frnd_
pic['picture']));
    imagecopymerge($image,$frnd,150,(80+($i*80)),0,0,50,50,100);
    $tags[] = array(
            'tag_uid' => $mutual_friends[$i]['id'],
             /*Current user's id*/
            'x' => (150/5),
            'y' => ((80+($i*80))/5)
        );


}
imagepng($image, './img/' . $me['id'] . '.png');
```

We use the `imagefttext()` function to print the rank and name of all of the five friends. Also, we retrieve the URL of their profile picture with the help of the `api()` function of the Facebook Graph API by making a GET request to `https://graph.facebook.com/user_id?fields=picture&type=square`. We have set the query parameter `fields` to `picture` and `type` to `square`. This means that we are requesting the URL of the square type profile picture of the user with the user ID `user_id` from Facebook. Once we get the URL from Facebook, then we use `file_get_contents()` to retrieve the image from this URL. Next, we pass this content to `imagecreatefromstring()` which creates an image from it. After this we use the `imagecopymerge()` function to merge the profile picture of each user to the main image at an appropriate location. This function takes the following parameters:

Meta properties	Description
dst_im	The destination image link resource.
src_im	The source image link resource.
dst_x	The x-coordinate of the destination point.
dst_y	The y-coordinate of the destination point.
src_x	The x-coordinate of the source point.
src_y	The y-coordinate of the source point.
src_w	The source width.
src_h	The source height.
pct	The level of alpha transparency for true color images.

For tagging the users, we create an array named `$tags`. This array contains sub-arrays where each sub-array carries the tag information for a particular user. This sub-array consists of three indices as listed:

Meta properties	Description
tag_uid	The ID of the user whom we want to tag in the picture.
x	The percentage from the left edge of the photo and decides the position of the tag box.
y	The percentage from the top edge of the tag box and decides the position of the tag box.

For each user we create a dynamic set of this sub-array containing a unique `tag_uid` and `x` and `y` coordinates. After looping through the top five friends, we save the final image using the `imagepng()` function. The first argument is the image identifier and the second argument specifies the path where to save the file. Here, we have saved the generated image to the `img` folder present in the root application directory. This `img` folder should have `777` permission assigned to it.

Finally, we post this photo in the user's album along with all his/her top five fast friends tagged in the photo. To do so, first we get the absolute path of the photo saved on our server by using `realpath()`. Next, we enable the upload and make the Facebook server ready to handle picture uploads. This has been done by the following line of code:

```php
$pic = realpath("/home/path/to/your/app/img/" . $me['id'] . '.png');
$facebook->setFileUploadSupport("http://" . $_SERVER['SERVER_NAME']);
```

The last step includes calling the `$facebook-api()` function with a POST request and passing an array to it, as its third argument, which contains the photo specific details (message, source of photo, and tag information) as shown:

```php
$pic_id = $facebook->api('/me/photos', 'POST', array('message' => 'My
Fast Friends' ,
  'source' => '@' . $pic,
  'tags' => $tags));
imagedestroy($image);
?>
<img src="./img/<?php echo $me['id']; ?>.png" />
```

After this we use the `imagedestroy()` function to free the memory associated with the main image identifier and finally we display this image to the user by using the HTML img tag.

Setting up a photo collage

This Facebook application will create an exquisite collage of pictures of the current user which are picked randomly from his/her albums. Also, it will create a new album in the user's profile and post the collage generated in it.

Getting ready

You should have created `index.php` and `config.php` as mentioned in the beginning of this chapter. Also, you should have provided `user_photos` extended permission to the application. Additionally, download a TrueType font of your choice as explained in the *Designing a "My Fast Friends" Facebook application* recipe.

How to do it...

The following steps will demonstrate how to set up a photo collage:

1. Open `index.php` and add the following PHP code before the `<html>` code. Here, first we define the `width` and `height` of each picture for the collage:

```php
<?php
  $cell_height = 140;
  $cell_width = 180;
```

2. Create a new image of appropriate dimensions by using the `imagecreatetruecolor()` function for the entire collage:

```
$image = imagecreatetruecolor(3*$cell_width+40,
                              3*$cell_height+110);
```

3. Create color identifiers for white and orange colors:

```
$white = imagecolorallocate($image, 0xFF, 0xFF, 0xFF);
$orange = imagecolorallocate($image, 0x00, 0x00, 0x00);
```

4. Create a new background image from the JPEG file `app3a.jpg`:

```
$bg = imagecreatefromjpeg('./app3a.jpg');
```

5. Set the image as a tile image for filling the background:

```
imagesettile($image, $bg);
```

6. Fill the image:

```
imagefilledrectangle($image, 0, 0, 3*$cell_width+40,
                     3*$cell_height+110, IMG_COLOR_TILED);
```

7. Specify the path of the TTF file:

```
$font_file = './TURNBB__.TTF';
```

8. Write text to the image using the specified font:

```
imagefttext($image, 30, 0, 90, 3*$cell_height+80, $white,
            $font_file, 'Photo Collage');
```

9. Create an empty array for handling the merged photos:

```
$merged_photos = array();
```

10. Retrieve all the albums of the user using the `api()` function:

```
$albums = $facebook->api('/me/albums');
```

11. Select random photos from different albums for creating a 3 x 3 matrix:

```
for($count=0;$count<9;$count++) {
  do {
    $album = $albums['data'][array_rand($albums['data'])];
    $photos = $facebook->api('/' . $album['id'] .'/photos');
    $photo = $photos['data'][array_rand($photos['data'])];
  } while(in_array($photo['id'],$merged_photos));
  $merged_photos[] = $photo['id'];
```

12. Store the `width` and `height` of the retrieved images:

```
$width = $photo['images'][1]['width'];
$height= $photo['images'][1]['height'];
```

13. Create an empty image of a size equal to each cell:

    ```
    $image_p = imagecreatetruecolor($cell_width, $cell_height);
    ```

14. Create an image from the photos retrieved:

    ```
    $image_o = imagecreatefromjpeg($photo['images'][1]['source']);
    ```

15. Copy all the retrieved photos to a fixed size:

    ```
    imagecopy($image_p, $image_o, 0, 0, 0, 0, $width, $height);
    $des_x = (10*(($count%3)+1)+(($count%3)*$width));
    $des_y = (10*(floor($count/3)+1)+(floor($count/3)*
    $cell_height));
    ```

16. Merge the copied image using the `imagecopymerge()` function to the main image and destroy the original and copied images:

    ```
    imagecopymerge($image,$image_p,$des_x,$des_y,0,0,$cell_width,
                    $cell_height,100);
    imagedestroy($image_p);
    imagedestroy($image_o);
    }
    ```

17. Save images to a file using the `imagepng()` function:

    ```
    imagepng($image, './img/' . $me['id'] . '.png');
    ```

18. Use the `realpath()` function to return the canonicalized absolute path name of the location of the image:

    ```
    $pic = realpath("/home/server/public_html/cookbook/img/" .
    $me['id'] . '.png');
    ```

19. Enable file upload to the Facebook server by using the `setFileUploadSupport()` function:

    ```
    $facebook->setFileUploadSupport("http://" . $_SERVER
    ['SERVER_NAME']);
    ```

20. Post the picture to the user's album:

    ```
    $pic_id = $facebook->api('/me/photos', 'POST', array(
      'message' => 'Photo Collage', 'source' => '@' . $pic,
    ));
    ```

21. Free the memory which is associated with the image:

    ```
    imagedestroy($image);
    ?>
    ```

22. Place the following code inside `fb-root` and render the image:

    ```
    <img src="./img/<?php echo $me['id']; ?>.png" />
    ```

23. Save the file. Also, create a folder named `img` inside the application directory and set its permission as `777`.

24. Now run the file. A collage containing random pictures from the user's albums will be displayed and will look something like this:

Along with this the a new album will be created titled **Photo Collage** and the collage will get posted in this album.

How it works...

The first task to do while creating a photo collage is to define the dimensions of it. Here, we have generated a 3 x 3 photo matrix where each photo in the matrix will be 180 x 140 px. This has been done in the following lines of code:

```
$cell_height = 140;
$cell_width = 180;
```

Next, we use the `imagecreatetruecolor()` function to create an image for the entire collage, and `$image` is our image resource identifier for this image, as shown:

```
$image = imagecreatetruecolor(3*$cell_width+40,
                              3*$cell_height+110);
```

After this we define some color identifiers, image to be used as background, font file and text to be written on the image as shown:

```
$white = imagecolorallocate($image, 0xFF, 0xFF, 0xFF);
$black = imagecolorallocate($image, 0x00, 0x00, 0x00);
$bg = imagecreatefromjpeg('./app3a.jpg');
imagesettile($image, $bg);
imagefilledrectangle($image, 0, 0, 3*$cell_width+40,
                     3*$cell_height+110, IMG_COLOR_TILED);
$font_file = './TURNBB__.TTF';
imagefttext($image, 30, 0, 90, 3*$cell_height+80, $white,
            $font_file, 'Photo Collage');
```

In this code, we set the resource identifiers for white and orange colors by using the `imagecolorallocate()` function. Then we create an image, which will be used as the background image, from an already existing image on our server named `app3a.jpg`. We pass the path of the JPEG image as an argument to this function. Next, we set this newly created image as the tile with which we will fill the background of our original image by using the `imagesettile()` function. We fill the background of our original image by using `imagefilledrectangle()`. This function takes the following arguments:

Meta properties	Description
image	The image resource on which this function will be applied.
x1	The x-coordinate of the starting point from where the rectangle will begin.
y1	The y-coordinate of the starting point from where the rectangle will begin.
x2	The x-coordinate of the end point to where the rectangle will end.
y2	The y-coordinate of the end point to where the rectangle will end.
color	The fill color to be used.

In our code, we have passed `IMG_COLOR_TILED` as the last argument of this function. This tells PHP to use the tile image, as defined by the `$bg` image resource identifier, for filling up the rectangle.

After this we write the name of our application, **Photo Collage**, on the bottom of the image by using the `imagefttext()` function. This function takes the following arguments:

Meta properties	Description
image	Represents an image resource.
size	The font size in points.
angle	The angle in degrees, with 0 being left-to-right reading text. Higher values represent a counter-clockwise rotation.
x	The x-coordinate from where the basepoint of the first character (roughly the lower-left corner of the character) will start.
y	The y-coordinate which sets the position of the font's baseline, not the very bottom of the character.
color	The index of the desired color for the text.
fontfile	The path to the TrueType font you wish to use.
text	The actual text to be inserted into the image.

Next, we retrieve random pictures from the albums of the user and make the collage as shown:

```
$merged_photos = array();
$albums = $facebook->api('/me/albums');
for($count=0;$count<9;$count++) {
  do {
    $album = $albums['data'][array_rand($albums['data'])];
    $photos = $facebook->api('/' . $album['id'] .'/photos');
    $photo = $photos['data'][array_rand($photos['data'])];
  } while(in_array($photo['id'],$merged_photos));
$merged_photos[] = $photo['id'];
```

In the code, first we use the Facebook Graph API to access http://graph.facebook.com/me/albums, retrieve all the albums of the current user and store in $albums. Next, for each photo cell we first choose a random album and then a random picture in that particular album by using the array_rand() function. Also, we create an empty array named $merged_photos which represents the photos already present in the collage. Next, we run the code to pick up a photo randomly inside a do while loop with the evaluation condition being that the photo ID is already present in the $merged_photos array. If it so, then we keep on choosing another picture randomly. This ensures that we don't put the same photo more than once in our photo collage. After choosing a unique photo we add its ID to the $merged_photos array so that when the loop runs next time we have the ID of all the photos already picked up.

After selecting a unique photo, we crop it to the fixed size of our predefined photo cell in the collage matrix. For this we first store the width and height of the selected photo as shown:

```
$width = $photo['images'][1]['width'];
$height= $photo['images'][1]['height'];
```

Now, we create two images with image identifiers as $image_p and $image_o where the former represents an empty image with its dimension the same as the photo cell and the latter represents the actual image from Facebook. By using the imagecopy() function we copy the selected photo to the $image_p image resource identifier and this image has dimensions as that of our predefined photo cell. Next, we use imagecopymerge() to merge this image to the main image at the appropriate coordinates. Finally, we free the memory allocated to the image identifiers by using imagedestroy(). All this is performed using the following lines of code:

```
$image_p = imagecreatetruecolor($cell_width, $cell_height);
  $image_o = imagecreatefromjpeg($photo['images'][1]['source']);
  imagecopy($image_p, $image_o, 0, 0, 0, 0, $width, $height);
  $des_x = (10*(($count%3)+1)+(($count%3)*$width));
  $des_y = (10*(floor($count/3)+1)+(floor($count/3)*$cell_height));
  imagecopymerge($image,$image_p,$des_x,$des_y,0,0,$cell_width,
              $cell_height,100);
  imagedestroy($image_p);
  imagedestroy($image_o);
```

Now, by using the imagepng() function we save the image inside a folder named img, present in the application directory, on our server. We then upload this image to the Facebook server. For this we use api() and finally the image is posted as shown:

```
imagepng($image, './img/' . $me['id'] . '.png');
$pic = realpath("/home/botskoco/public_html/cookbook/img/" . $me['id']
. '.png');
$facebook->setFileUploadSupport("http://" . $_SERVER['SERVER_NAME']);
$pic_id = $facebook->api('/me/photos', 'POST', array(
        'message' => 'photo collage', 'source' => '@' . $pic,
        ));
imagedestroy($image);
?>
```

Finally we display the photo collage to the user by using the HTML img tag as shown:

```
<img src="./img/<?php echo $me['id']; ?>.png" />
```

See also

For more information on how to post a picture to an album you may refer to the *How to post a picture to a specific album of the user* recipe in *Chapter 2*

Building a birthday calendar

This Facebook application will provide users with a calendar which will show the birthdays of all their friends for a specific month. Here, we will illustrate, step-by-step, how to make this application.

Getting ready

You should have created index.php and config.php as mentioned in the beginning of this chapter. Also, you should have provided friends_birthday extended permission to the application. Additionally, download a TrueType font of your choice as explained in the *Designing a "My Fast Friends" Facebook application recipe*.

How to do it...

The following steps will demonstrate how to create a birthday calendar:

1. Open index.php and append the following code after the HTML `<body>` tag. Create a combo box to enable users to select a month:

```php
<?php if (!isset($_REQUEST['selection'])) : ?>
<form name="myForm"
onsubmit="http://apps.facebook.com/[your_app_url]/ ">
  <select size="1" name="selection">
    <option value="1"> Jan </option>
    <option value="2"> Feb</option>
    <option value="3"> Mar </option>
    <option value="4"> Apr </option>
    <option value="5"> May</option>
    <option value="6"> Jun </option>
    <option value="7"> Jul </option>
    <option value="8"> Aug</option>
    <option value="9"> Sep </option>
    <option value="10"> Oct</option>
    <option value="11"> Nov </option>
    <option value="12"> Dec </option>
  </select>
```

2. Create a `submit` button:

```
<input type="submit" name="submit" value="Go !" />
</form>
<?php
  exit;
  endif;
?>
<?php
```

3. Store the submitted month in the `$month` variable:

```
$month = $_REQUEST['selection'];
```

4. Use FQL to retrieve the birthdays of all friends of the user:

```
$friends = $facebook->api(array('method' => 'fql.query',
    'query' => "SELECT birthday_date, name, uid, pic_square FROM
    user WHERE uid IN (SELECT uid2 FROM friend WHERE uid1= me())"));
```

5. Create an empty array `$ordered_friends`:

```
$ordered_friends = array();
```

6. Loop through the `$friends` array:

```
foreach($friends as $friend){
  if(isset($friend['birthday_date'])){
```

7. Split birthdays into dates, months, and years:

```
$dt = split("/",$friend['birthday_date']);
```

8. Check for the month matching with the one entered by the user and store the corresponding friend's birthday:

```
if($dt[0] == $month){
    $ordered_friends[ltrim($dt[1],'0')][] = $friend;
    }
  }
}
```

9. Retrieve the number of days present in the month selected:

```
$last_day = date("d", strtotime("-1 day",
    strtotime(date("Y-" . ($month+1) . "-01"))));
```

10. Set the background image and colors for the text to be written on the background:

```
$image = imagecreatetruecolor(450, 700);
$white = imagecolorallocate($image, 0xFF, 0xFF, 0xFF);
$orange = imagecolorallocate($image, 0xF5, 0xA9, 0x53);
```

11. Create a background image from an already existing file, `app2_bg.jpg` on the server:

    ```
    $bg = imagecreatefromjpeg('./app2_bg.jpg');
    ```

12. Set the image as a tile image for filling the background:

    ```
    imagesettile($image, $bg);
    ```

13. Fill the image:

    ```
    imagefilledrectangle($image, 0, 0, 450, 700, IMG_COLOR_TILED);
    imagedestroy($bg);
    ```

14. Provide the path of the TTF file:

    ```
    $font_file = './TURNBB__.TTF';
    imagefttext($image, 16, 0, 15, 50, $orange, $font_file,
                'Friends Birthday Calender');
    imagefttext($image, 16, 0, 150, 80, $orange, $font_file,
                date("F", strtotime(date("Y-" . ($month) . "-01"))));
    $day = 1;
    ```

15. Copy the user's friends' images to their respective birthdays in the calendar:

    ```
    for($i=0;$i<ceil($last_day/5);$i++) {
      for($j=0;$j<5&&$day<=$last_day;$j++,$day++) {
        imagefilledrectangle($image, 30+($j*80), 100+($i*80),
                             30+($j*80+70), 100+($i*80+70), $white);
        imagefttext($image, 22, 45, 40+($j*80+15), 150+($i*80+15),
                    $orange, $font_file, $day);
        if(count($ordered_friends[$day])) {
            for($col=1;count($ordered_friends[$day])>($col*$col);
                $col++);
            $side = 50;
            $cell_side = floor($side/$col);
            for($count=0;$count<count($ordered_friends[$day]);$count++)
              {
              $image_p = imagecreatetruecolor($cell_side, $cell_side);
              $image_o = imagecreatefromstring(file_get_contents(
                      $ordered_friends[$day][$count]['pic_square']));
              imagecopyresized($image_p, $image_o, 0, 0, 0, 0,
                               $cell_side, $cell_side, $side, $side);
              $des_x = 30+($j*80)+(5*(($count%$col)+1)+(
                          ($count%$col)*$cell_side));
              $des_y = 100+($i*80)+(5*(floor($count/$col)+1)+
                          (floor($count/$col)*$cell_side));
              imagecopymerge($image,$image_p,$des_x,$des_y,0,0,
                             $cell_side,$cell_side,100);
              imagedestroy($image_p);
    ```

```
            imagedestroy($image_o);
        }
      }
    }
  }
```

16. Save the image file on the server:

```
imagepng($image, './img/' . $me['id'] . '.png');
```

17. Retrieve the image from the server and post it to the user's album:

```
$pic = realpath("/home/botskoco/public_html/cookbook/img/" .
  $me['id'] . '.png');
$facebook->setFileUploadSupport("http://" .
  $_SERVER['SERVER_NAME']);
$pic_id = $facebook->api('/me/photos', 'POST',
  array('message' => $message);
```

18. Free the memory which is associated with the image:

```
imagedestroy($image);
?>
```

19. Place the following code inside `fb-root` and render the image:

```
<img src="./img/<?php echo $me['id']; ?>.png" />
```

20. Save the file and run it. A screen displaying the combo box will appear and would be something like the following:

21. Now, if we select any month from the drop down and click on the **Go** button we will be shown a calendar having user's friends' birthdays falling into that month as shown:

How it works...

In this application, we display the profile pictures, date-wise, of all the friends whose birthdays lie in the month selected by the user. Initially, we provide the user with the option to choose a month for which he or she wants the birthday calendar to be displayed. We do this by creating a form which contains a combo box providing a drop down menu to the users with all the months of a year. This has been done via the following lines of code:

```
<?php if(!isset($_REQUEST['selection'])) : ?>
<form name="myForm" onsubmit="http://apps.facebook.com/[your_app_
url]">
  <select size="1" name="selection">
    <option value="1"> Jan </option>
    <option value="2"> Feb</option>
    <option value="3"> Mar </option>
    <option value="4"> Apr </option>
    <option value="5"> May</option>
    <option value="6"> Jun </option>
    <option value="7"> Jul </option>
    <option value="8"> Aug</option>
```

```
        <option value="9"> Sep </option>
        <option value="10"> Oct</option>
        <option value="11"> Nov </option>
        <option value="12"> Dec </option>
    </select>
    <input type="submit" name="submit" value="Go !" />
</form>
<?php
    exit;
    endif;
?>
<?php
$month = $_REQUEST['selection'];
```

Here, we first check whether the user has already chosen a month or not and if not we display a form to him/her. When the user selects a particular month and clicks on the **Submit** button, the form gets submitted and we store the selected month in $month variable. We now run an FQL query to retrieve the birthday of all the friends of the users falling in this selected month. It is done by making a call to the api() function as shown:

```
$friends = $facebook->api(array(
    'method' => 'fql.query',
    'query' => "SELECT birthday_date, name, uid, pic_square FROM user
        WHERE uid IN (SELECT uid2 FROM friend
            WHERE uid1= me())"));
```

We pass an array as an argument to the api() function. In this array the method parameter is set to fql.query which specifies that we want to run an FQL query. The query parameter contains the actual query. The data returned is stored in $friends.

Next, we create an empty array $ordered_friends to store the information of only those friends whose birthday falls in the month selected by the user. For this we first split the birthday of each friend using the split() function into days, months, and years with the following code:

```
$dt = split("/",$friend['birthday_date'])
```

Then we check the month of this birthday with that requested by the user. If the months match we remove the preceding zeroes from the dates by using the ltrim() function and store it in the $ordered_friends array as shown:

```
if($dt[0] == $month){
        $ordered_friends[ltrim($dt[1],'0')][] = $friend;
    }
```

After this, we calculate the total number of days present in the month selected by the user. For this we retrieve the first day of the next month and subtract "1 day", by using the `strtotime()` function, from it and again form a date from this new timestamp as shown:

```
$last_day = date("d", strtotime("-1 day", strtotime(date(
    "Y-" . ($month+1) . "-01"))));
```

Now, we create our main image on which we will print the calendar and merge profile picture of all friends present in the `$ordered_friends` array. We use the `imagecreatetruecolor()` function for creating our main image. Additionally, we use the `imagecolorallocate()` function to create color identifiers for various colors that we will use in our image as shown in the following:

```
$image = imagecreatetruecolor(450, 700);
$white = imagecolorallocate($image, 0xFF, 0xFF, 0xFF);
$orange = imagecolorallocate($image, 0xF5, 0xA9, 0x53);
```

Then, we create a background image by using the `imagecreatefromjpeg()` function. We set this image as a tile to fill up the background of the main image by using the `imagesettile()` function. We then use `imagefilledrectangle()` to fill up the background of the main image with this tile image. It takes the following arguments:

Arguments	Description
image	Defines the image resource on which this function will be applied.
x1	The x-coordinate of the starting point from where the rectangle will begin.
y1	The y-coordinate of the starting point from where the rectangle will begin.
x2	The x-coordinate of the end point to where the rectangle will end.
y2	The y-coordinate of the end point to where the rectangle will end.
color	Defines the fill color to be used.

After this we use our TTF font to write text on the birthday calendar using the `imagefttext()` function. This function takes the following arguments:

Arguments	Description
image	An image resource, returned by one of the image creation functions, such as `imagecreatetruecolor()`.
size	The font size to use, in points.
angle	The angle in degrees, with 0 being left-to-right reading text. Higher values represent a counter-clockwise rotation. For example, a value of 90 would result in bottom-to-top reading text.
x	The coordinates given by x and y will define the basepoint of the first character (roughly the lower-left corner of the character). This is different from the `imagestring()`, where x and y define the upper-left corner of the first character. For example, "top-left" is 0,0.
y	The y-coordinate: This sets the position of the font's baseline, not the very bottom of the character.
color	The index of the desired color for the text.
fontfile	The path to the TrueType font you wish to use.
text	Text to be inserted into the image.

So the overall code becomes:

```
$bg = imagecreatefromjpeg('./app2_bg.jpg');
imagesettile($image, $bg);
imagefilledrectangle($image, 0, 0, 450, 700, IMG_COLOR_TILED);
imagedestroy($bg);
$font_file = './TURNBB__.TTF';
imagefttext($image, 16, 0, 15, 50, $orange, $font_file,
   'Friends Birthday Calender');
imagefttext($image, 16, 0, 150, 80, $orange, $font_file, date
   ("F", strtotime(date("Y-" . ($month) . "-01"))));
```

Next, we draw cells by using the `imagefilledrectangle()` function corresponding to all the days for the selected month. We use a nested `for` loop to ensure that each row contains five cells in the birthday calendar. Additionally, we print the date at an angle of 45 degrees, by using the `imagefttext()` function, on each cell as shown:

```
for($i=0;$i<ceil($last_day/5);$i++) {
    for($j=0;$j<5&&$day<=$last_day;$j++,$day++) {
        imagefilledrectangle($image, 30+($j*80), 100+($i*80),
                             30+($j*80+70), 100+($i*80+70), $white);
        imagefttext($image, 22, 45, 40+($j*80+15), 150+($i*80+15),
                    $orange, $font_file, $day);
```

For each day we check whether any friend of the user has a birthday and if it so we print the profile picture of all such friends with appropriate x and y coordinates as shown:

```
if(count($ordered_friends[$day])) {
  for($col=1;count($ordered_friends[$day])>($col*$col);$col++);
  $side = 50;
  $cell_side = floor($side/$col);
  for($count=0;$count<count($ordered_friends[$day]);$count++) {
    $image_p = imagecreatetruecolor($cell_side, $cell_side);
    $image_o = imagecreatefromstring(file_get_contents(
      $ordered_friends[$day][$count]['pic_square']));
    imagecopyresized($image_p, $image_o, 0, 0, 0, 0,
                    $cell_side, $cell_side, $side, $side);
```

Here, we count the total number of friends who share the same birthday, because then we will have to show more than one profile pictures in a cell. This requires us to resize the profile pictures accordingly to a smaller size. The new size is calculated and stored in `$cell_side`. We retrieve the profile pictures by using the `imagecreatefromstring()` and `file_get_contents()` functions. After this, we resize the profile picture of all friends, who share the same birthday, using `imagecopyresized()`. After resizing the image we merge it with the appropriate location on the main image whose x and y coordinates are represented by `$des_x` and `$des_y` respectively, as shown:

```
$des_x = 30+($j*80)+(5*(($count%$col)+1)+(
        ($count%$col)*$cell_side));
$des_y = 100+($i*80)+(5*(floor($count/$col)+1)+(floor(
        $count/$col)*$cell_side));
imagecopymerge($image,$image_p,$des_x,$des_y,0,0,$cell_side,
            $cell_side,100);
imagedestroy($image_p);
imagedestroy($image_o);
      }
    }
  }
}
```

Finally, we use the `imagecopymerge()` function to merge the resized profile picture with the main image. After the loop execution is over our main image is ready and we save it using the `imagepng()` function as shown:

```
imagepng($image, './img/' . $me['id'] . '.png');
```

Now, we can post this image in the user's album. We do so by using `api()` as shown:

```
$pic = realpath("/home/botskoco/public_html/cookbook/img/" . $me['id']
. '.png');
$facebook->setFileUploadSupport("http://" . $_SERVER['SERVER_NAME']);
$pic_id = $facebook->api('/me/photos', 'POST', array('message' =>
$message
);
```

Finally, we free the associated memory with image resource identifier and render the image with the following code:

```
imagedestroy($image);
?>
<img src="./img/<?php echo $me['id']; ?>.png" />
```

Now, the user will see a customized birthday calendar for the month requested by him/her as output and it will be posted as an image in his/her album as well.

Developing an application to classify friends according to the cities they live in

In this application a user will be able to classify all of his/her friends according to the cities in which they currently reside.

Getting ready

You should have already created `index.php` and `config.php` as mentioned in the beginning of the third chapter. Additionally, you should also provide `friends_location` and `user_location` extended permission to the application.

How to do it...

The following steps will demonstrate the creation of this application:

1. Open `index.php` and append the following code after the HTML `<body>` tag. Select the location, name, user ID, and profile picture of the user's friends by using FQL:

```
<?php
    $friends = $facebook->api(array('method' => 'fql.query',
        'query' => "SELECT current_location, name, uid, pic_square
        FROM user WHERE uid IN (SELECT uid2 FROM friend WHERE uid1=
        me())"));
```

2. Create an empty array, `$cities`, to maintain a count of the number of users in a city:

```
$cities = array();
```

3. Create another empty array `$cities_frnds` to store the city wise friends' information:

```
$cities_frnds = array();
```

4. Loop through the `$friends` array:

```
foreach($friends as $friend) {
```

5. Check, if for the current friend's city, whether an index exists in `$cities` array and if so increment its count by one:

```
if(isset($friend['current_location']['city'])) {
    if (array_key_exists($friend['current_location']
    ['city'],$cities)) {
        $cities[$friend['current_location']['city']]++;
    }
```

6. Otherwise create a new key and initialize it to 1:

```
    else {
        $cities[$friend['current_location']['city']] = 1;
    }
```

7. Store the city-wise friends' information in `$cities_frnds`:

```
    $cities_frnds[$friend['current_location']['city']][] =
    array('name' => $friend['name'], 'pic_square' =>
    $friend['pic_square']);
    }
}
```

8. Sort the cities in descending order using the `arsort()` function:

```
arsort($cities);
?>
```

9. Place the code given below inside `fb-root`:

```
<?php
echo '<table width="100%" border="1">';
foreach($cities as $key => $value) {
```

10. Display the result in a table:

```
    echo '<tr><td width="15%">' . $key . '</td>
                <td width="15%">' . $value . '</td>
                <td width="70%">';
    foreach($cities_frnds[$key] as $city_frnd) {
        echo "<img width='40' src='{$city_frnd['pic_square']}' />";
    }
```

```
      echo '</td></tr>';
   }
   echo '</table>'
?>
```

11. Now save and run the file. A list will appear on the screen containing the city name, the number of friends in that particular city, and profile pictures of the users who share the same city:

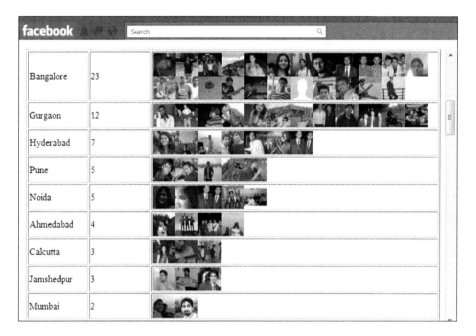

How it works...

In this application, we have classified user's friends according to their current residing location. To retrieve the current location and the city of each user's friend we use the FQL query over the **user** table. To execute the FQL query we use the api() function which contains an array as an argument. This array has a key named method which we set to fql.query. This denotes that we want to execute an FQL query. Similarly, the value of the key query contains the actual FQL query to be executed. We store the returned data in the $friends variable as shown:

```
$friends = $facebook->api(array(
 'method' => 'fql.query',
 'query' => "SELECT current_location, name, uid, pic_square FROM user
   WHERE uid IN (SELECT uid2 FROM friend
     WHERE uid1= me())"
));
```

Next, we create two more arrays, `$cities` to store the count of users in each city and `$cities_frnds` to store the city wise friends information. For this we have the following code:

```
$cities = array();
$cities_frnds = array();
```

Now, we loop through all the elements in the `$friends` array by using the `foreach` loop and we check whether, for the current friend's city, an index exists in `$cities` array and if so we increment its count by one. Otherwise we create a new key for the current friend's city and initialize its value to 1. We also store the friend's details in the form of a sub array with his/her city as key in `$cities_frnds`. The complete code for this is shown:

```
foreach($friends as $friend) {
  if(isset($friend['current_location']['city'])) {
    if (array_key_exists($friend['current_location']['city'],$cities))
  {
      $cities[$friend['current_location']['city']]++;
    }
    else {
      $cities[$friend['current_location']['city']] = 1;
    }
    $cities_frnds[$friend['current_location']['city']][] =
array('name' => $friend['name'], 'pic_square' => $friend['pic_
square']);
  }
}
```

Finally, we use the `arsort ()` function to sort the `$cities` array in the descending order so that the city having the maximum number of users appears at the top. The final result is then displayed inside a table as shown:

```
arsort($cities);
echo '<table width="100%" border="1">';
foreach($cities as $key => $value) {
   echo '<tr><td width="15%">' . $key . '</td>
             <td width="15%">' . $value . '</td>
             <td width="70%">';
   foreach($cities_frnds[$key] as $city_frnd) {
      echo "<img width='40' src='{$city_frnd['pic_square']}' />";
   }
   echo '</td></tr>';
}
echo '</table>'
?>
```

The table contains the profile pictures of all friends grouped city-wise in descending order, that is, the city having the maximum number friends as their current location is displayed at the top.

11
Using Facebook Open Graph Beta

In this chapter, we will cover:

- ▶ Setting up your application for using Facebook Open Graph Beta
- ▶ Defining actions, objects, and aggregations for your application
- ▶ Customizing the Facebook Auth Dialog box
- ▶ Requesting permission for publishing to the user's timeline
- ▶ Defining your web page as a Facebook graph object
- ▶ Publishing actions of user to Facebook

Introduction

Recently, Facebook has come up with an innovative way to make its users feel more at home. With the introduction of **Open Graph Beta** and **Timeline**, Facebook has changed the concept of social interaction. Now, to share our activities with others, we don't need to like corresponding objects/pages. We can tell people exactly what we are doing at a particular moment. It may be simply reading an article on a website, or listening to music from an online store or virtually anything. The best part is that it gives others the ability to interact with the same content instantaneously. This is a wonderful opportunity for Facebook developers giving them the ability to virally spread their content on Facebook. We will show you how to capitalize on this idea in this chapter.

With Open Graph Beta, Facebook has introduced the concept of actions and objects. Actions are basically verbs which define your lifestyle such as cook, read, listen, dance, and so on, whereas Objects are the nouns which are associated with those verbs. For example food, article, news, and music respectively, in response to the actions defined above. The sole purpose to define these is to make others know what exactly your end users are doing on your application. Aggregation displays the data, related to action and object, of an application specific to a user after filtering based on specified criteria.

Setting up your application for using Facebook Open Graph Beta

In this recipe, we will show you how to integrate your website with Facebook Open Graph Beta. This will help us to post the user actions on your website to Facebook. Here, the user actions refer to the activities that an end user might perform on your website. For example, reading an article, listening to a song, and so on.

How to do it...

The following steps will help set up your application for using Facebook Open Graph Beta:

1. Go to the following URL: `http://developers.facebook.com/`.

2. Click on the **Apps** tab present on the Facebook top bar navigation:

3. Next, click on the **Create New App** button present on the right corner.

4. You will be presented with a pop up asking you for the **App Display Name** and **App Namespace**. It will appear as shown in the following screenshot:

5. Enter a suitable display name and namespace for your application. Now, check the **I agree to the Facebook Platform Policies** checkbox and click on **Continue**.

6. You may be prompted with a Facebook **Security Check** dialog box. Complete the CAPTCHA and click on **Submit**, as shown in the following screenshot:

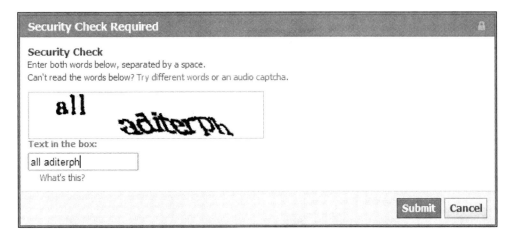

7. Next, the page containing the basic settings of the application will load:

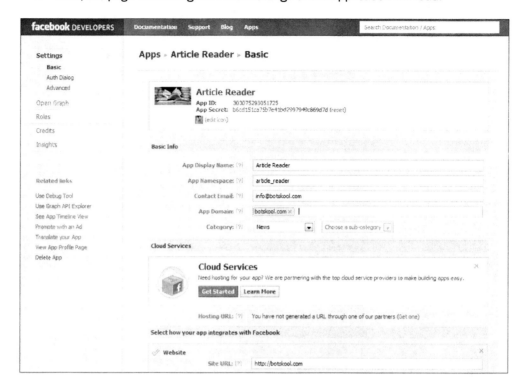

8. You will notice that the **App Display Name** and **App Namespace** are already populated with the values you had entered earlier. Also, our unique **App ID** and **App Secret** will be shown.

9. Fill in the **Contact Email** and **App Domain** fields. Also, expand the **Website** tab and enter your **Site URL**. You may also set a suitable **Logo** and **Icon**.

10. Click on **Save Changes**. If everything is fine, you will see a message, as shown in the following screenshot, at the top of the page:

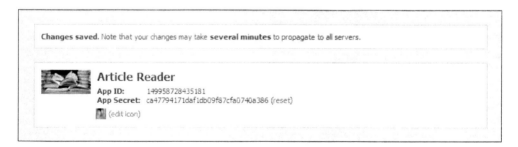

Thus, we are done with the initial step of integrating our website with Facebook.

How it works...

The first step in integration of any third-party website or page with the Open Graph Beta of Facebook is to create a new custom application. Initially, we mention the display name and namespace of our application as **Article Reader** and **article_reader** respectively. The **App Display Name** is the name which appears to the application users, whereas the **App Namespace** is a unique machine name of your application which is used to manage the app's actions and objects.

Next, we mention the domain name and the base URL of the website which we want to integrate with Facebook. This enables Facebook to track down the actions that a user performs on our website.

See also

▸ *Defining actions, objects, and aggregations for your application*

Defining actions, objects, and aggregations for your application

The actions, objects, and aggregations form an integral part of Facebook Open Graph Beta. Here, we will show you how to define them.

Getting ready

You should have created an application as explained in *Setting up your application for using Facebook Open Graph Beta* recipe.

How to do it...

The following steps will demonstrate how to define actions, objects, and aggregations:

1. Go to `https://developers.facebook.com/apps`. Locate your application and click on the **Edit App** button present on the top right-hand side.

2. Next, click on the **Open Graph** tab present on the left sidebar. By default, the **Getting Started** option will get selected in the sub menu and the corresponding page will load as shown in the following screenshot:

3. Here, mention our application's action (**read**) in the first textbox next to the **People can** label. Also, mention the object (**article**) corresponding to this action in the second textbox. Click on the **Get Started** button.

4. Next, we will be directed to **Edit your Action Type** page, where we can configure our newly created action. It will appear as shown in the following screenshot:

5. The **Past Tense** label contains a drop-down list box. Choose **via Article Reader** from it. Click on **Save Changes and Next**.

6. Next, we will be directed to the **Edit your Object Type** page. Here, we enter sample values for **Title**, **Image**, and **Description** of our newly created object type—**article**. This allows us to preview how our objects will appear in the Facebook news feed. Also, under the **Advanced** section, we change the meta tag for our object type. Now, click on **Save Changes and Next** button:

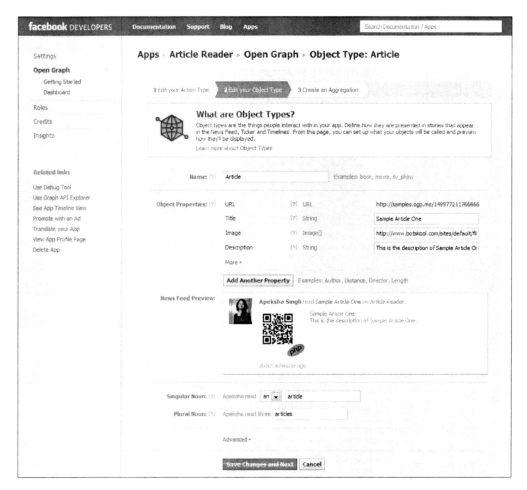

7. Finally, we are directed to **Create an Aggregation** page. It will look as shown in the following screenshot:

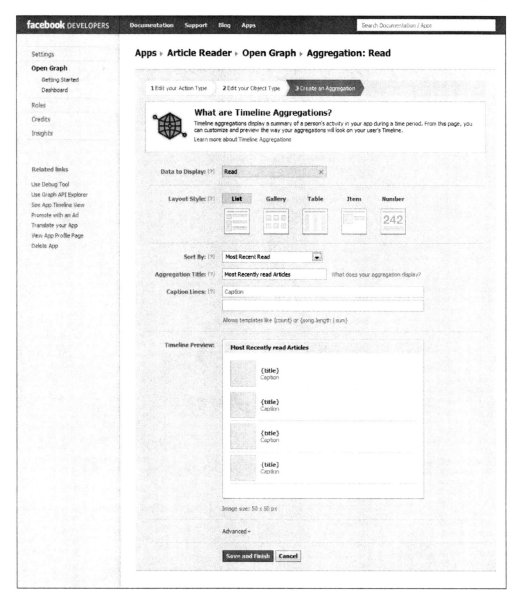

8. Set the value of the **Sort By** label as **Most Recently Read** and **Aggregation Title** as **Most Recently read Articles**. Click on **Save and Finish**.

9. Now, you will be redirected to the **Open Graph Dashboard** and it will appear, as shown in the following screenshot:

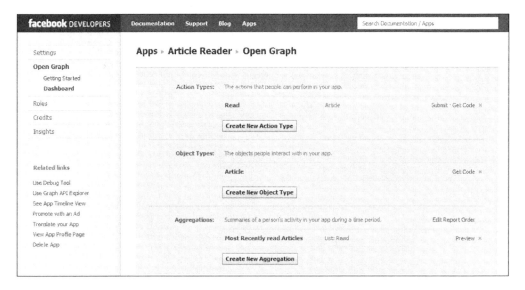

10. Click on the **Preview** link of the **Most Recently read Articles** aggregation. A pop up will appear.

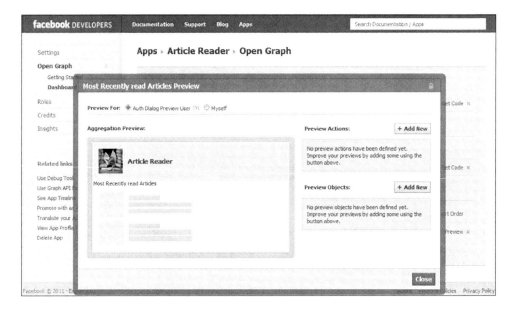

11. Click on the **Add New** button under the **Preview Objects** section. A pop up like this will appear:

12. Enter a suitable title and description for the dummy object. Also, provide a valid image URL and click on the **Save Changes** button. Similarly, create another dummy object and finally the aggregation preview dialog box will look as shown in the following screenshot:

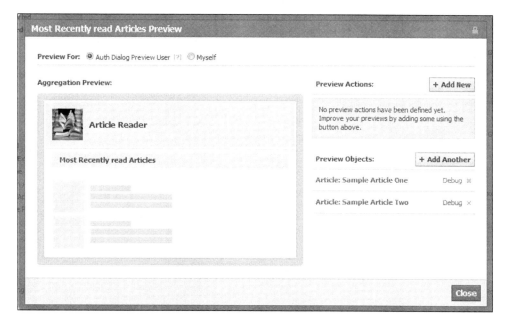

13. Click on the **Add New** button under the **Preview Actions** section. A pop up will appear:

14. Choose one of the dummy articles created earlier in the **Article** section and click on the **Create** button. Similarly, create another preview action corresponding to the other dummy object and finally your aggregation preview dialog box will look as shown in the following screenshot:

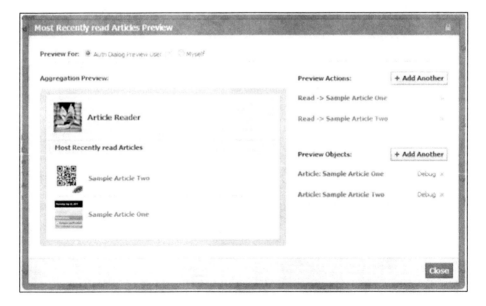

15. Click on the **Close** button.

How it works...

Here, we define a new action named **read**. We configure this action on the **Edit your Action Type** page. Similarly, we create a new object named **article** and this object is related to the action **read**. We configure this object as shown in the previous section.

Finally, we create an aggregation where the data is sorted by the most recently performed read actions. We also add the preview data for this aggregation. We do so by creating two dummy objects and creating corresponding actions for them. This preview data of the aggregation is used in various places such as in the **Add to Timeline** plugin, **Auth Dialog** box, and so on.

See also

▶   *Customizing the Facebook Auth Dialog box*

Customizing the Facebook Auth Dialog box

We can make the Facebook Auth Dialog user-friendly and more appealing by configuring it as explained in this recipe. This includes setting up the logo, content, description, and other properties.

Getting ready

You should have created your application as described in the previous two recipes.

How to do it...

The following steps will help customize the Facebook Auth Dialog box:

1. Go to `https://developers.facebook.com/apps`. Locate your application and click on the **Edit App** button present on the top right-hand side.

2. Next, click on the **Basic | Auth Dialog** on the left sidebar.

3. Set the **Headline** as **Article Reader**.

4. Set the **Description** as **An application for reading articles**.

5. Provide the **Privacy Policy URL** and **Terms of Service URL**. Also, provide the landing URL where the user should be directed after authorization is complete. This can be the home page of your website.

6. Under the **Authenticated Referrals** section, add the **publish_actions** permission in the **User & Friend Permissions** textbox. Finally, the page will look as shown in the following screenshot:

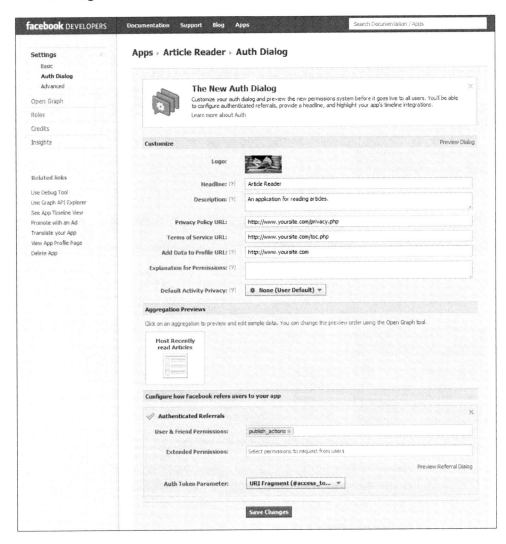

7. Click on the **Preview Referral Dialog** link to see the preview of the Auth Dialog:

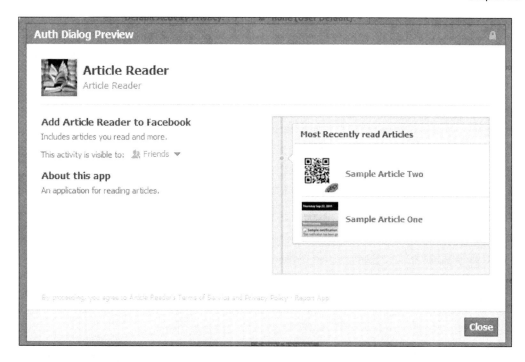

8. Click on the **Close** button. Finally, click on the **Save Changes** button.

How it works...

Here, we can configure various properties of the Auth Dialog which determines its layout. We can use the following properties to theme the Auth Dialog box:

▶ **Logo**: We can upload a logo for our application.

▶ **Headline**: This is a one line description of our application.

▶ **Description**: This is a longer description of our application. It is shown under the **About this app** section.

▶ **Privacy Policy URL**: It is the URL to the privacy policy.

▶ **Terms of Service URL**: It is the URL to the terms of service.

▶ **Add Data to Profile URL**: The URL to which the user should be later on directed to for engagement and action publishing.

▶ **Explanation for Permissions**: If our application requires extended permissions other than `e-mail` and `publish_actions`, a second Auth dialog screen will appear after the user authorizes the initial Auth Dialog. The text here is used to explain why we need the additional permissions.

▶ **Default Activity Privacy**: This field is used to set the Auth Dialog with a default application action visibility setting. By default, this value is **None**, which means our application specific actions published will follow the user's default privacy permissions. Valid values are: **None, Friends, Me only**, or **Public**. The user can change the Activity Privacy on the Auth Dialog.

After setting the values of the above fields, we next specify the permission to be requested by the Auth Dialog in the **Authentication Referrals** section. In order to use Open Graph, we request for the `publish_actions` permission.

 In order to request the `publish_actions` permission, make sure that an aggregation is defined and populated with some preview data, as explained in the *Defining actions, objects, and aggregations for your application* recipe.

Finally, we preview the Auth Dialog box before saving the changes.

See also

▶ *Requesting permission for publishing to the user's timeline*

Requesting permission for publishing to the user's timeline

In order to publish application specific actions to a user's timeline, we need to request the `publish_actions` permission from the user. This can be easily accomplished with the help of the **Add to Timeline (Beta)** plugin.

Getting ready

We should have created our application for our website as defined in the *Setting up your application for using Facebook Open Graph Beta* recipe.

How to do it...

The following steps will demonstrate a request for permission:

1. Open `index.php` and copy the following code to it:

```
<html xmlns="http://www.w3.org/1999/xhtml"dir="ltr"
lang="en-US" xmlns:fb="https://www.facebook.com/2008/fbml">
  <head>
  </head>
  <body>
```

```
    <div id="fb-root"></div>
    <script src="http://connect.facebook.net/en_US/all.js">
    </script>
    <script>
      FB.init({
        appId:'your_app_id', cookie:true,
        status:true, xfbml:true, oauth:true
      });
    </script>
    <fb:add-to-timeline></fb:add-to-timeline>
  </body>
</html>
```

2. Replace the `your_app_id` in the code above with your application ID. Now save and run this file. A screen, as shown in the following screenshot, will appear:

3. On clicking on the **Add to Timeline** button, the following Auth Dialog box loads:

4. Next, if the user clicks on the **Log In and Add to Facebook** button, then the application gets the authorization and finally the following screen appears:

How it works...

The `publish_actions` allows us to publish application specific actions to the user's timeline. The easiest way to request this permission is by using the **Add to Timeline** plugin.

We use the `fb:add-to-timeline` XFBML tag of FB JavaScript SDK in order to render this plugin. This plugin has two display modes—**box** and **button**. We can configure the plugin with the help of the following attributes:

- `data-show-faces`: This specifies whether to show faces underneath the login button.

- `data-mode`: This defines the mode of the plugin—**box** and **button**. The default mode is **box**.

- `data-perms`: It is a comma separated list of extended permissions.

When a user clicks on the **Add to Timeline** button, the user is present with an Auth Dialog box informing about the application and requesting the permission to access the timeline of the user.

If the extended permissions are specified, then a second dialog box loads (after the initial auth dialog box) requesting these permissions from the user.

There's more...

If we want to use the **button** display mode, along with an extended permission `publish stream`, then the XFBML tag will be:

```
<fb:add-to-timeline data-show-faces="true" data-mode="button" data-
perms="publish_stream"  />
```

It will appear as shown in the following screenshot:

See also

- *Defining your web page as a a Facebook graph object*

Defining your web page as a a Facebook graph object

In this recipe, we will show you how, with the help of various meta tags, you can define a web page as an object of Facebook Open Graph Beta.

Getting ready

You should have configured your application to be used with Facebook Open Graph Beta, that is, you should have set up objects, actions, and aggregation. If you haven't already done so, refer to the all the recipes discussed earlier in this chapter.

How to do it...

The following steps will demonstrate how to define your web page as a Facebook graph object:

1. Go to `https://developers.facebook.com/apps`. Locate your application and click on the **Edit App** button present on the top right-hand side.

2. Next, go to the **Open Graph | Dashboard**, present on the left sidebar, as shown in the following screenshot:

3. Now, under the **Object Types** section, click on the **Get Code** link on the right-hand side corresponding to the **Article** object. A pop up will appear:

4. This pop-up box contains sample meta tags for the article object of our application. Copy this code.

5. Open the web page which you want to define as an object, say `index.php`. Paste this code in the `head` section of the page as shown:

```
<head prefix="og: http://ogp.me/ns# fb: http://ogp.me/ns/fb#
article_reader: http://ogp.me/ns/fb/your_app_name#">
  <meta property="fb:app_id"
    content="your_app_id" />
  <meta property="og:type"
    content="your_app_namespace:your_object_name" />
  <meta property="og:url"
    content="http://your_web_page_url"/>
  <meta property="og:title"
    content="your_object_title" />
  <meta property="og:description"
    content="your_object_description." />
  <meta property="og:image"
    content="http://your_object_image_url " />
</head>
```

6. These meta tags help Facebook interpret this web page as an object of Facebook Open Graph Beta.

How it works...

Facebook uses certain meta tags to determine whether a web page is an object of its Open Graph. These meta tags are used to specify values of some parameters through which Facebook categorizes a web page into an object. These object-specific meta properties are as follows:

Meta properties	Description
`fb:app_id`	This is the application id to which our web page refers to.
`og:type`	This defines the type of the object the current web page is.
`og:image`	This is the image which will be associated with the current object when published/ previewed in the Facebook news feed. It will appear in news feeds, ticker, and timeline.
`og:description`	This is the description of the current object.
`og:url`	This is the URL of the current web page.

After adding these meta tags to our web page, we can associate an action to it, as defined in the next recipe—*Publishing actions of a user to Facebook*.

See also

▸ *Publishing actions of a user to Facebook*

Publishing actions of a user to Facebook

Facebook Open Graph Beta gives us the capability to publish actions to Facebook whenever a user interacts with our Facebook Open Graph objects. Here, we will show you how to publish actions.

Getting ready

You should have configured your application to be used with Facebook Open Graph Beta, that is, you should have set up objects, actions, and aggregation. If you haven't already done so, refer to the all the recipes discussed earlier in this chapter.

How to do it...

The following steps will demonstrate how to publish user actions:

1. Open `index.php` and add the following code to it:

    ```
    <html xmlns="http://www.w3.org/1999/xhtml" dir="ltr"
    lang="en-US" xmlns:fb="https://www.facebook.com/2008/fbml">
    ```

2. Add the following meta tags, in order to define this web page as an article to Facebook:

```
<head prefix="og: http://ogp.me/ns# fb: http://ogp.me/ns/fb#
  article_reader: http://ogp.me/ns/fb/article_reader#">
  <meta property="fb:app_id"
    content="your_app_id" />
  <meta property="og:type"
    content="article_reader:article" />
  <meta property="og:url"
    content="http://yoursite.com/index.php" />
  <meta property="og:title"
    content="The title of the article" />
  <meta property="og:description"
    content="The description of the article." />
  <meta property="og:image"
    content="http://yoursite.com/image1.png" />
</head>
```

3. Next, add the content of your article:

```
<body>
  <div id="fb-root"></div>
  <div id="teaser">Some teaser about the article here.
    <a href="#" onclick="readArticle();">Read full article</a>
  <br/></div>
  <div id="full-content" style="display: none">Full Content
  Here</div>
```

4. Include FB JS SDK and jQuery:

```
<script src="http://connect.facebook.net/en_US/all.js"></script>
<script type="text/javascript"
  src="https://ajax.googleapis.com/ajax/libs/jquery/
  1.5.2/jquery.min.js"></script>
```

5. Next, add the `FB.init()` function:

```
<script>
  FB.init({
    appId:'149958728435181', cookie:true,
    status:true, xfbml:true, oauth:true
  });
```

6. Add the `readArticle()` function which will publish the read action to Facebook for the current object:

```
function readArticle()
{
$('#teaser').hide();
```

```
        $('#full-content').show();
        FB.api('/me/article_reader:read' +
          '?article=http://yoursite.com/index.php','post',
          function(response) {
          if (!response || response.error) {
            alert('Error occured');
          } else {
            alert('Post was successful! Action ID: ' +
              response.id);
          }
        });
      }
    </script>

  <fb:add-to-timeline></fb:add-to-timeline>
  </body>
</html>
```

7. Save the code and run it. A screen similar to the following screenshot will appear:

8. Click on the **Read full article** link. A pop up, displaying the message that the post has been successful along with action ID, will appear:

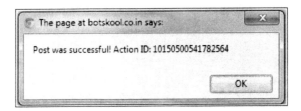

9. Also, the action will be published to Facebook and will appear on the ticker of the user and friends, as shown in the following screenshot:

How it works...

Here, first we have added some meta tags in order to define the current web page as a Facebook object. This we do with the help of the following code:

```
<meta property="fb:app_id"
  content="your_app_id" />
<meta property="og:type"
  content="article_reader:article" />
<meta property="og:url"
  content="http://yoursite.com/index.php" />
<meta property="og:title"
  content="The title of the article"
  />
<meta property="og:description" content="The description of
  the article." />
<meta property="og:image"
  content="http://yoursite.com/image1.png" />
```

The meta tag `fb:app_id` is used to specify the application ID. Similarly, the meta tags `og:type`, `og:url`, `og:title`, `og:description`, and `og:image` correspond to object type, object URL, object title, object description, and object image respectively.

After this, we include the content of the article inside the div `full-content` and have marked it as hidden. Also, we have a `teaser` div which contains the short description of the whole article along with a link to read the full content.

When the user clicks on this link to read the full article, the JavaScript function `readArticle()` is called. This function hides the short description of the article and shows its full content with the help of the following code:

```
function readArticle()
  {
    $('#teaser').hide();
    $('#full-content').show();
    FB.api('/me/article_reader:read' +
      '?article=http://yoursite.com/index.php','post',
      function(response) {
        if (!response || response.error) {
          alert('Error occured');
        } else {
          alert('Post was successful! Action ID: ' +
            response.id);
        }
    });
  }
```

Also, after showing the full content to the user, we publish the action **read** for the current **article** on behalf of the active logged in user.

To publish an action on Facebook, we need to make a POST request to the following URL – `https://graph.facebook.com/me/YOUR_APPNAMESPACE:action`. Along with this, we need to specify some additional parameters such as the Object URL and the access token. So the complete URL becomes:

`https://graph.facebook.com/me/YOUR_APPNAMESPACE:action?object=OBJE CT_URL&access_token=ACCESS_TOKEN`

To make this POST request, we make use of the `FB.api()` function of FB JS SDK. It takes the following three parameters:

- The first parameter is appended to the URL—`https://graph.facebook.com` and then a request is made to the complete URL. Here, the value of this parameter is `'/me/article_reader:read' + '?article=http://yoursite.com/index.php'`.

- The second parameter is the type of request. For example, GET or POST request. Here, it is `post` request.

- The third parameter is the callback function which we use to inform the user about the final outcome, that is, whether the action was published successfully or not.

If the action is published successfully to Facebook, then it appears in the ticker of the current user and his/her friends.

Index

Symbols

$cities array 312
$decodedSignedRequest array 28
$.each() function 164
$events variable 113
$facebook 252
$facebook->api() function 56, 75, 166, 278
$facebook-api() function 292
$facebook->getLoginUrl() 76, 278
$facebook->getSession() function 34, 75, 278
$friends array 244, 282
$me variable 34
$multi_queries array 114
$.post() function 52
$_REQUEST array 218
<div> element 119
<fb:comments> tag 187
<fb:login-button> XFBML tag 193
<html> element 119
<meta> tags 197
<script> element 26, 119, 149
XFBML
  using, for Send button integration 187-190

A

access_token 236
action attribute 172
actions
  defining 317-324
  working 325
action tag 24
Activity Feed plugin
  about 177
  configuring 178, 180

customizing 178, 180
  working 178
ad
  creating, for Facebook application 269-274
  working 274
Add bookmark button 141
Add New button 324
Add to Timeline (Beta) plugin 328
Add to Timeline button 330
Add to Timeline plugin 325, 331
administration interface, page
  Facebook URL Linter 207
  log in 207
  working with 204-206
Admin URL 207
aggregations
  defining 317-324
  working 325
Allow button 19
api() function 68, 75, 78, 113, 116, 166, 228, 256, 310
append() function 248
app_id attribute 151, 182, 223
appId, meta properties 279
app_id parameter 155
application callback setup, Facebook Credits
  about 215
  canceled, meta properties 220
  Data 219
  Description 219
  image_url 219
  item_id 219
  Price 219
  product_url 219
  refunded, meta properties 220
  setting up, steps 215

settled, meta properties 220
steps 215-218
Title 219
working 218-221
application, Facebook
birthday calendar, building 299
Body parameter 274
city-based friends classification application,
      developing 308
configuring 13, 14
creating from scratch 275-279
destination parameter 274
My Fast Friends, creating 284
new ad, creating 269-274
photo collage, setting up 292
Title parameter 274
type parameter 274
URL parameter 274
working 14, 274
Your Good Luck Charm of the Day, creating
      279-281
application permission status
checking 100, 101
permissions table, working 102
application setup, Facebook Credits
Callback URL, working 214
steps 212
application setup, for Open Graph Beta
steps 314-317
working 317
**application specific actions, publishing to
      user timeline**
publish_actions permission, requesting 328-
      331
Apps tab 314
arguments, imagefilledrectangle() function
color 305
image 305
x1 305
x2 305
y1 305
y2 305
arguments, imagefttext() function
angle 290, 306
color 290, 306
fontfile 290, 306
image 290, 306

size 290, 306
text 290, 306
x 290, 306
y 290, 306
array_rand() function 297
to 282
arsort() function 312
attributes, XFBML tag
autologoutlink 143
max-rows 143
perms 143
show-faces 143
width 143
audio data
integrating 200-203
meta properties 202
Auth Dialog box
theming, properties used 327, 328
authentication
obtaining, in Facebook 17
auth.login event 134, 135, 144
auth.logout event 135, 145
authorization
obtaining, in Facebook 15, 17
working 16, 17
auth.prompt event 135
auth.sessionChange event 135
auth.statusChange event 135
autocomplete() function 248
autocompleteselect event 249

B

batch request
using, for page's stream views retrival 258,
      259
using, for page's wall post retrival 258, 259
working 259, 260
birthday calendar
about 299
building 299-302
working 303-308
bookmark functionality 139
bookmarks
adding, XFBML used 139, 140
working 141

border_color attribute, Activity Feed plugin 178

box_count attribute 171

button_count attribute 171

button display 331

C

callCredit() function 240, 247

canceled 220

Canvas Page 10

Canvas URL 10

caption attribute 151

cb_fn parameter, FB.api() function 130

chco 258

chd 258

chs 258

cht 258

chtt 258

chxl 258

chxt 258

city-based friends classification application
  creating 308-310
  working 310, 312

click() event 49, 128, 137, 151

click() method 154, 222

client_id parameter, OAuth Dialog 160

cmp() function 289

college namespace 200

colorscheme attribute 172

colorscheme attribute, Activity Feed plugin 178

comment
  deleting 43

Comment box
  integrating, XFBML used 185-187
  working 187

comment.create event 135

comment.remove event 135

cookie, meta properties 279

count() function 288

Create an Ad button 270

Create button 324

create_event permission 55

Create New App button 314

Credits Callback URL 214

credits_purchase 223

cURL 8

curl_exec() function 70, 227

curl_init() function 227

CURLOPT_HEADER attribute 64, 228

CURLOPT_POST attribute 64, 228

CURLOPT_POSTFIELDS attribute 64, 228

CURLOPT_RETURNTRANSFER attribute 64, 228

curl_setopt() function 64, 69, 235

current user's friendlist
  $facebook , working 45
  deleting 46
  members, obtaining 45
  new friendlist, creating 45
  new member, adding 46
  retrieving 44, 45

current user status
  obtaining 121-124

custom offers
  about 229, 230
  DealSpot, integrating 232
  DealSpot integration, parameters 233
  implementing 230-232
  working 232

D

data-mode attributes 331

data-perms attributes 331

data-show-faces attributes 331

DateTime PHP class 256

description attribute 151

dev_purchase_params 223

display parameter, OAuth Dialog 156, 160

document.ready function 240

downloading
  PHP-SDK 8

E

edge.create event 135

edge.remove event 135

Edit App button 325, 332

Edit your Action Type page 318

event change
  subscribing to 133-135
  unsubscribing 135, 136
  working 137

event details
  retrieving 111, 112
  working 113
events
  auth.login 134, 135
  auth.logout 135, 145
  auth.prompt 135
  auth.sessionChange 135
  auth.statusChange 135
  click() 126, 137
  comment.create 135
  comment.remove 135
  edge.create 135
  edge.remove 135
  eventclick() 49
  eventonclick 21
  fb.log 135
  onclick() 123
  xfbml.render 135
events, Facebook
  creating 55, 56
  deleting 57
  working 56
event subscription 133
explode() function 64, 70, 228, 235
extended permission
  about 124
  authenticating, XFBML 142-145
  setting up 124
  setting up, XFBML 142-145
  working 125

F

Facebook
  about 5, 6
  application, configuring 13
  application, creating from scratch 275
  benefits, for developers 7
  events, creating 55
  Facebook Dialogs 147
  features 6
  Graph API 32
  Facebook Insights 251
  JavaScript SDK 117
  page liking by user, determining 27
  pages followed by user, obataining 86

  querying 74
  social plugins 169
Facebook Auth Dialog box
  customizing 325-328
  working 327, 328
Facebook class 17, 75, 262, 276
Facebook Credits
  about 211
  application callback, setting up 215
  application setup 212
  frontend, creating 221
  obtaining, without purchase 226
Facebook Credits frontend
  creating, JavaScript SDK 221-223
  meta properties 223
  working 223-225
Facebook Dialogs
  about 147
  prerequisites 148, 149
  story, publishing 150
Facebook Graph API
  about 32
  features 32
  prerequisites 32-34
  URL 16
Facebook graph object
  web pages, defining 332-334
Facebook Insights
  about 251
  prerequisites 252, 253
Facebook Open Graph Beta. *See* **Open Graph
    Beta**
Facebook page
  application's tab based content, customizing
    29
  liking by user, determining 27
  signed_request parameter 28
  working 28
Facebook Query Language. *See* **FQL**
Facebook social graph
  web pages, unifying 195
Facebook URL Linter
  URL 207
fb:profile-pic
fb:height attribute 138
fb:linked attribute 138
fb:size attribute 138

fb:uid attribute 138
fb:width attribute 138
FB.api() function
  about 130, 338
  parameters 130
FB.Canvas.setAutosize() parameter 27
FB.Canvas.setSize() function 128
FB.Data.query() function 132
FB.event.subscribe() function 144
FB.Event.subscribe() function 134, 137, 142
FB.Event.unsubscribe() function 137
FB.getLoginStatus() function 121, 122, 131, 132
FB.init() function
  about 121, 133, 149, 222, 279, 335
  cookie parameters 120
  xfbml parameters 120
fb.log event 135
FB.login() function 122, 123, 134
FB.logout() function 126
fb:profile-pic XFBML tag
  height attribute 138
FB.ui() function 283
FB.XFBML.parse() function 135
features, Facebook 6
features, Facebook Graph API
  analytics 32
  authorization 32
  deleting 32
  publishing 32
  reading 32
  searching 32
Feed Dialog Box, configuring
  caption 283
  description 283
  link 283
  message 283
  name 283
  picture 283
  to 283
file_get_contents() function 307
filter attribute, Activity Feed plugin 178
font and border_color attribute, Activity Feed plugin 178
font attribute 172

font attribute, Activity Feed plugin 178
foreach() loop 111, 311
foreach() PHP loop 78, 113
form submission
  handling, in iFrame Facebook application 23, 24
FQL
  about 74
  application permission status, checking 100
  event details of user friends retrieving, multi-query method used 114
  event details, retrieving 111
  friends retrieving, from specific friend list 95, 96
  group information, retrieving 91
  group members, retrieving 93
  important points 74
  message, obtaining in thread 98
  notification, retrieving 102
  prerequisites 74-76
  user associated video details, retrieving 104
  user following pages, obtaining 86
  user friendship, determining 89
  user information, returning 76
  user posted link, obtaining 84, 85
  user published photos, retrieving 109
  user's friend profile pictures, retrieving 81
  user status message, obtaining 78
  user tagged photos, obtaining 106
FQL multiquery
  visitors statistics, obtaining 263-269
fql.multiquery method 114
FQL query
  executing 131, 132
  working 132
fqlQuery() function 131, 132
fql.query method 114
FQL user table
  retrieving 78
friend details, user
  retrieving, multiquery method used 114, 116
friend request
  processing 164-167
  sending, by user 161-164
  sending, Facebook Dialog used 153-155
FROM clause 74

G

Get Code button 192
getFriendId() function 47, 48
getLoginUrl() function 16, 19
GET parameters
  chbh 258
  chco 258
  chd 258
  chs 258
  cht 258
  chtt 258
  chxl 258
  chxt 258
getSession() function 16, 33, 75, 253
getSignedRequest() 28
Getting Started option 318
Google Chart API
  using, for chart creation 257, 258
Graph API call
  making 129
  working 130, 131
group information
  FQL query, executing 92
  retrieving 91, 92
group members
  retrieving 93, 94
  working 95, 97

H

hash_hmac() function 219
header attribute, Activity Feed plugin 178
header() function 19
height attribute, Activity Feed plugin 178
height attributes 138
href attribute
  colorscheme attribute, using 191
  font attribute, using 191
  href attribute, using 191
  layout, specifying 171
href parameter 21, 173
href value 181
href value attribute 182
http_method parameter, FB.api() function
  130

hub_challenge parameter 67
hub_mode parameter 67
hub_verify_token parameter 67

I

id parameter 156
iFrame Facebook application
  about 21
  dynamically resizing 24-27
  FB.Canvas.setAutosize() parameter 27
  JavaScript SDK, working 26
  navigation, handling 22
  working 22
iframe size
  resetting 127
  working 128
imagecolorallocate() function 305
imagecopy() function 298
imagecopymerge() function 307
imagecreatefromjpeg() function 305
imagecreatetruecolor() function 305
imagedestroy() function 292
imagefilledrectangle() function
  about 306
  arguments 289, 305
imagefttext() function
  about 306
  arguments 290, 306
imagepng() function 298, 307
imagesettile() function 305
img attributes 138
img HTML tag 138
img tag 83
index method 82
Insight Dashboard 252

J

JavaScript SDK
  about 26, 118
  prerequisites 118-120
  source URL 118
json_decode() function 68
json_encode() function 114, 116, 248, 260,
  269

K

key named method 310

L

layout attribute 171
Like box
about 173
adding 174, 175
working 175-177
Like Box plugin
chart creating, Google Chart API used 257, 258
impressions, retrieving 254-256
working 255, 256
Like button
about 170
setting up, on your web page 170
Like button, integrating with websites
action attribute, specifying 172
colorscheme, specifying 172
font attribute, specifying 172
href attributes, specifying 171
layout attibutes, specifying 171
ref scheme, specifying 172
sendscheme, specifying 172
show_faces attribute, specifying 172
steps 170
width attribute, specifying 172
working 171-173
LIMIT clause 111
link attribute 151
link table
link_id field 85
owner_comment field 85
summary field 85
title field 85
url field 85
list() function 219
Live Stream plugin
about 183
integrating, XFBML used 183
working 185
Log In and Add to Facebook button 330
login plugin
about 192

max-rows attribute 193
using 192, 193
width attribute 193
working 193

M

Manage Permissions link 205
max_rows attribute 182
max-rows attribute 193
Message 236
message attribute 151
meta properties, audio data
og:audio:album 202
og:audio:artist 202
og:audio:title 202
og:audio:type 202
meta properties, Facebook Credits frontend
app_id 223
credits_purchase 223
dev_purchase_params 223
order_info 223
purchase_type 223
redirect_uri 223
meta properties, imagecopymerge() function
dst_im 291
dst_x 291
dst_y 291
pct 291
src_h 291
src_im 291
src_w 291
src_x 291
src_y 291
meta properties, order
access_token 236
CURLOPT_HEADER 235
CURLOPT_POST 235
CURLOPT_POSTFIELDS 235
CURLOPT_RETURNTRANSFER 235
Message 236
order_id 236
refund_funding_source 236
refund_reason 236
Status 236
meta properties, order details
CURLOPT_HEADER 228

CURLOPT_POST 228
CURLOPT_POSTFIELDS 228
CURLOPT_RETURNTRANSFER 228
meta properties, video data
  og:video:height 203
  og:video:type 203
  og:video:width 203
method attribute 163
multiple application installation
  FQL, using 261, 262
  working 262, 263
multiquery method
  using, for details retrieving 114, 115
  working 116
my_app directory 14
My Fast Friends application
  color, meta properties 289
  creating 284-287
  image, meta properties 289
  working 288-291
  x1, meta properties 289
  x2, meta properties 289
  y1, meta properties 289
  y2, meta properties 289
mysql_connect() function 246
mysql_fetch_array() function 246
mysql_select_db() function 246

N

name attribute 151
new Facebook application
  about 10
  application ID, working 12
  application secret key, working 12
  developer account, verifying for 10
  registering 10-12
  sandbox mode 13
  secret key, resetting 13
  secure connection 13
  working 12
notification, user
  obtaining 102-104

O

OAuth Dialog
  meta properties 161

parameters 160
uisng, for application permission 160
using, for application permission request
    157-161
objects
  defining 317-324
  working 325
object-specific meta properties
  fb:app_id 334
  og:description 334
  og:image 334
  og:type 334
  og:url 334
offset parameter 58
og:audio:title, meta properties 202
og:audio
  album, meta properties 202
  artist, meta properties 202
og:audio, meta properties 202
og:audio:title, meta properties 202
og:audio:type, meta properties 202
og:description property 198
og:image property 198
og:site_name property 198
og:title property 197
og:type property 197
og:url property 198
og:video:height, meta properties 203
og:video, meta properties 203
og:video:type, meta properties 203
og:video:width, meta properties 203
onclick() event 21, 123
Open Graph Beta
  about 313, 314
  application, setting up 314
Open Graph tab 318
order
  refunding 233, 234
  status, updating 236
  working 235, 236
order details
  about 226
  configuring, curl_setopt() function used 228
  retrieving, steps 227, 228
  working 228, 229
order_id property 219, 236
order_info property 219, 223

P

page
about 63
administration interface 204
Page Tabs settings 27
parameters, OAuth Dialog
client_id 160
display 160
redirect_uri 160
response_type 160
state 160
Params 236
parse_signed_request() function 216, 218
payment_status_update method 220
period() function 268
permissions 36, 63
photo collage
about 292
setting up 292-295
working 295-298
PHP cURL extension 8, 9
PHP JSON (JavaScript Object Notation) extension
about 8
installation 9
PHP-SDK
downloading 8
facebook.php file, working 9
setting, on server 9
PHP-SDK, downloading
environment, setting up 8
picture
deleting 43
picture attribute 151
post
comments, placing 38-40
creating, on user's friends wall 46-48
creating, on user's friend wall 47
deleting 43
link, deleting 38
linking 36, 37
post, commenting on
comments, deleting 40
posted link, user
obtaining 84
post request 338

prerequisites, Facebook Dialogs
appID parameter 149
basic configuration, performing 148
cookie parameter 149
status parameter 149
xfbmlparameter 149
prerequisites, Facebook Graph API 32-34
prerequisites, FQL 74-76
print_r($results) 116
print_r() function 260
profile picture
retrieving, XFBML used 137, 138
profile pictures of friends, user
retrieving 81-83
property, Facebook
fb:admins 198
og:description 198
og:site_name 198
property, Open Graph protocol
og:image 198
og:title 197
og:type 197, 198
og:url 198
publish_actions permission
about 328
requesting, for publishing to user's time line
328, 330
working 331
published photos, of user
retrieving 109
working 111
publish_stream permission 102
purchase_type 223

Q

query_param parameter 131
query_param parameter, FB.api() function
130
query variable 132

R

readArticle() function 335, 338
read_mailbox permission 102
ready() function 51
realpath() function 52, 62, 294
real time updates, handling

callback, creating 65, 66, 68
    working 67, 68
**recommendations attribute, Activity Feed
    plugin 178**
recommendations plugin 180
redirect_uri attribute 151, 223
redirect_uri parameter 155
redirect_uri parameter, OAuth Dialog 160
ref attribute 172
ref attribute, Activity Feed plugin 178
refunded 220
refund_funding_source 236
refund_reason 236
req_perms 76
Request for Permission dialog box 122
response_type parameter, OAuth Dialog 160
retrieve method 216
RETURNTRANSFER method 234

S

Save Changes button 323
scope parameter, OAuth Dialog 160
SELECT clause 104
Send a Gift application
    developing 236-241
    frontend, sections 244
    integrating, with Facebook Credits 238-242
    meta properties 247
    working 244-249
send attribute 172
Send button
    customizing, attributes used 191
    integrating, stand-alone Send button 190,
        191
    integrating, with Like button 188-190
    integrating, XFBML used 187-190
    working 191
session validation
    performing 121-124
setFileUploadSupport() function 61, 294
settled 220
show_faces attribute 172, 193
Show faces option 192
signed_request key 218
signed_request parameter 28
site attribute, Activity Feed plugin 178

size attributes 138
sms permission 102
social graph
    video data, attaching 203
    web pages defining, Facebook Open Graph
        protocol used 199
    web pages, integrating 196-199
split() function 304
SQL 74
standard attribute 171
state parameter, OAuth Dialog 160
Status 236
status message
    likes by friends, retrieving 53, 55
    setting 41, 42
    working 42
status, meta properties 279
story, publishing
    Facebook Feed Dialog box, working 151-153
    steps 150
stream updates
    publishing, to user 208, 209
strtotime() function 305
Structured Query Language. *See* **SQL**
subscriptions
    deleting 69, 70

T

tabs() function 248
tagged photos, of user
    obtaining 106, 108
    photo_tag table, working 108, 109
tag_uid, meta properties 291
target attribute 23
target parameter 21
thread messages
    about 98
    obtaining 98, 99
    working 99
Timeline 313

U

uid attributes 138
unset() function 245
user
    about 63

data parameter 163
Facebook Feed Dialog box, configuring 151-153
friend profile pictures, retrieving 81
friend request, sending 161-164
information, returning 76, 77
links posted, obtaining 84-86
logging out 126, 127
message parameter 163
notification, obtaining 102-104
sent friend request, processing 164-167
status messages, obtaining 78, 80
story, publishing 150
title parameter 163
to parameter 163
usergetLoginUrl() function, working 19
usergetLogoutUrl() function, working 21
userlogging out 20
userspecific permissions, requesting 17-19
userstatus message likes by friends, retrieving 53, 55
user actions, publishing to Facebook
starting with 334
steps 334-337
working 337, 338
user album
picture, posting 49-53
user_birthday permission 76
user_checkins permission 102
user following pages
retrieving 86-88
working 88
user friendship
determining 89, 90
working 90
user information
retrieving 76, 77
returning 76, 77
user table, working 77
user object-related real time updates
attributes configuring, curl_setopt() function used 64
subscription, adding 63, 64
working 64, 65
users
tagging, in picture 60-62
user's feed

searching through 59
working 60
user's friend profile pictures
retrieving 81
user's friends
paging through 57-59
user's information
about 34
retrieving 34, 35
working 35, 36
user status message, obtaining
about 78
api() function, working 80
steps 78
usort() function 288

V

val() function 128, 249
valid user session
obtaining, in Facebook 15
working 16, 17
video data
attaching, to social graph 203
integrating 200-203
meta properties 203
video details, of user
retrieving 104, 105
video_tag table, working 106
visitor statistics
end_time parameter 268
metric parameter 268
object_id parameter 268
obtaining, FQL multiquery used 263-267
period parameter 268
value parameter 269
working 267-269

W

web page
Facepile plugin, setting up 180-182
Facepile plugin, working 182
Like button, setting up 170
web page definition, as Facebook graph object
steps 332, 333
working 334

web pages

    integrating, into social graph 196-199

web pages defining, Facebook Open Graph
        protocol used

    contact information, defining 200

    custom object type, defining 200

    local information, defining 199, 200

WHERE clause 74, 89

width attribute 172, 182, 193

width attribute, Activity Feed plugin 178

width attributes 138

window.fbAsyncInit function 149

X

XFBML

    bookmarks, adding 139, 140

    extended permissions, setting up 142-145

    profile picture, retrieving 137, 138

    using, for Comment box integration 185-187

    using, for Live Stream plugin integration 183-
        185

xfbml attribute 138

xfbml, meta properties 279

xfbml.render event 135

XFBML tag

    attributes 142

x, meta properties 291

Y

y, meta properties 291

Your Good Luck Charm of the Day application

    creating 279-282

    working 282, 283

Thank you for buying
Facebook Application Development with
Graph API Cookbook

About Packt Publishing

Packt, pronounced 'packed', published its first book "*Mastering phpMyAdmin for Effective MySQL Management*" in April 2004 and subsequently continued to specialize in publishing highly focused books on specific technologies and solutions.

Our books and publications share the experiences of your fellow IT professionals in adapting and customizing today's systems, applications, and frameworks. Our solution based books give you the knowledge and power to customize the software and technologies you're using to get the job done. Packt books are more specific and less general than the IT books you have seen in the past. Our unique business model allows us to bring you more focused information, giving you more of what you need to know, and less of what you don't.

Packt is a modern, yet unique publishing company, which focuses on producing quality, cutting-edge books for communities of developers, administrators, and newbies alike. For more information, please visit our website: www.packtpub.com.

Writing for Packt

We welcome all inquiries from people who are interested in authoring. Book proposals should be sent to author@packtpub.com. If your book idea is still at an early stage and you would like to discuss it first before writing a formal book proposal, contact us; one of our commissioning editors will get in touch with you.

We're not just looking for published authors; if you have strong technical skills but no writing experience, our experienced editors can help you develop a writing career, or simply get some additional reward for your expertise.

Flash Facebook Cookbook

ISBN: 978-1-84969-072-0   Paperback: 388 pages

Over 60 recipes for integrating the Flash applications
with the Graph API and Facebook

1. Work with the key Graph API objects and
   their social connections, using the Facebook
   ActionScript 3 SDK

2. Create new Checkins at Facebook Places and plot
   existing Checkins and Facebook Places on Flex
   mapping components

3. Upload image files or generated images to
   Facebook

4. Packed full of solutions using a recipe-based
   approach

Facebook Graph API Development with Flash

ISBN: 978-1-84969-074-4   Paperback: 324 pages

Build social Flash applications fully integrated with the
Facebook Graph API

1. Build your own interactive applications and games
   that integrate with Facebook

2. Add social features to your AS3 projects without
   having to build a new social network from scratch

3. Learn how to retrieve information from Facebook's
   database

4. A hands-on guide with step-by-step instructions
   and clear explanation that encourages
   experimentation and play

Please check **www.PacktPub.com** for information on our titles

Flash Game Development by Example

ISBN: 978-1-84969-090-4   Paperback: 428 pages

Build 9 classic Flash games and learn game development along the way

1. Build 10 classic games in Flash. Learn the essential skills for Flash game development

2. Start developing games straight away. Build your first game in the first chapter

3. Fun and fast paced. Ideal for readers with no Flash or game programming experience

4. The most popular games in the world are built in Flash

CryENGINE 3 Cookbook

ISBN: 978-1-84969-106-2   Paperback: 324 pages

Over 90 recipes written by Crytek developers for creating third-generation real-time games

1. Begin developing your AAA game or simulation by harnessing the power of the award winning CryENGINE3

2. Create entire game worlds using the powerful CryENGINE 3 Sandbox

3. Create your very own customized content for use within the CryENGINE3 with the multiple creation recipes in this book

Please check **www.PacktPub.com** for information on our titles

CPSIA information can be obtained at www.ICGtesting.com
Printed in the USA
LVOW122307171111

255473LV00004B/14/P